Being Different: The Autobiography of Jane Fry

Being Different: The Autobiography of Jane Fry

collected, compiled, and edited
with an introduction
and conclusion by

ROBERT BOGDAN

A WILEY-INTERSCIENCE PUBLICATION

JOHN WILEY & SONS, New York • London • Sydney • Toronto

Library of Congress Cataloging in Publication Data:

Fry, Jane.
  Being different: the autobiography of Jane Fry.

"A Wiley-Interscience publication."
   1. Sexual deviation—Personal narratives.   2. Psychiatric hospitals.
3. United States—Social conditions.   4. Fry, Jane.   I. Bogdan, Robert, ed.   II. Title.

RC557.F78   362.2'092 4 [B]   73-20155

ISBN 0-471-08570-7

Printed in the United States of America

10 9 8 7 6 5 4 3 2 1

*"In the animal kingdom, the rule is, eat or be eaten;
in the human kingdom, define or be defined."*

THOMAS SZASZ*

* Thomas Szasz, *The Second Sin* (Garden City, N.Y.: Anchor Press; Doubleday and Company, 1973), p. 20.

Foreword

Dr. Bogdan has provided us with a biography which turns out to be, and in surprising ways, a commentary on various aspects of American society and culture. Surprising because we learn even more about "ordinary" aspects of social living than we do about sexuality and its vicissitudes. For example, we learn about the effects of war, geographical mobility, and vocational instability on family organization. We get a picture of how our schools can be amazingly insensitive to a child's talents and needs. We learn a good deal about how the less privileged youngsters in our society are haphazardly introduced into the world of work. And, of course, we are again informed about institutional psychiatry and how it degrades and depersonalizes the caretakers as well as the cared for. Make no mistake about it: The detailed picture we get about mental hospitals is independent of who provided the description. I congratulate Dr. Bogdan for using the life history to illustrate compellingly what these "humane" institutions are. Obviously, the uniqueness and power here resides in who is telling the story, and to whom.

This, then, is not a "clinical" case history containing lurid details about sexual deviancy. It is not an exposé. In this narrative one person—an obviously intelligent, reflective, courageous, troubled individual—describes her encounters with the major institutions of our society. A sophisticated reader's understanding of sexual deviancy and personality disorder (their origins and development) may not be technically increased by this account, but it will surely deepen his comprehension of how our culture exacerbates the consequences of what it views as atypical. What this book does or can do, if one does not unduly focus on the fact that this is the life history of a transsexual, is to illuminate some important characteristics of our society and its institutions.

The life-history as an investigative social science methodology, developed and used so productively by the Chicago School of Sociology earlier in this century, has not become fashionable. Social science has deprived itself of an important way of gaining knowledge about man and society. Hopefully, through Dr. Bogdan's effort, we will see the life-history accorded its rightful place as a productive social science technique.

SEYMOUR SARASON
New Haven, Connecticut

Preface

In one sense my interest in compiling this book stems from a history of disillusionment with social science research which all too often presents the world in such a way that it does not resemble what it is to those who are in it.

I became extremely disillusioned when, after having lived in West Africa for two years, I returned to graduate school to complete a doctorate in sociology. The literature I read and the discussions in my seminars were not totally without worth, but there seemed little connection between what I was supposed to be learning and the social processes I had observed. The theory and discussion were not grounded in the people I had known, their problems, and their situation. The frustration of experiencing a mismatch between the world I had experienced and the world as presented in my graduate training was partly relieved by my contact with people who represented the tradition of the Chicago School of Sociology and who encouraged me to conduct research. After my first year back I started my first field work study and began reading the studies representing that tradition.

My first job after completing my degree brought me in contact with many people who had been declared either "mentally ill" and were or had been in state mental hospitals, or "mentally retarded" and were similarly institutionalized or had a high potential for becoming so. I supervised many students as they did field research among these people, and spent time with them also. During this period I had an opportunity to talk to many mental health professionals and to read the literature in the field. The disillusion that I had felt after returning from Africa and the disillusion I had on reading the "mental health" literature was similar. By this time I had become more sophisticated in analyzing my frustration, and I was a member of the profession that I was disillusioned with. I had come to see that social science studies

ix

produce and create their own realities and that it was a very legitimate and important professional pursuit to engage in research that would present reality as experienced by those we call subjects. That was my intent when I began this project.

The book is organized in three parts. Part I discusses the autobiography as a method of understanding social life and tells the story of the book's creation. Part II consists of the autobiography of Jane Fry, which I collected using tape-recorded interviews. Part III consists of a discussion of Jane's story and the presentation of data from her medical records, which allows the reader to put in juxtaposition Jane's story with the perspectives of professionals who have come in contact with her.

I would like to thank those who helped me with this book. Blanche Geer and Irwin Deutscher introduced me to the approach I have used. My wife, Janet Bogdan, Burton Blatt, and Douglas Biklen provided me with the kind of support, encouragement, and stimulation that made the work less of a struggle. They, along with Sandy Haynes and Steve Taylor, read the first draft of the manuscript and made useful comments. Beverly Warren transcribed the tapes, and Jean Gilman typed the manuscript. Of course, Jane Fry contributed more than anyone.

Finally, in keeping with social research practices and to preserve the privacy of those who have participated in Jane Fry's life, I have changed the names of all people and places mentioned in her narrative and in my own comments on it. "Jane Fry", too, is a pseudonym.

ROBERT BOGDAN

Center on Human Policy
Syracuse University
Syracuse, New York
October 1973

Contents

CONTENTS

Being Different:
The Autobiography
of Jane Fry

Introduction

This book is the autobiography of a person we shall call Jane Fry. She is a high school "dropout," a veteran of the Navy, a former resident of five psychiatric facilities, and although she has the organs of a man, she dresses and lives as a woman, and feels that she is one.

This narrative, dealing with one person's life as she tells it, is presented as more than just a story. It may be engaging, personal, moving and enjoyable, as stories are, but its aim is one common in the social sciences: a better understanding of society, its institutions, and those who pass through them. It is a "sociological autobiography,"[1] that is, it was collected and edited by one trained to ask and be concerned with sociological questions. Here, as in similar works, the sociologist partner in the enterprise guides the narrator to give details and to elaborate in areas of interest to his discipline. In compiling and editing as well, the concern is to present materials of sociological importance rather than to focus on materials that might serve other purposes, such as entertainment or popular market value.

A Promise from the Past:
A Short History of Personal Documents

Personal documents such as diaries, letters, and autobiographies, although not very popular, have always been used in the social sciences.[2] Typical of these publications were the works of W. I. Thomas. The depth of his attachment to this form of data is best indicated by a quotation from his classic, *The Polish Peasant in Europe and America,* which he wrote with F. Znaniecki: "We are safe in saying that personal life-records, as complete as possible, constitute the perfect type of sociological material. . . ."[4]

Between 1918, when these words were written, and the 1940's numerous sociological autobiographies and monographs employing personal documents were published; these included the well-known works of Shaw and of Sutherland.[5] Even during this period of their greatest popularity, however, autobiographical materials did not obtain a position of prominence as a source of sociological understanding. Thomas and Znaniecki's statement appeared ironic in light of the growing interest in quantitative research to the exclusion of other methods.

In the late 1930s and early 1940s the importance of the personal document was enhanced by the publication of a series of monographs by the Committee on Appraisal of Research of the Social Science Research Council. These works provided an appraisal of the usefulness of such materials, and Gordon W. Allport's *The Use of Personal Documents in Psychological Science,* part of the series, still stands as one of the most comprehensive, examinations of the nature and use of autobiographical material.[6] In concluding his book Allport strongly advocated the increased experimental use of personal documents, but his remark, quoted below, indicates the type of criticism to which this research approach was subjected and that a decline in its popularity would occur in the decades that followed:

> Strong counter measures are indicated against theorists who damn the personal document with faint praise, saying that its sole merit lies in its capacity to yield hunches or to suggest hypotheses, or that mental operations brought to bear upon a single case are merely a matter of incomplete and inadequate statistical reasoning. Although these points of view do reflect the prevailing empirical climate of our times, they fail to express more than a small part of the value of personal documents in the social sciences.[7]

A few works relying heavily upon personal documents and related material, including the works of Oscar Lewis,[8] and nonsociological autobiographies which have gained attention in the academic community, such as *Manchild in the Promised Land*[9] and *The Autobiography of Malcom X,*[10] were produced in the three decades following Allport's statement. His words, however, forecast the death of the autobiography as a social science technique, rather than its rebirth.

The acceptance of the autobiography as a source of social science data has had a bleak history. Reading through the various works based on such materials, for example, Shaw's *The Jack-Roller,* and Sutherland's *The Professional Thief,* one cannot help but realize that much understanding is to be gained from their pursuit. Perhaps our failure to develop this research approach is less a reflection on its worth than it is an indication of the fads and norms that tend to dominate the field.

In the 1960s, and now in the 1970s trends have emerged which suggest a change in social science. These include increased use of labeling theory in the study of deviant behavior, more frequent use of participant observation and development of ethnographic techniques, growing interest in theoretical approaches that emphasize the social construction of reality and interest in existential psychiatry. Perhaps the climate is right for exploration of the usefulness of the personal document again. It is with that hope that this book has been written.

The Uses of the Autobiography

Before we examine Jane's story, we look briefly at the nature of an autobiography and its value to the social scientist. In doing so I hope to make the reader who is not familiar with this form of data cognizant of its uses, hence a more sensitive observer of the story that follows.

The autobiography is an important approach to social science understanding simply because it acquaints us with people we would not otherwise know. As the author speaks about himself and his experiences, we develop an empathy which allows us to see the world from his point of view. The subjective nature of the personal document is one of its most important values—it enables us to develop an understanding of the subjective nature of reality.

Observing the world from the viewpoint of someone who may have opinions that differ from ours allows us to examine our commonsense assumptions about the nature of the person who is revealing his life. Howard Becker points out:

> . . . we can feel and become aware of the deep biases about such people that ordinarily permeate our thinking and shape the kinds of problems we investigate. . . . we can begin to see what we take for granted (and ought not to) in designing our research—what kinds of assumptions . . . are embedded in the way we set the questions we study.[11]

The autobiography can contribute to the effectiveness of professional groups which claim to be interested in "the search for basic knowledge," or in "acting in the best interest of the client," because it can provide a platform for the individuals they serve to express their own opinions. That is, the autobiography adds to theory construction and diagnosis another viewpoint which provides the professionals with an opportunity to examine the possibility that they are not doing what they profess to be doing, or that they are misrepresenting those whom they claim to be telling us about. This reality confrontation cannot help but be productive.

The author's own story provides a view of organizations and agencies from the perspective of one who has dealt with them. While there are social science reports describing a wide variety of agencies, including public schools, prisons, hospitals, factories, and welfare agencies, these studies, by and large, do not deal with the experiences of clients served by these organizations. Many times, with the help of research deals with formal and informal organizational structure, we forget there is a subjective side to organizational life which has as much, if not more, to do with the effects of these agencies as their structural and economic nature. Through various field work studies, the internal functioning of such institutions as large state mental hospitals and local jails is being understood. The autobiography can reveal the significance of institutions that may not appear to us to be important in people's lives. They can do this by giving us a feeling of what it was like to have been there.

Because the author of a personal document, be he a juvenile delinquent or a plumber, has been a member of various subcultures during his life time, he can provide us with a description of the day-to-day activities of segments of society we know nothing about. While an autobiography cannot provide a complete ethnography, it can supplement enthographic materials already collected.

The autobiography is unique in allowing us to view an individual in the context of his whole life, from birth to the point at which we encounter him. Because of this it can lead us to a fuller understanding of the stages and critical periods in the process of his development. It enables us to look at subjects as if they have a past with successes as well as failures, and a future with hopes and fears. It also allows us to see an individual in relation to the history of his time, and how he is influenced by the various religious, social, psychological, and economic currents present in his world. It permits us to view the intersection of the life history of men with the history of their society, thereby enabling us to understand better the choices, contingencies, and options open to the individual.[12]

The life history contributes to our understanding of the struggle between man and his society, in that it permits us to experience with the author his attempt to make sense of a world that is not always congruent with what he thinks it is and should be. Through the autobiography we can see an individual in the process of developing definitions of the world (perspectives or social constructs), as well as how the individual affects the definitions of reality of groups he comes in contact with. We see the struggle between the demands society makes on man and the demands he makes on it. It makes vivid what W. I. Thomas noted long ago:

> Every new invention, every chance acquaintanceship, every new environment, has the possibility of redefining the situation and of introducing change, disorganization or different types of organization into the life of the individual or even of the whole world.[13]

Because of its subjective nature, the personal document can be used to explore concepts whose essence is lost in the application of research techniques that rely on operationalized variables. Such phenomena as beauty, faith, pain, suffering, frustration, hope, and love can be dealt with in the autobiography as they are defined and experienced by real people in their world.

The author's own story is an especially valuable tool for training students. In most cases students have limited experience dealing with the realities of lives that are very different from their own. The personal narrative can provide them with a "reality shock," that is, "the surprising and jolting experience of being confronted by the irreality of something previously 'known' to be real '(their own assumptions)' or by the experience that others do not view our reality as real."[14] By doing this it can provide an experience which can free the student to be more open in his exploration of society.

Another characteristic of the personal document that makes it so valuable as a pedagogical device is that it is interesting as a literary form. The courses listed in university catalogs that fill the student with hope of finding relevance are those listed under the social sciences; yet they rarely fulfill their promise. Students often see these courses as "ego trips" of men obsessed with the history and instruments of *their* discipline, rather than as insightful and relevant in terms of revealing a new understanding. The autobiography provides a touchstone with reality which can excite students and maintain their interest by grounding the course content in the bedrock of human experience.

In addition, the autobiography can serve as a "devil's advocate" in examining theories and concepts in common use among sociologists, and can provide vivid illustrations of those that meet the test. Also, a detailed description of one person's life can provide us with a real-life starting point from which we may generate new ideas and hypotheses to pursue in future research. It can also provide a data base for constructing items on standardized instruments. By letting these instruments develop inductively out of the self-told experiences of a person who knows the substantive area of the researcher's interest, one can be sure that the instrument is relevant to the subject and that it uses the vocabulary of the person he wishes to understand.

The media through which we view an individual cannot help but affect how we feel about him and how we define him. When we present subjects in the form of numbers produced by the reduction of data gathered in mass, we do not engender in the reader a feeling of respect for or closeness to the people being discussed. Such views of human beings are not evil or unnecessary, but they comprise only a single view, and overemphasis on this view without presenting the subjective side distorts our knowledge of man in a dangerous way. We can manipulate statistical aggregates in a manner in which we cannot manipulate the people to whom we have spoken. The autobiography keeps us from reducing human forms to numbers, and from forgetting that the particulars of individuals' lives are as important to them as they are to social science knowledge.

Traditionally, social scientists have studied "deviants" as a separate category of human beings, and by doing this have accepted commonsense definitions. It is assumed that "deviant" behavior is basically different from other kinds of behavior, and that it needs to be explained by special theories distinct from those used to explain the behavior of "regular" people. Social scientists, by studying these phenomena as if they belonged to a unique, inherently different category, reify and legitimize commonsense classification of individuals as "normal" or "deviant." The autobiography, as a form of data and a source of understanding, permits us to know a "deviant" intimately, and by sharing his or her life we can approach the subject matter closely and see it in its more human dimensions rather than as a scientific category. It is through this intimacy that how the subject views himself and what he has in common with all of us becomes clear, and his differences take on less importance. The autobiography forces us to think of subjects as people, and categories of all kinds become less relevant.

Each person's life experiences are somewhat unique, and yet we all share certain experiences and developmental processes. By looking carefully at one life history, we can examine the nature of all human life, and by looking at life histories of authors who have had certain very unique experiences, we can observe clearly the dynamics of certain processes that appear only subtly in other lives. Each life history provides a laboratory in which certain aspects of human experience can best be studied and, hopefully, illuminated.

The Story of the Book

It was the spring of 1971 that I first met Jane, the narrator of this book. She had recently been discharged from the psychiatric ward of the Veterans Administration (VA) Hospital in Central City and had just joined a chapter of a homosexual liberation group which had a speaker's bureau. One of its first engagements was to address a "Social Problems" class at a nearby college. I sat in on the class, and subsequently asked the group to speak to two of my classes. Jane was one of the members of the group, and she stood out in several ways, mostly because of her ability to conceptualize her life and present situation.[15] The following fall I asked the group to address an advanced graduate methodology course. Sometime between spring and fall I first thought of working with Jane in compiling her story, although I did not seriously pursue the idea until the following spring. During the period between conception of the idea and its pursuit, I reread some of the early autobiographical materials of the Chicago School and was further impressed by their usefulness—this fanned my enthusiasm for the project.

By late winter I was ready to seek Jane out, but I postponed contacting her for several reasons, mainly because I did not know her very well and did not know how she would react to this possible intrusion in her life. In early March I visited the Crisis Center where Jane had been doing volunteer work and inquired about her. I was surprised and shocked to be told nonchalantly that she had been involuntarily committed to Central State Mental Hospital a few days earlier.

Toward the end of March I attended a meeting at the Crisis Center, and to my surprise Jane was there. I spoke to her after that meeting, mainly about her stay at Central State Hospital. We also conversed at two later meetings. In a sense, we had already established a rapport when I finally mentioned the project to her and asked if she would meet with me and discuss it. She knew that I was a college instructor, but she also knew that I was interested in the concerns of the Crisis Center, which were also of great interest to her.[16]

Our first arranged meeting was held at my office which was located in an old one-family house in a deteriorating residential setting. Other community-based researchers and practitioners worked there according to flexible schedules and with little formality. The congenial atmosphere perhaps facilitated development of the rapport Jane and I established during our talks over the next few months.

At our first meeting I told Jane of my interest in working with her on her autobiography and explained that I wanted to produce a work that would make a contribution to sociological understanding. I explained the book would be useful in giving sociologists and their students an understanding of her life and the world as she saw it. Jane was enthusiastic about working as a partner, and told me that she had thought about writing her story on several occasions but had never been able to work on it for any prolonged period of time. She had at one time started writing and had completed 15 pages but had not returned to it. She also told me that at two periods in her life she had written "self-analysis" pieces, a few pages in length which were reflections on her experiences and feelings. She also shared with me the letters from her correspondence with two doctors; they have been used at various points in her story.

Jane's motivation for participating in the project was many-faceted. She was interested in presenting her story to others, so that they might better understand what it means to be different and to grow up in the United States. This was the same reason that had led her to accept a few speaking engagements. Another reason was that she simply wanted to write a book. We first planned to identify Jane by her real name, but as we progressed further there were legal matters to consider, as well as concerns about protecting friends, relatives, and Jane from possible harm. Therefore, fictitious names have been used and places have been disguised. According to Jane, "The names have been changed to protect the guilty." Another possible motivating factor was monetary gain, although it was made clear from the beginning that when and if the book were published it would be for an academic rather than a popular audience, thus making the possibility of a large profit unlikely.

A few weeks elapsed between our first discussion of the project and the start of our work. Most of our meetings were held during the months of April, May, and June of 1972 at my office, and consisted of unstructured interviews which were tape-recorded. We started with informal conversations, pursuing various topics and discussing different phases of her life as they came up. If Jane brought up topics during a taping session that she was unable to finish, I would mention them the next day. We did not attempt to record her life story chronologically, but skipped around from day to day. There was an advantage in this method: It allowed a relationship to develop between us so that experiences that were difficult for her to talk about were dealt with at later sessions. I replayed certain tapes and at later taping sessions asked Jane questions regarding the chronology of events, and so on. Early in the interviewing I asked her to list the main events in her life chronologically, and this listing was used as a guide in organizing the material, as well as, in directing later taping sessions.

During the three-month period the material was recorded, we met from one to five times a week, and our meetings lasted from one to five hours. I did not keep an accurate count of the number of hours we spent recording our sessions; an estimate is about 100. Over 750 pages of transcribed material was the result of our effort.

It is difficult to describe the rapport that developed between us. Jane had spent three years in psychotherapy, prior to this project so she was accustomed to talking about herself to someone else, which probably facilitated the flow of information. However, she had been used to talking to probe her memory for answers to her difficulties, which was quite different from what we were doing. The effect of the psychotherapy on what Jane focused on in talking with me, and the degree to which it affected her story, is difficult to determine. Clearly, I was not her therapist; she did not relate to me as such, nor I to her.

Because of my marginal professional position in her eyes and because of my lack of affiliation with any service facility that might help her, there was no reason for Jane to distort her story in any particular direction in the hope of obtaining professional services.[17] Our relationship was an equalitarian one in which two people had made a serious commitment to accomplish a particular objective. I had done enough participant observation field work[18] to be familiar with researcher-subject relations, and did not worry about developing a friend-ship relationship with Jane. I knew the advantages of seeing her outside the research setting, and on afternoons that we worked she shared dinner with me and my family. She came to a picnic one afternoon with us and our friends, and we celebrated the completion of the interviewing by dining out. During the interviewing Jane took me to her parents' home on a social occasion and I had an opportunity to meet and talk with them. I have visited her home since that meeting, and have met other relatives.

At first I was not sure how Jane viewed me, and then one day during a session she used the word "freak" two or three times and I asked her exactly what she meant by it. She said that it did not have so much to do with drugs or that kind of thing, but with how open and tolerant a person was and whether they were "hung-up" on how other people looked. Then she said, "Like you, you're a freak, though you probably don't think of yourself as one." In a sense, a relationship evolved in which we both accepted each other, and this relationship was important to the quality of the material presented here. In retrospect, research partnerships seem to be much more productive in terms of the quality of data than the master-peasant relationships that seem to be so characteristic of many researcher subject undertakings.

I grew to trust Jane over the time we worked on the project, and I believe she learned to trust me. While I trust that she had not deceived me in purpose-fully misrepresenting herself, trust is not enough for "social science." One obligation a researcher has is to question his data, and I have made numerous checks on mine. First, in recording the interviews there was a good deal of skipping around from one time in Jane's life to another, and on many occasions Jane repeated incidents from her life two or three times, forgetting that we had previously recorded them. In reading through the material, however, I have found no contradictions. It would have been extremely difficult for her to lie so well and so consistently. Since meeting Jane, I have had opportunities to meet with other people who knew her at different times in her life. I have questioned some of them and have received no information that substantively contradicts what Jane has told me. During the interviews Jane showed me documents that support parts of her story. I have questioned a Navy officer extensively about various aspects of the Navy and am convinced that someone must have lived the experiences Jane did in order to have the knowledge of the Navy she has. This is also true of a wide variety of other experiences, including those involving psychiatric facilities, beauty school, door-to-door selling, and mechanics. I have visited many of the places Jane mentions in her story, and her descriptions and my observations clearly match. The most elaborate check of the accuracy of the "facts" as she related them was in my reading of Jane's medical records after having completed the interviewing.

How the material in this volume came to be arranged in this order is my own story. After the many pages of transcript had been typed, I read all the material once and then went through it all again, coding it for chronological order. After sorting out this information, I organized the chapters one at a time. With minor exceptions I kept the work in Jane's words, and attempted to convey the meaning she had intended. I eliminated materials that did not seem central to sociological concerns. For example, originally, there was much more detailed information about Jane's work experiences after leaving the Navy than that which appears in the book. And in the raw data much of the material was repetitious. In editing I have combined this material in order to provide the fullest description possible. In order to make the material more readable, I have edited some of the material for wordiness and tense, but by and large the work represents Jane's story as it was told to me.

NOTES

1. The phrase "sociological autobiography" is not intended to suggest that autobiographies written without social science guidance are not valuable sources of data. To the contrary, I believe that one of social science's most important unused resources is the virtually thousands of autobiographies produced over the ages by authors who have been moved to commit to paper what they have experienced. Little use has been made of this huge data bank. One way to encourage its use would be to develop an indexed, annotated bibliography.

2. Among these are the works of William James, G. Stanley Hall, and Sigmund Freud. See Gordon W. Allport, *The Use of Personal Documents in Psychological Science* (New York: Social Science Research Council, 1942), Chapters 1 and 2, for a discussion of the history of their use.

3. See Robert E. L. Faris, *Chicago Sociology, 1920–1932* Chicago (University of Chicago Press, 1970), and Howard S. Becker's introduction to the 1966 edition of Clifford Shaw's *The Jack-Roller* (Chicago: University of Chicago Press, 1966), for a discussion.

4. William I. Thomas and Florian Znaniecki, *The Polish Peasant in Europe and America* 2nd ed. (New York: Alfred A. Knopf, 1927), p. 1832. For other works of Thomas that make use of personal documents, see *The Unadjusted Girl* (New York: Harper and Row, 1967, origi-

nally published in 1923 by Little, Brown and Company, Boston), and W. I. Thomas and Dorothy Swaine Thomas, *The Child in America* (New York: Alfred A. Knopf, 1928).

5. Clifford Shaw, *The Jack-Roller* (Chicago: University of Chicago Press, 1966, originally published in 1930), *The Natural History of a Delinquent Career* (Chicago: University of Chicago Press, 1931), *Brothers in Crime* (Chicago: University of Chicago Press, 1936). Edwin Sutherland, *The Professional Thief* (Chicago: University of Chicago Press, 1937).

6. Gordon Allport, *The Use of Personal Documents in Psychological Science*. (New York: Social Science Research Council, 1942) The other volumes in the series were Herbert Blumer, *Critiques of Research in the Social Sciences I: An appraisal of Thomas and Znaniecki's The Polish Peasant* (New York: Social Science Research Council, 1939), and Louis Gottschalk, Clyde Kluckholn, and Robert Angell, *The Use of Personal Documents in History, Anthropology and Sociology* (New York: Social Science Research Council, 1945). The personal document as a form of data is discussed in John Dollard, *Criteria for the Life History* (New Haven: Yale University Press, 1935).

7. Allport, *op cit.*,p. 191.

8. Oscar Lewis, *Five Families* (New York: Basic Books, 1959), *The Children of Sanchez* (New York: Vintage Books, 1963), *La Vida* (New York: Vintage Books, 1966), and so on. For a more recent contribution, see Bruce Jackson, *Outside the Law* (New Brunswick, New Jersey, Transaction Books, 1972).

9. Claude Brown, *Manchild in the Promised Land* (New York: New American Library, 1965).

10. Malcolm X, *The Autobiography of Malcolm X* (New York: Grove Press, 1966).

11. Howard S. Becker, introduction to the 1966 edition of Clifford Shaw's *The Jack-Roller* (Chicago: University of Chicago Press, 1966), p. xv.

12. C. Wright Mills' writings indicate a strong concern for understanding this interface. The *Sociological Imagination* (New York: Oxford University Press, 1959), he observes: "The over-all questions of the social sciences come readily to the mind that has firm hold of the orienting conception of social science as the study of biography, history, and of the problems of their intersection within the social structure. To study these problems, to realize the human variety, requires that our work be continuously and closely related to the level of historical reality—and to the meanings of this reality for individual men and women" (p. 134).

13. W. I. Thomas, *The Unadjusted Girl* (New York: Harper Torch Editions, 1967), p. 71.

14. Burkart Holzner, *Reality Construction in Society* (Cambridge, Massachusetts: Schenkman Publishing Company, 1972), p. 2.

15. To some readers Jane may appear extremely exceptional in these areas. While I do not wish to suggest that she is not an exceptionally talented person, she may appear exceptional because we tend to think that people in positions such as hers have only limited intellectual abilities. We must be careful not to malign others and support stereotypes about others by praising Jane. I have come to believe, through listening to people talk about their lives and by reading personal documents, that everyone has at least one good story in them—his own. This is as true of those we believe to have only the most limited literary talent as it is of everyone else. If one takes the time to establish a relationship with a person, and encourage him to discuss his life, one can find this kind of exceptionality in anyone.

16. The Crisis Center was a street clinic which focused on drug and psychiatric problems. It offered limited, short-term crisis services, mainly to young people in the university area.

17. This is in contrast to Garfinkel's experience: Harold Garfinkel, *Studies in Ethnomethodology* (Englewood Cliffs, N.J.: Prentice Hall, 1967), Chapter V.

18. Robert Bogdan, *Participant Observation in Organizational Settings* (Syracuse: Syracuse University Press, 1972), "Learning to Sell Door to Door," *The American Behavioral Scientist* Sept./Oct. 1972, *A Forgotten Organizational Type* (Ann Arbor: University Microfilm, 1971), "Youth Clubs in a West African City," in Paul Meadows and Ephraim Mizruchi (Eds.), *Urbanism, Urbanization, and Change* (Reading, Massachusetts: Addison-Wesley Publishing Company, 1969), "A Qualitative Method for Studying Mental Retardation Facilities," a paper presented at the annual meeting of the American Association of Mental Deficiency, Atlanta, Ga., May 1973.

PART

II

*The Autobiography
of Jane Fry*

Chronology of Events in the Life of Jane Fry

July 4, 1945	Born in Brooklyn, New York.
1945–1946	Lived in Brooklyn, New York.
1946–1947	Lived in Boston, Massachusetts.
1947–1950	Lived in Marple, Massachusetts.
July 4, 1950	Fifth birthday.
1950–1956	Lived in Chester, New Jersey; first childhood memories; lived with aunt; father off to Korean War; developed TB; first school experiences; first dressed in sister's clothes; childhood memories of wanting to be a girl and being teased; father had a "breakdown"; left back in school.
June 4, 1954	Was baptized.
July 4, 1956	Eleventh birthday.
1956–1961	Lived in Watershire, Vermont; met Jimmy; went to Rickland Junior High School; puberty.
Spring 1961	Moved to Central City (end of ninth grade).
July 4, 1961	Sixteenth birthday.
Fall 1961	Started Brian High School; had problems with school authorities; bought women's clothes for the first time.
Summer 1962	Summer school.
July 5, 1962	Joined Navy Reserves.
September 1962	Left high school.
October 9, 1962	Enlisted in the Navy.
December 1962	Gun fell on head while in bootcamp.
December 20, 1962	Went home for Christmas leave—near the end of bootcamp.
January 1963	Left for Hawaii.

15

Spring 1963	Passed high school equivalency; visited home; started diesel mechanic school.
Summer 1963	Bought clothes while in diesel school while on weekend pass; acquired tattoo.
1963–1964	Submarine school; affair with man after being picked up hitch-hiking;dressed in public for first time on trip to New York City; cruise to Puerto Rico; requested transfer from submarine service.
May 20, 1964	Admitted to psychiatric ward at Naval Hospital.
June 4, 1964	Given psychiatric discharge from the Navy.
August 5, 1964	Admitted to VA Hospital in Central City complaining of headache.
August 20, 1964	Discharged from VA Hospital with a diagnosis of "headache of undetermined etiology."
December 1964	First job (elevator operator) after being discharged from the Navy.
February 1965	Started Manpower nurses aid training school.
September 1965	Sold magazines cross-country.
1965–1966	Worked at Mark's Decorating and Omega Industries; rented own apartment; interviewed by IBM.
Summer 1966	Took job in restaurant as manager trainee; after this went to cooking school and then to baking school.
January 9, 1967	Admitted to VA Hospital for "abdominal pains"; examined by endocrinologist.
February 17, 1967	Discharged from VA Hospital with diagnosis of "abdominal pains of unknown cause" with suggestion that they were psychosomatic.
May 16, 1967	Admitted to VA Hospital with diagnosis of "psychotic reaction to scopolamine."
May 23, 1967	Discharged from VA Hospital with secondary diagnosis of "schizoid personality—marked."
Summer 1967	Worked at Marshall Scientific Supply Company.
September 1967	Found out Joan was pregnant.
October 9, 1967	Married Joan.
February 19, 1968	Admitted to VA Hopsital seeking help for "emotional problems."
February 26, 1968	First suicide attempt (cut wrists in psychiatric ward at VA).
April 11, 1968	Son born.
August 19, 1968	Wrote first letter to Dr. Campbell.
September 16, 1968	Received a reply from Dr. Campbell.
November 1968	First visit to Dr. Campbell.
January 10, 1969	Second trip to New York City to see Dr. Rider.

October 1969	Tattoo removed.
April 1970	Dressed in front of other patients.
January 24, 1971	Discharged from VA Hospital.
April 15, 1971	Admitted to the Medical Center for overdose of Mysoline and Valium. Transferred to VA Hospital.
April 4, 1971	Neurologist reported seizure disorder.
April 21, 1971	Attended first Gay Liberation Meeting.
July 21, 1971	Admitted to Medical Center for abdominal pains.
Summer 1971	Worked at Crisis Center.
August 5, 1971	Appendix operation at Medical Center.
September 1971	Moved from Adler Street to apartment with three women.
December 1971	Moved out of apartment with three women and into house near the Crisis Center.
January 27, 1972	Admitted to psychiatric ward of Medical Center.
March 8, 1972	Involuntarily committed to Central State Mental Hospital.
April 1972	Visited Boston and started interviews for the book.
July 1972	Moved to Boston.

1

Prologue: Purgatory

Being referred to as a "transsexual" doesn't bother me too much. I would rather be thought of as a person first, but it doesn't make me angry because that's what I am. A transsexual is a person who wishes to change sexes and is actively going about it. Which is exactly what I am doing.[1]

I have the physical organs of a man, but I feel that I am a woman. For a long time I fought these feelings, but I don't anymore. I take female hormones and dress and live as a woman, and I have for two years. I understand my transsexualism for what it is. Basically, it boils down to this: What is a person? Is a person what he is on the inside? Or what he is on the outside? I know what I am on the inside, a female. There is no doubt there. I could spend 50 years of my life trying to change, but I doubt if that would do anything. I know what I am. I like it, and I don't want to change. The only thing I want to change is my body, so that it matches what I am. A body is like a covering; it's like a shell. What is more important? The body or the person that is inside?

As you will read, I went for three years of psychotherapy and I couldn't find anything in my childhood to pin this thing down on, nothing that would be different from your background or anybody else's. Sure, if you look hard enough into my childhood you would find things, just like if I looked into yours I could find things, if I wanted to. You might say that there were psychological reasons for my state if my father was a superdrunk, or if my mother made me sleep with her, or if she wanted a girl so much she dressed me in girls' clothes; but there was nothing like that. My father said to me once that there were a few males on his side of the family way back that were fairly feminine. I don't know whether heredity is part of it or not. For sure, my father isn't feminine.

I spent three years searching for psychological reasons and other kinds of reasons, because I was expected to. I'm not interested in reasons anymore. I don't give a damn what caused it. God could have poked his finger in by belly button and said, "You're going to think of yourself as a girl," and that could have caused it. All I want to do is get it fixed. I just want to be myself. But in order to get it fixed you have to convince God knows how many people that you're sane, convince people that you really want the operation, find someone to do it, and come up with the money.

I stopped looking for reasons two years ago. Every doctor you see gives you a different explanation, and you just come to the point of knowing that they just don't know what the hell they are talking about. One thing that I did learn in meeting all the doctors is that you have to give a little—pretend a little. Any one of them can kill you physically or emotionally. They can put the dampers on everything. If they decide that I am totally insane because I want to be a female, who knows what they can do. I nod when they tell me their theories now. You have got to learn to give and take, which I took some time in learning.

Before I go on and tell you about the operation and transsexualism and the hassle involved in that, let me tell you a little about the way I look at life and analyze myself. There is this story I heard once about Freud that pretty much sums it up. He was at a meeting with some colleagues, and he lit up this hugh stogey. His colleagues around the table started snickering because of his writing about oral complexes and phallus symbols. Freud just looked at it and said, "Yes gentlemen. I know this is a phallic symbol but it is also a god damned good cigar." That's a good way to look at life. If it's enjoyable, do it as long as it doesn't harm anybody, and don't worry about analyzing everything. That is my philosophy. I am the only one responsible for what I do, and as long as I don't harm another human being mentally or physcially, I'm being a good person. I think that I'm a good person because I operate according to my principles. I may break the law, but I'm not breaking my law which seems like the sensible one to me. I also think people should help each other, which I try to do. I think people should help me. They shouldn't sit down and try to analyze me, or try to figure out why I am the way I am or whether I am eligible for a sex change.

There are two laws that I know of that affect transsexuals—one the police can pick you up for. It's about impersonation. I don't know the actual law, but it was put on the books in the 1700s. The reason they had it was that farmers were dressing up as indians in order to avoid paying taxes—some would even dress as women. So they passed this law not allowing people to dress up in public and to paint their faces. That's the law they now arrest transsexuals and transvestites on.

The other law keeps surgeons from doing the operation. That one comes from England. There was a war going on there and the people were trying to get out of the draft by cutting off their fingers and toes, and they would have a surgeon do it. So the law states that no surgeon can take away any part of your body that would make you ineligible for the draft. So cutting off my genitals is making me ineligible for the draft. I think the draft board could afford to lose a few, but anyway that's the law that the surgeons are afraid of. I've heard of a couple of times where doctors were ready to perform the operation and were notified by the DA that if they did they would press charges.

The doctors usually back off. They don't want to get involved. They don't have the time to get in a test case, and most of the time they don't want that kind of publicity. The hospitals especially don't like that kind of publicity. They don't get donations, I guess, if the public finds out they are doing sexual change operations. The board of directors and contributors jump down their throats for doing such an atrocious thing, and if the word gets out that a hospital is doing the surgery, they get besieged by transsexuals wanting to get one.

Most people don't know the difference between transvestites, homosexuals, and transsexuals, so I think I ought to clear that up before I go any further. Most people just lump them all together. I saw one Archie Bunker show on homosexuals that really pointed out how Americans think about people who have different sexual practices. People don't realize how prejudiced they are about homosexuality and transsexuality, because they aren't even at a point of knowing that it's something that you can be prejudiced about. They are so sure that the rest of the world is supposed to be the way they are that they don't even think the people who are different have an opinion. They just lump them all together as nuts or perverts. That's the way Archie was on this program.

Well, anyway, a transvestite only wants to dress like a woman. They don't want to go all the way and have an operation and live as a woman. The transsexual wants an operation. It's a difference in the way you think about yourself. The way of thinking of a transsexual is: "I am a female with a birth defect. I am a woman, but I have the organs of the other sex. I want to be a whole person again." The term is also used to refer to people who are physiologically women who want to be men. The way of thinking of a transvestite is: "I am a man, but I want to play the role of a female. I know that I am a male, but I get kicks out of dressing like a woman." The transvestite gets emotional gratification and psychological good feelings from dressing. A transsexual doesn't. There is an interest in clothing, but it's much like a woman's interest. No erotic stimulation or anything like that. Like, I am just as happy bumming around in a pair of jeans and a blouse as in some type of fancy low-cut gown with heels.

The difference between a homosexual and a transsexual or a transvestite is that the homosexual knows that he is a man, let's say, but he is sexually attracted to those of the same sex and has sex with them. He says: "I know that I am a man, but I want to have sex with a man." Some transvestites are not homosexuals, because they don't want sex. Transsexuals are not homosexuals because they don't want to have sex with those who are of the same sex as they are; they want sex with the opposite sex.

I used to be down on homosexuals. Homosexuals and transsexuals usually don't hit it off. I happened to relate well with a group a few years ago, and I was able to get over my prejudices and start seeing what we had in common rather than what we differed over. I found it easy to relate to this group, because what we had in common was that we were suppressed. We both share some of the dangers of being brutalized because of our beliefs. We can be picked up for impersonation, or for vagrancy, or anything else they want to pick us up for. We also share being made jokes of or beat up at any time. Like, just last week I had a seizure in the middle of the street, and someone called an ambulance. The first thing that I remember was being the in the ambulance strapped to a stretcher. I looked up, and there are these two guys laughing and joking. One says to me, "Don't worry, *dearie*. We've got you figured out." I was so angry I almost couldn't control myself, but that is typical of what we have to watch out for.

When you're like me, you have always got to be on your guard that you don't get into a position that is going to get you into a jam. Like, I went downtown and picketed the recruiting center as part of the antiwar demonstration. I had decided that I was going to perform an act of civil disobedience with a group if they tried to clear us out of the road. But standing around down there, all of a sudden it hit me. If I get busted and get taken to jail, they might throw every charge in the book at me if they found out I was physically a man. I have to be more careful than anybody else that goes on a march like that. I went in the front of the parade in this particular march, carrying a banner—but that wasn't smart to do. If people were to ever find out and if it was in the papers, the reporters and the readers would zero in on the fact of what I was, and that would have blown the whole issue. Immediately, all the hard hats would go back to their favorite sayings: "Look at all those faggot queers with the long hair marching around. They got a real beauty out in front this time." People like me aren't sincere about those issues, according to them. We don't count.

It's hard for transsexuals, because you don't have many allies. I'm almost totally dependent on white, middle-class doctors to give me a fair shake. There are so few doctors that will see me, that I have to scrape to get what I want. They are in control. They told me that I have to conform to their standards or I don't get the operation.

I'm probably different from other transsexuals, but they probably think the same about themselves. One thing is that it is usually hard for transsexuals to talk about themselves, especially after the operation. I'm going to tell you a lot about myself. Talking about it opens up a lot of old wounds. I haven't had the operation, so it's a lot easier because the wounds are still in the open and I get new ones every day.

I don't think very many transsexuals have gone through three years of psychotherapy, as I have. Most phase it out after 50 sessions or so. I'm different, too, in that most transsexuals don't go to psychiatric hospitals. Why that is I don't know. Most transsexuals are also very introverted. They want to stay totally undercover, outside the public eye. They don't want to upset the apple cart. They have to keep low profiles so as to keep respectable. This is because they don't depend on each other so much as on their physicians.

Your doctor is the most important part of your life. He takes precedence over fathers and mothers, in some cases. That is the person who prescribes the hormones and may be able to help you get the operation. You've got to keep him happy. Doctors are gods to them Which is why I don't think I get along too well with some doctors, because I don't think of them or treat them like God, not anymore anyway—I think they are as fucked up in some respects as me. When you talk to another transsexual, the first thing they will talk about is what their doctor is doing for them. I don't think it's healthy or that you can be a person, if your whole life is so dependent on someone else who can cut you off any time.

I am talking about the transsexuals I know. I haven't known that many. Maybe I've met a total of 30. There aren't too many in the United States. Dr. Benjamin's book say there are 100,000, or something like that, in the United States. Maybe I should just talk for myself.

The vast majority of transsexuals try to make it in the straight world, as the gay community calls it. The reason for that is because the operation is not very well advertised. I mean, you don't see many articles in popular magazines about it, so people don't know about it. People who are transsexuals and don't know about operations are trying to live the role that society says they have to. Like myself—everybody used to say, "You have got to be a little boy." I knew I wasn't, but they said I had to. As you will read in this book, I went into the Navy to try to be. I went into submarine service trying to be. I even got married trying to be. I underwent psychotherapy, but that didn't work either. Then I heard about the operation, and that's what I have been working toward ever since.

I am presently living in purgatory. A little between heaven and hell. I am working my way upwards, slowly, but when you have to fight the whole damn system single-handed, it's hard. Usually, you look for help and people turn their backs on you. I tell them what I want, and they say, "He's really a *sick* person." They don't get it through their heads that they are the ones that have made me sick and are keeping me sick. Most transsexuals have had hassles, but they don't have the hassles over being a transsexual; they have them over the way society fucks over them. After it fucks over you, it asks, "What can we do to help?" So to help they stick you into an institution for the mentally ill that gives you more hassles. It's a cycle. When I went into the VA psychiatric ward, I was in hell. Now that I am getting hormone shots and living and working as a female, it's purgatory. Once I get the operation, although I know it's not going to be perfect, it will kind of be like heaven. I am not going to say that the operation is going to cure everything—I don't consider it a cure-all. I have a lot of hassles to clear up, just like most people. It's not going to be a cure-all, but it will sure as hell get rid of many of the pressures and tensions I am under.

The cost of the operation is twice what it would be if it weren't so controversial. You feel that you're being taken advantage of. The cost in Casablanca is about $8000, and they go between $3500 and $5000 in other places. That is not the cost of the operation—that is just the surgeon's fees. That is not counting the anesthesiologist, the operating room, the recovery time, medication, and so on. Since when does a person get over $3500 for less than a day's work? What they do is remove parts of the male organ and use part of it to build a vagina. The vagina has the nerve endings from the penis and scrotum, so there are sexual feelings.

There are two doctors in the world today who are working toward perfecting the male-to-female surgery. One is a doctor in Casablanca; the other is in Tijuana. They have their own clinics with operating suites and the whole thing. They are both expensive. You have to deposit the right amount in their Swiss bank account prior to the operation. He gets out of paying the taxes and the hassle of taking that much through customs. These are the men who are doing most of the surgical research.

There are people in the United States doing research, but it is mostly statistical or psychological. A couple of places out West did some operations and have decided to wait between 12 and 20 years to find out the results before they do any more. Johns Hopkins did a lot, but I don't think they are doing any now either. They were supposed to be doing one every three months or so. There are other places here and there that do them, but it's hard to find out for sure who's doing them.

According to Dr. Benjamin, who studied over 100 people who had the operation, only one was considered unsatisfactory. They had all made a better adjustment to life than before the operation. The one that was unsatisfactory was a medical thing, not psychological. So the operation seems pretty fool-proof. By the way, psychotherapy has never been known to "cure" a transsexual.

The reason the cost is so high is part of the old supply and demand thing. Transsexuals need one thing, the operation, and there is only a small group of doctors who will do it. If these people stick together in the price they charge, the only thing someone can do is pay their price. You can't very well boycott or picket, or stuff like that. There is no recourse but to pay it or not get it done.

People who do the operation have this informal rule, that in order to be eligible for it you have to be living as a female for two years. That includes working as a female. You also have to have a recommendation from a psychiatrist you have been seeing for two years. They say that, if you can work as a female successfully enough to make the money, then you'll make a good adjustment after the operation. It's the kind of a situation where you're so concerned about the operation that it's hard to concentrate on working—if you had the operation, you might settle down. Besides, it's almost impossible to get any kind of a job that pays enough for you to save on. The other thing is: Who is going to write you a recommendation in the first place to get a job, and what name are they going to put down, your old one or your new one? Also, what about when they ask you for your social security card and it has a man's name on it? Medicaid won't pay for it, and Blue Cross and Blue Shield get upset when you even suggest it. They consider it cosmetic surgery.

The operation is a vicious circle. I want to have the operation so bad that I am under great pressure and strain. The pressure makes it hard to find or keep a good job. The fact that you can't keep a job and that you're uptight is used as evidence that you're not sane. They tell you, "If you really wanted it, you could do it." I can see their reasoning, but I don't agree with it. I don't know what I can do about it though. They tell you getting the money is part of the therapy.

What people don't understand is that transsexuals, myself included, think of this whole operation in the same way you would think of having a wart removed, or having plastic surgery done on your nose. If you think your nose is ugly and you want it fixed, if it's bothering you, instead of worrying about it and while your head is thinking about it the way it is and all that stuff, you go out and get it fixed. That's the way I think of it, but most physician's don't. Most people are so uptight about sex in general, and about penises and vaginas, that they have to find something psychological to worry about. It's funny.

I don't know how you're taking this so far, but the majority of people hear about me and they automatically think I have problems—super head problems. Even if I don't have them, they think I'm crazy. You just try to avoid people like that. After I get to know people it works out. If I make them uptight, I leave.

People usually find out that I'm a transsexual not from me, but from my "friends." It makes me angry to have to explain it to people because, I don't know, how would you like to have to explain yourself to everyone you met? Explain how you think you're a man or a woman. Why the hell do I have to be explained? I mean to hell with the transsexualism, I'm a human being first, and female second, and a transsexual third. But people can't respond to it like that. Society doesn't want to know me as a human being. I have to be a transsexual first to do anything. It's almost, "Forget Jane Fry and let's talk about the transsexual." It's almost like when I went to get my appendix out. They were so much into looking at me as a transsexual that they didn't do anything about my appendix. When I was in the psychiatric hospitals, they concentrated so much on me being a transsexual that they weren't willing to help me with what I needed help with.

I have come to automatically distrust people because of this. I want to be accepted as a human being, and people won't do it; they make it so you can't be a human being. This combined with the operation being so hard to achieve that you have to concentrate on being a transsexual 24 hours a day instead of being a person. All your hopes ride on the operation, and that's what you keep striving for and that's what you fight for. So you think of it all the time, and people treat you like one all the time, and there you are.

It actually makes it more frustrating for me when people don't know about me before I meet them, because you have to jump over a hurdle—I have to explain more or less what I'm all about. Sometimes I blow people's minds intentionally. I get a horror or a fear reaction from people who are set in their ways, who haven't run across this kind of thing before.

Men get particularly uptight around me. They just don't know how to handle it. Some guys, the first time they see me, like all males who see a female, look at me as a female and then all of a sudden they find out; it blows their image of themselves. They say to themselves, "God, I must be queer." A lot of people seem to go through that, but I don't know what to do about it. I get along with women a lot better. They don't seem so threatened.

The biggest problem I face is dealing with society in a way that it accepts me and I can accept myself. I have done that to some extent, but I feel I'm kind of doing it the easy way by living on the fringes in the freak culture. Most of my friends are either students or hang out in the University section. People are much more open in their thinking—they don't care if you're different or not. It makes life a lot easier than if I was to try, say, to play the role of the supermiddle-class secretary that lives in the suburbs. The majority of transsexuals do that. They are superstraight. Maybe that's easy for them, dealing with it that way, but I just couldn't make it. By living on the fringe I don't have to face the head hassles they do every day. The majority of transsexuals don't have the time or energy left after fighting the hassles to understand what society is like. They are so busy trying to join in and at the same time fight it that they don't see what it's all about.

Being a transsexual, it seems like you're fighting all society and everybody in it. If you don't have psychological hang-ups after all that fighting, there is something wrong with you. I've got problems now, quite a few emotional hang-ups right now. It doesn't mean that I have to be locked up. I recognize them, but I also recognize the reason I got them. I spend half my time worrying about what society thinks, instead of worrying about me. So you have to end up with problems. Anybody can relate the emotional problems that I have now to my childhood and say that my transsexualism is the reason for it, but it's nothing about the transsexualism itself that causes hang-ups—it's fighting society.

This doctor told me that my father was a very violent man and in rejecting him I rejected masculinity and violence, so I had to be a female. I think that's bullshit. What he didn't stop to think was that I probably was a transsexual right from the beginning and I was so worried about the problems that it caused with others I didn't know how to relate to them. You get so wrapped up in your emotions that you can't relate.

I don't think my transsexualism is the direct cause of my emotional problems, but I have to let psychiatrists keep saying it is or else they won't treat me. I have got to get back on the road to getting my operation, so I have to see one. When I see a psychiatrist now, I just ignore it when they start rapping on about my transsexualism. If it gets too bad, I just won't see them anymore.

A lot of people can't even imagine the shit I go through. It's the same thing that they go through, except I go through it to a greater extent. They are forced to become one thing or the other; they have to conform to a certain set of standards, even though they don't think it fits them. With me it's just more obvious that's all. A normal guy, if he likes to cut flowers or wants to be a hairdresser or something like that, his masculinity is questioned and he has pressure on him not to do it. Or a woman who wants to drive a truck—it's the same thing. The male/female thing is just part of it. There are other roles we play too. Masks—that's what I call them. By the time a person is 20 years old you can't see the person for the masks. If someone tries to go against the masks, they are schizophrenic or something else. That's what they are called. That's what's on my medical records.

With the masks society tries to hide human sexuality. What I mean is that society has taken and stereotyped masculinity and femininity so you don't get a full and real picture of what it is. Everybody is trying to live up to the stereotype image.

It's hard to live away from the stereotype a little, but it is a thousand times harder to go away from it as radically as I have. I am doing what most people can't even think of, going from a man to a woman. My father's first comment when I told him was, "Why can't you pick an easier one, like being a homosexual?" Which makes a good point. At least if I was a homosexual, I would be the same sex, but to do something so obvious like changing dress and everything is something that you can't hide. Women who want to go to work are thought to be crazy—if a normal person wants to change roles, he has to fight a lot, but if he wants to change sex, that's a lot more.

I guess you can think of transsexualism as more or less a mask, too. Or it can be. I'm a transsexual, but people try to force me into a stereotype—they try to exaggerate the importance of what I am. It's a part of you, granted, but they make it more a part of you than it really is. I am trying not to make it that way. I'm trying not to fall into the slot, but I'm forced into it.

NOTES

1. Jane's definition of transsexualism closely parallels the one found in most modern dictionaries and those used by the professional community. Harry Benjamin, the doctor who first used the term, states, "The transsexual male or female is deeply unhappy as a member of the sex (or gender) to which he or she was assigned by the anatomical structure of the body, particularly the genitals. To avoid misunderstanding: this has nothing to do with hermaphroditism. The transsexual is physically normal (although occasionally underdeveloped) .... True transsexuals feel that they belong to the other sex, they want to be and function as members of the opposite sex ...." (*The Transsexual Phenomenon,* New York: The Julian Press, 1966, p. 13).

2

Family Album

My father was a cook in the Navy; my mother was in the Navy, too. That's how they met—it was in the service during World War II. As a matter of fact, they were married at the Naval Station on the river in Maryland. They were about 21 at the time.

He is an interesting man, very open to people and very jovial. My friends like him very much. A couple of times he came up to the Crisis Center that I worked at with a case of beer and sat around with the group and bullshitted with everybody. They said that he could speed rap better than anyone they had ever known, and it's true. He is kind of a happy-go-lucky person. He smoked grass a couple of times, too. He's about five foot eight and about 190 pounds. He kind of accepts my situation now—he didn't at first. It was hard on him because he wanted a son. The trouble he has now is remembering my name—"Jane, not John, Dad." Good old John is what he used to call me. It's hard on him. He is pretty open, but he can't stand blacks. As a matter of fact, when I use the term "black" at the house, he says, "You mean nigger," but I think that's about his only real prejudice.

My mother is a very puritanical person; not domineering, but fairly set in her ways. She had only two jobs since the Navy; one was a clerk for Anchor in the book division and the other as a sales clerk. My father has had hundreds of jobs. He never stayed on one until last year after his breakdown. It wasn't actually a breakdown, more a drinking problem. He isn't an alcoholic or anything like that; he just likes his beer. He was assigned to the psychological research department of the hospital as part of his vocational rehabilitation. He liked it so much and he did such a good job that they hired him to build rat mazes and just about everything you can think of. He is head of his department now. He is really intelligent, and he needed something to challenge him.

My mother and father used to knock themselves out trying to figure out why I am the way I am. They went through a period of blaming themselves, but now they say things like, "I don't think John wanted to play with dolls or anything when he was young—at least he never did." Mostly, they don't remember because I did things before they took notice of them, and like a lot of parents they didn't want to see it. They don't want to remember it. When they did see it, they blocked it out of their minds because they didn't want to see me as different—like a homosexual or something.

I don't think I ever saw my parents fight in my whole life. I've seen them argue, maybe two or three times, but never call each other names or anything like that. They have a philosophy of living together, which is when one of them is upset the other one doesn't bug them. It works beautifully. When my mother's nerves were uptight, my father just left her alone, and the same with my mother. It is a good relationship—I've never seen two people get along like that, with no tension between them like you can sense in other marriages.

My mother kind of smooths the water around my father and keeps things really nice around the house. My father was king of the castle, but since my mother takes care of the castle, she had quite a bit over father, but you don't ever say that, though. She sort of soothes tattered nerves, and stuff like that. She would keep him on jobs longer than he normally would have stayed. She sometimes would go along with him on things that he wanted to do but she thought weren't good, like changing jobs. She loves my father very deeply, as my father loves my mother. I've been out with my father when he makes jokes about girls that he would like to go out with, and things like that, but he wouldn't—he loves my mother too much. He would joke and egg me on, but he wouldn't do anything himself.

I identify with him in some things, and my mother in others. Both are extremely intelligent people. My mother was heading for college when the war broke out, and then she joined the Waves.

My grandfather on my mother's side was Scotch and my father is Irish, which didn't settle too well as far as family relations went. My mother said that he was really mad when a fat, red-headed Irishman married into the household. My father is mostly Irish, but we have some Swede.

I have one brother Tom and three sisters, Harmony, Sharon, and Denise. I can never remember anyone's ages so I will probably get them all wrong, but Tom and Harmony are fraternal twins and are about 25. Both are married, and both have a child. Harmony is expecting her second, or she might already have had it. Sharon is 16, and Denise is 13. By the way, I am 27. Denise is the only one in the family who doesn't know about me, but I think she suspects. That's one reason my mother and father want me to be careful around the house. They don't want me to wear makeup or obvious clothing. They say they don't want to upset Denise or her friends. Sharon knows, though. My brother and sisters think it's pretty weird. They always thought I was better off as a girl than a boy, anyway.

Harmony is living close by in Lansing, and Tom in Seneca River, at least I think it's Seneca. The two girls are living at home in Brighton (a suburb of Central City).

I don't know the facts about my brother's suicide attempt, but he tried about a year ago. He's having trouble with his marriage. I saw him once at the house awhile ago, but that was only for an hour. That's what's wrong with my family. You can't sit down and have a long talk with anybody, because something is always going on. I just hear pieces about Tom from my father. My brother's wife doesn't like my family, so she refuses to allow my brother to come over and see us. She is a very domineering type, and that upsets him. My father was very shook-up about the suicide attempt. I have tried it too. His comment to me was, "At least your brother can do a better job on it than you can." My father is really not that vulgar. He probably meant it as a joke and didn't realize what he was saying. That comment upset me, but I kept it all inside me like a person shouldn't.

I haven't seen any of my relatives since this whole thing came to the surface. Actually, I saw one, my cousin and his wife. He is a service manager in one of the cafeterias at Baker College. He accepted me; thought it was really cool; but then of course he is at least half freak.

My family is okay now—they are trying to accept things. It was hard for them to understand. I broke the news to them with a lie. I told them that there was something wrong with me physically, and let them work out the implications. After a few months I worked around to how it affects me mentally, and then worked into what it was really all about. I played it kind of by ear. I knew they couldn't stand the whole thing at once, so I tried to find the easiest way. I didn't tell them until I became a psychiatric patient at the VA.

The reason I went to the VA, according to them and according to what I told my parents, was that I was having a nervous breakdown. I told them that they examined me and found that I was not fully a male, and that in some ways it was affecting my head. There was shock, but they didn't quite understand so they wanted a full explanation. But I played the mental patient role—stupid, not understanding, and saying things like, "The doctors didn't tell me anything." After awhile I came right out and told them that I wanted to be a female, that I was a female mentally. That dropped the floor right out from under them, but at least I had prepared them a little.

When I told them they said, and I remember this distinctly, "Well, don't tell your brothers and sisters. They mustn't know." To hell with my brothers and sisters. I mean, I was in a psychiatric hospital and I wanted help—forget what everybody thinks. After they got to know a little more about what it involved, my mother comes out with things like, "Well, you're not going to come home in a dress. What would the neighbors think?" They were worried about themselves, not me. That really hurt me, but I didn't tell them. I was just very angry and ignored them and didn't write them. I did go home that Christmas, but I didn't talk to them much.

My mother cried when I told her. She said, "My son, the girl." My mother was raised in a Jewish neighborhood in Brooklyn, and when she gets excited she comes out with phrases like that. That's typical of my mother, "My son, the girl."

I was more direct with my brother and sister. I came right out and said that I want to be a girl, and that I always thought that I was one. I was relieved to tell them all. I could talk to people now; before I couldn't talk to anybody.

My second youngest sister I didn't tell until right after I got out of the VA, which was two years after I told the others. I was living on over by the University, and I asked her over for supper. My father and mother said it was okay. She was 14 or 15 then, so it was no big deal. They didn't expect me to tell her, though. When she got over, I said to her, "I might as well tell you a few things. I want to be a girl." She said, "Yeah." Just like that, "Yeah." I said, "Well, that's what I am working for—to live and work as a girl. I'm looking forward to an operation." She said that was great, and we got back to eating. I didn't bother her. Little kids are like that—nothing bothers them. They are all wrapped up in themselves at that age, I guess.

Ever since I was little I hated Christmas; it's the worst time of the year. People would give me shirts, ties, fire engines, and other masculine things. I used to destroy them. I wanted so much to be given girls' things. The Christmas after I told them, my mother and father gave me a shirt and tie, and I walked out the door. I think they got the hint—the next Christmas I got money but that even pissed me off. This Christmas they gave me money, but they put on the card, "To Jane" which is very considerate of them, considering where they came from. I don't like getting money for a present. It seems so commercial. Give me something that represents me. Something that says I am a female. There are things I need. I need a lot of clothes because I don't have much money and very few clothes, but they can't fully accept me as a female yet. I guess one time my sister gave me candles, which is a little better.

Christmas is still lousy for me though. In my own home I've got to play a role. I have to be something I am not. It's a strain on me and a strain on my parents, and I don't want to bother them anymore. Some people have said to me that I am too considerate. I don't know; that's just the way I am. I'm looking out for everybody else's troubles, and I shouldn't. I should be looking out for me as number one. I've been changing, though.

I had the best Christmas of my life while I was at the VA. When I got back after being home, some friends, a few nurses, and myself, had a Christmas party down in my room. We swapped gifts and just had a good time. Just to be accepted; it was beautiful. It was the best Christmas I ever had.

I love my mother and father and like to see them, even though it's a hassle. They do love me. Just because they can't accept this factor of my life completely, there is no reason why they should hate me. They don't. I just try to go along with them as much as I can. Although my mother used to tell me to keep it cool with the neighbors, she wouldn't be too shook-up now if I came home in a skirt and blouse.

This Christmas I wouldn't go home unless I dressed as myself. My father called me up and said, "What time do you want to come to the house?" I said, "I'm not coming home." He said, "What do you mean you're not coming home?" I said, "You heard me. I'm not coming home this Christmas." So a half-hour later my mother called back and said, "Well have you made up your mind about coming home?" I said, "Yes, I'm not coming." She said, "Why?" I said, "I just don't want to play your silly games anymore. I want to be me." She said, "I don't care what you wear, just don't be obvious." I said, "Get lost." He got on and was kind of angry. "Well, at least you can have the common courtesy not to wear a skirt and blouse." I said, "Bullshit. I'm not coming home, then." So my mother called back again and said, "Look, I don't care what you wear, as long as you come home." I said, "Okay."

The funny thing is that I went home in jeans and a pullover. The idea that they told me not to wear something is what bugged me. I wouldn't have worn anything home to embarrass them. I knew I had to play the role, but I had to get them to a point where they said, "I don't care how you come, just come. Just as long as you're there." I wouldn't embarrass them, but they embarrass me.

I was referred to as "it" this weekend. I went home for a steak dinner, and we were at the table. My mother said, "He wants more mashed potatoes." My father said, "She wants more potatoes." My sister pipes in with, "No, *it* wants more." I said, "I do." That wasn't funny to me, but things take time.

Every time I hear someone call me "him" or "it" it hurts me. It's hard to change your family's opinion over night. I never forget that I grew up with them as John Fry, and it is awful hard for them to stop thinking of me as their oldest son home from the Navy, and that kind of bullshit.

Sharon said, "it." Denise doesn't even know. She knows my name is Jane, though. Sharon told me that one time Daddy called and asked for me as Jane, Jane Fry, and then Denise asked who Jane Fry was. She told her, "Your brother," and that I had decided to change my name. That's all she knows, but I think she knows more because she is pretty swift.

I guess I feel somewhat accepted at home now. At least they don't try to treat me as a male. I don't think I will get neckties for Christmas again, which is a step up the ladder.

3

Early Memories

I don't know when it all started. As far back as I can remember, when I was four or five years old, I knew I was a female and was angry for not being built like one. At the time I didn't have the sense to say, "Why am I different?" or "How am I different?" I just knew I was different; mostly I got the feeling that I was different from people around me. Very few families in America sit down and tell their sons at a very early age that homosexuality is very bad and people who are sexually different are freaks, but it's such an ingrained thing that you learn it from snide comments and jokes that you hear. You're riding down the street with your father and you see someone walking down the street dressed differently, and he'll make comments like, "Look at that queer," and things like that. You may hear your father or mother or some men talking about it over the bar—about the queers and perverts. A lot of the jokes that you hear are about feminine men, and things like that.

On Saturday mornings one of my best excursions was going with my father in the truck to the dump to get wood for the furnace. He would stop off at a bar and we would go in, and he'd sit us down with a coke in a booth with potato chips and he would have a couple of beers and talk with the men. When you're in a bar like that, listening to them talk, it doesn't take long to know what is acceptable and what isn't. It was through a slow process that I learned what a homosexual was and that it was not acceptable. I knew I wasn't a homosexual, but I knew I was different. Before I got off on a tangent, I should start with when and where I was born and go through my life.

I was born on July 4, 1945, at 8:30 a.m. in Brooklyn, New York. We didn't live there long. We lived in Boston for a year or two, and Marple, Massachusetts, for a couple of years. And then, when I was five, we moved to Chester, New Jersey, which is where I have my first childhood memories.

The reason that we went to Chester is my father went to war—the Korean War—and we went to live with my mother's sister and family. After World War II my father stayed in the reserves, so when Korea broke out they called him back. He was in for two years. My uncle was the manager of a night club in New York City and he made fairly good money, so they had this guest house out back where we stayed. He commuted to the city. Most of the people around us were airline pilots, company executives, and people like that—very well-to-do people.

I played with my cousin, and when we got into mischief my uncle spanked me just like I was his own son. He took over as a substitute father. I spent a lot of time with my cousin. I slept in their house a lot, instead of with my mother and younger brother and sisters.

I remember visiting my grandfather, who lived close to my aunt. I used to sit on his lap, and he would give me butterscotch candies and tell me about the time he was with Teddy Roosevelt's Rough Riders. He was great. They had a big scrapbook in their house. The house was beautiful, with a big fireplace in the living room. He died right after my father came back from Korea, and we moved into his place.

My grandfather died from TB. He went to this big hospital near New York and caught pneumonia there and died. They gave us all tests and found out my four-year-old brother had it, so he went into the hospital for nine months. He had part of his lung cut out and developed complications. They also gave him an operation for his crossed eyes. They found out I had developed TB, but I had fought it off or it enclosed itself.

After we lived there for awhile we moved to a different house close by. My father kept his same job, which was driving the school bus and being a mechanic. That was when my mother got her first job for *Anchor* and that's when we went to parochial school. My father is Catholic and my mother Protestant. Neither of them practiced, but my father thought it would be good for our morals. That's also where I have some of my sharpest childhood memories. That's also where I used to get into fights.

It was living there that I first remembered wanting to be a girl. There were other boys around to play with if I had wanted to, but there were some girls that lived down the road that I would walk to play with. I felt that I should be a girl instead of a boy. I mentioned it to those kids, and they teased me about it. I found out quickly that you shouldn't mention it. I remember the girls fairly vividly, but not enough to tell you their names. Half of them were bigger than me, because I remember having to look up at them. I was a short kid, rather skinny at first, and then that one summer I became quite fat—just over the summer.

It was at this house that I first dressed in my sister's clothes. We used to play house, and I played the mother. It was during this time that my father had a mental breakdown. He wasn't right for six months and spent a couple of weeks in the hospital. It wasn't in the psychiatric ward though. I remember him coming home, and I was very glad to see him. He was very much thinner. Before he went in he just loafed around the house and used to get angry for no reason. He was a domineering person, anyway. My memory during this time is kind of jumbled, but there are some parts that are supervivid, like him coming home.

I remember that my father used to beat us. He was every bit a physical man. If he was mad at one of us kids, he belted us—usually not hard, but sometimes hard depending on what you did wrong. I think it was good. I don't have any super traumas about him hitting us. I just don't consider him a bad person. I was kind of afraid of him—especially through the period when he had the breakdown.

I remember that was the house that I broke my arm in. My father was playing horsey with me, and he reared and I fell backwards. So I had a cast on my arm. My sister used to pull some dirty tricks on me, like egg me on to swiping pies and emptying perfume bottles, and then we would get in trouble.

The only actual rules in our house were about table manners. I used to get rapped across the knuckles for reaching across the table. We used to have a lot of fun at the table, though. My father used to joke by taking what everybody said literally. If he was in a joking mood, you had to be careful of your speech. One time my mother said, "Toss me a roll," and he did. We would get in trouble if we did that. He would say to me things like, "What did you do at school today?" I'd say, "I went to gym", and he would say, "Jim who?" and I'd say, "You know." He would say, "Jim You Know? Never met him." Then the conversation would just go on like that.

I used to spend a lot of time outside. We used to ride with my father on the school bus—get up at 5:00 a.m. to get the bus out by 6:00 a.m., and then get to school by 8:30. It was lots of fun.

After school I went home and was kind of the babysitter, since my mother was working. Actually, there was a woman next door who kept an eye on us, but I kind of babysat and did things around the house until my mother got home—like starting dinner. I remember I used to send my brother and sisters next door to play with the woman's kids, and I would put on an apron and play house—pretending I was the mother. A few times I went up and got one of my sister's dresses and put it on just to see how it would feel and what I would look like. It's a wonder I never got caught, because my father would come home once in awhile early without notice. I remember my sister and me surprising my mother by cooking cookies that turned out wrong, and going down to the basement and cracking nuts with a hammer so they were smashed apart.

It was kind of nice with our family having a little money because of the two salaries. I did the normal running away a couple of times. I'd get into arguments with my mother and tell her I was going to run away, and then I would go across the road and hide in the tree.

I kind of stayed away from people as I got a little older. I had a bicycle, and I used to go to the library and get science fiction books and read them. I also joined the Cub Scouts. I joined the Cub Scouts because I thought that if I couldn't lick them I'd join them.

In the Cub Scouts we used to sit around and make diddly things. I got my Webelo badge, and all that stuff. I was a real goodie Cub Scout. I think the only reason they gave me badges was that I was consistent—I always came to meetings. There were only two things that I used to do outside the house—ride my bike to the library and go to those meetings.

There are two incidents that stand out in my mind about this time. There was a back road off the main highway that went past my house. It was dirt, and I was sitting off to the side of it one day playing with a doll of my sister's. My father went by and bitched me out because I was acting like a baby playing with a doll. The other thing that stands out is out in back of our house there was a large dollhouse that was all handmade with a roof that lifted up on hinges. It was like a real house, with concrete walls. My brother and sister were allowed to play in it, but I got yelled at because I was playing in the dollhouse. This one time I got so mad I busted it all up—the furniture and the wooden roof. I got a real good spanking, which I deserved, but I thought they deserved something, too, because I couldn't play in the dollhouse.

There was another event like the ones I just told you about, only it happened a little later. It was at a Christmas party at school, and they were handing out gifts. I got a big red truck. This is around when I was nine years old. The thing that hurt the most was that a girl said as she gave it to me, "Here is something to play with the *boys* with." I remember running out of the school and throwing the truck into a creek that ran nearby.

To this day my father and mother say that they didn't see anything wrong with me at that time. By wrong, I mean feminine acting or anything like that. They just never saw me acting that way, or they just didn't relate things that I did to being feminine. I remember being very conscious of the differences between males and females, and of the different roles they had to play. I was very conscious of the games I had to play to deceive people about me being feminine. I felt that I was a girl then, but who do you talk to about that? You just don't come right out and tell people.

I started getting beat up everyday on my way home from school. My father saw a couple of those fights, but he didn't stop them—he figured it was best for me to settle my own battles, which I wasn't very good at. Kids taunted me, teased me, and called me names; they pushed me around. When I got the chance, I would run from them, but they would chase me and yell things like "sissy" and "little girl." One of the first times it happened was in the schoolyard. I used to play with the girls before school and during recess. I played hopscotch and jump rope. I used to swing one of the ropes, because I wasn't a very good jumper. The play yard wasn't marked off for boys and girls, but all the girls used to play in this one corner. So this one time it was time to line up to go into school and I was standing there talking to a girl who was in line. I just wound up in the girls' line, and that's when the boys started yelling at me. I went over to the boys' line, crying, which made them tease me more. It got so that I dreaded going to school. I used to come down with all these illnesses that I made up so I wouldn't have to go.

I played with girls before this, but I was never teased about it. I was physically a little shorter than most kids my age. I had put on weight, so I was dumpy, but I couldn't defend myself, and I would cry a lot. I never won any fights and never had any friends.

There was one kid in school who kind of liked me. His father was a judge, and we went up to his backyard playground which had all kinds of swings and rocks in it and things. I remember once the kids were really tormenting me, and he butted in and took my side and got into a fight over me. We became friends, but I didn't see him that often—maybe four times I went to his house. I kind of stayed away because I was afraid. The house was so big and they were rich, and we weren't poor then but we didn't have anything like he had.

When we first moved to Chester, I could play with girls, but it started to get toward that time when girls got uptight having a boy around. I think it was in the fourth or fifth grade. The girls didn't tease me—they just wouldn't let me get close to them. I kind of got afraid of most people and stayed by myself. I read science fiction—I was reading at a tenth grade level when I was in the fourth grade.

I always did poorly in school, or at least my report cards were lousy. The main reason I did poorly is that I couldn't hack the people. It wasn't that I wasn't smart—I just couldn't function in the school system. The nuns used to rap you on the knuckles with a ruler. They wore this black habit with a razor strop going down the side, which I was on the receiving end of a couple of times.

It used to frustrate the nuns to no end that I couldn't spell. When I first went to school, they taught phonetic spelling, and when I went to Catholic school, they did it the other way. Instead of them trying to sit down and straighten me out, they belted me. When it was time for me to go into the third grade, they said that I couldn't do the work. So they put me back in the second, and I stayed one year behind all through school.

The thing that used to really get my father mad when I went to that school was my report cards. He hit me in the face a couple of times because of this one card. I remember that distinctly because I had a black eye and a cauli-flower ear. I went to school the next day, and the nuns said, "Oh, what happened?" I told them that I fell down a flight of stairs. They didn't give a damn to stop and find out what the hell was going on—they didn't give a damn.

The only fear I had of my father was in relation to my school work. He was not the kind of person that got angry over anything—just specific things. When I brought my report card and tests home, I was afraid. The 25's in spelling used to make him the angriest—and I had those for three or four years running. There were notes put on the back to the effect of, "John is a bright student, but lazy." Now if that wouldn't piss off a father, I don't know what would. It seemed like a giant conspiracy between the nuns and the Almighty to get me in trouble with my father. I always knew my father loved me. I had no doubts about that. The only bone between me and him was my school work; otherwise, we got along perfectly.

I was baptized on June 4, 1954, and received my First Holy Communion June 17, 1954. I used to freak the sisters out because I would get 90 and 100 in my religion exams, while getting 25 on my spelling. That's why they said I was lazy on my report card. I could always see what they wanted on the religion tests. I knew what they wanted me to say, and I would give the nuns what they wanted. I could make four paragraphs out of what could be said in a sentence, and it used to tickle them pink. I was going to be an altar boy, and all that. I would have been, too, if it weren't for my poor grades on everything else.

There was one nice nun in the school. She wasn't my teacher: she was my brother's and sister's. My brother and sister are twins, and even though he lost a year of school because of the TB, they put them back together. They were so inseparable that my sister refused to work without her brother in the class. The teacher was Sister Mary something. She was a big woman—I don't know—I just liked her whenever I saw her. I don't remember any of my teachers, thank God, but I can picture the classroom. It was off a corridor and we had open top desks. There was a platform up in the front of the room with the teacher's desk on it. There were blackboards behind the desk, and a cru-cifix right in the middle. There weren't any windows, and it used to get so hot in there. It's funny how I remember it. I used to sit, coming in from the back, two rows over on the left about three seats from the rear. That was *my* seat. I remember every Friday we used to have spelling tests.

I was in that school for three years, and the teasing went on all through that time. It is very vivid in my mind—it just kind of pops out in my thoughts. My brothers and sisters could fight like demons, but they didn't protect me. I was the oldest son, so I was supposed to protect them. I used to get into fights with my brother and sister. I could handle one at a time but they were always together, and when someone picked on one, the other one would clobber them from the back. That's the way they worked—they would have made a beautiful tag team. The fights were always just brother-and sister kinds of fights. They never seriously teased me or beat me, or anything like that.

Mostly rich kids went to the school, and although we were in pretty good shape financially at the time, I felt kind of poor in relation to the others. That was one reason that I didn't keep up my relationship with the judge's son. They had this big house on the top of the hill, with a maid and a cook.

It makes me angry at this point to look back on my schooling, because I think the only ones who could have done anything for me—the nuns— wouldn't do anything. I don't know what they could have done, but perhaps try to help me a little bit so I would have been a better student, They could have given me some individual attention and tried to find out what was bothering me. If they could have looked into the kids tormenting me, maybe they could have figured out what was in back of it. They might have tried to get me out of what I was doing, which was withdrawing to the privacy of my house to get away from people.

Society is funny—first people put you in a position to make you withdraw, and then people get angry because you are withdrawing. That getting angry with you builds a higher wall between you and the society. The person who is pushed out has a tough time seeing what is happening. That's what was happening to me at this point. I was being tormented by the kids for being feminine so I withdrew, but the more I tried to withdraw the odder I became, and the more they tormented me the more I withdrew. An eight-year-old kid doesn't have the knowledge to understand what is happening to him—why he does what he does. Somebody might have pointed it out to me, and that might have helped. Well anyway, these are my first feelings of being pushed out of society.

CHAPTER

4

Coming of Age

We left Chester in 1956 and moved to Watershire, Vermont, I remember before we moved my parents talking about it and me looking forward to going. We had made visits there a couple of times to my grandfather's, who owned some land. Summers we used to drive up, which was a treat in itself because we use to stop at Howard Johnson's and have fried clam dinners. They used to get the adult size for me, because the kid's size wouldn't fill me. I liked the idea of going to Vermont. I didn't have anything worthwhile to stay in New Jersey for—no friends or anything. It just seemed fine with me. I thought by moving I would make some friends and maybe meet some people who would understand me. I thought that maybe I wouldn't have the hassles I had been having. That was wrong in some respects, but in some ways it was better. I learned to hide my feelings and to put up a front and to stay away from people. I started a whole lot of habits of ways of protecting myself and watching out for other people and being superself-conscious of how people reacted to me. I developed a kind of tactics for self-preservation.

When we moved, my father was broke and the family was somewhat destitute. That was new to me then, but it got to be more familiar as I got older. We went to Catholic Charities to get some help—my mother and father didn't want it for them, just for us kids until my father could get a job. They just turned him down bluntly. My aunt Bell, who is really my grandfather's second wife, was an officer in the Salvation Army, so we figured we'd hit them up. They had a pretty big operation in Watershire, and my father had grown up there so he knew most of the officers. They helped us out, and we became Salvationists for awhile. We started going to church, and all that stuff. My mother went to church services, but my father never really practiced. It was my sister who really got into it heavy—almost gave up Catholicism completely. She joined the Girl Guards, which is equivalent to the Salvation Army Girl Scouts. My brother learned to play the bugle, but he never could play for anything. I just trucked along with the whole thing. I was put in a play there. As a matter of fact, I was made a woman in that play. Every Halloween as far back as I can remember, I dressed as a female. That was more or less my own doing, but in the play they chose me to be a woman.

Bell was a very devout Salvationist, and she used to go out all dressed up with her tamborine and collect money, and stuff. She didn't approve of drinking and smoking, which my grandfather liked to do. She wouldn't let him keep his beer in the refrigerator, so he had to put it down in the cellar. I never heard him swear around her; she just wouldn't put up with anything like that. Every once in awhile he would give it to her, but it was always very calm and controlled. She kind of accepted my father, who is her stepson, like she accepted my grandfather. She doesn't try to convert either of them, because she knows it's useless. She gave up trying to convert me, too, a long time ago. When I was about 13, I told her I was an agnostic and not to bother me with her religion. My mother and father went through the roof.

In Watershire we lived in a lot of different places. When we first arrived, we lived in this cabin that didn't have any cooking or anything. We ate at my grandfather's most of the time, but I found out how to cook in hub caps. I remember cooking hamburgers in hub caps and then scouring them out in the river. We had a Studebaker—the ones that looked like they had two fronts. We were there for my birthday, I remember, but we didn't stay long. We moved into a house in East Watershire and stayed there for a few months. Nothing sticks out in my mind about that place, except I remember going down to a park and there was a baseball game going on. I thought that I would play, and the kids made fun of me because I didn't know how to play well. There was a lot in back of the house, and I went there and played games by myself.

Then we moved to School Street, which is where I met Jimmy. I was at White Park, and there was this kid who came up to me and started bad-mouthing me, like kids that age do—I was bad-mouthing him too. In fact, we even pushed and shoved each other's chest, like kids do. I was very uptight because I thought I was getting into another fight, but I didn't. He started walking home, and I did too, and we were walking the same way. I told him that he was following me and he said I was following him, and I came to find out he lived right behind me. That's how I got involved with Jimmy, and we became close friends.

I started school in the fall; I had only a year of grade school to go. Things worked out fairly well, even though I still did lousy. Jimmy and I joined the Boy Scouts together, and I continued to go to the library and read science fiction. I used to take out 10 to 15 books a week. I kind of stayed away from everybody except Jimmy. I was a loner, and in some respects he was, too. He had friends, but we just stayed together a lot. We were always together. Summertimes he used to go to Cape Cod. One summer he took me along. We would go down for two weeks, and then come home for one and then go back down. It was fun playing on the wharves and in the sand dunes and swimming in the ocean.

We were philosophers, Jimmy and myself. We used to have long talks about the system and how we should change it. I remember sitting on the back porch or in the fort we built in the apple tree, rapping about what we would do if we got a lot of money and how we would change the system. We knew about socialism and communism and all the "isms", and we just used to talk. This was when we were only in the sixth grade, which is kind of phenomenal. The majority of the kids at the school were well-to-to, and Jimmy and me were broke most of the time because we both came from fairly poor families. We used to get frustrated with the rich kids, and that's what we talked a lot about. We were only about 11, and we were talking about dividing up the wealth.

My early years in Watershire were really nice. I have some very happy memories of going out bike riding and going to the quarries. I had never had a friend before this, and I could at least relate to one person, whereas before I didn't have anybody. I couldn't tell Jimmy everything, but at least I could tell him some things about me—stuff like what I wanted to be and that I wanted to go to college. I remember I wanted to be a mathematician at that time, which probably blew my teacher's mind. I always used to come up with big words like that, which were hard to pronounce. I was about four or five years ahead of my class in reading skills.

I was involved with one other person besides Jimmy; it wasn't for long, and I think it was right before junior high school. He was a boy that was superfeminine and didn't mind showing it. For some reason I can't remember his name, but he was going to a special clinic up at the hospital—it was a child psychology clinic or something like that. I used to go with him and sit around the waiting room until he got through. We used to go to his mother's house and have dinner and go down in his basement, and he would show me the projects he was working on—sewing and things like that. I thought that was really great, but everybody kept knocking me because I was hanging around with him. My folks even started to get down on me because I was with this person who was "sick." He wasn't that sick. His mother and father were divorced, and I spent a lot of time at his house. His mother invited me out with them to concerts and stuff like that. I saw the opera for the first time, and I went to hear the symphony play for the first time. It was my first really good experience with classical music, although I had heard records before. I really enjoyed it.

They used to rib him a lot, and they started ribbing me when I was around him. They called me "fairy," "faggot," and "queer." I still was seeing Jimmy during this time. My mother told me that she didn't want me hanging around with this person at all, and Jimmy said that I had better cool it or I would get into trouble. Certain things are acceptable, and others aren't. I tried to weasel out of the relationship. I stopped seeing him, but I feel very bad about it.

Jimmy was my first childhood love—I was very much infatuated with him. It was kind of puppy love. There were lots of things we did together, like swim in the quarries and go up to the mental hospital and steal apples. I never came out and told Jimmy about it, even though we were close. It's a wonder that I concealed it the way I did, but I did. Funny, when I used to think about Jimmy, I wanted to marry him. It was kind of like Schroeder and Lucy in *Peanuts*. He is married now and has two or three kids; he works for the telephone company. Funny how you change. I was going to marry him when I grew up—that was my life's dream. I never told him that, of course. I was feeling very angry with myself, because I couldn't tell Jimmy because I didn't want to lose him as a friend. He was so close a friend and I could talk to him about so many other things, that I was afraid he would have rejected me. Looking back on it now, I know he wouldn't have.

In the early years the knowledge that I was not a female, although I felt like one and wanted to be one, was with me, but I didn't dwell on it then as I do now. I wasn't so wrapped up in it, like I became later. When I was 10 and 11, it was important and I thought about it, but it wasn't all that important. It was like in the back of my mind all the time, but it didn't interfere with my everyday activities.

I forget the name of it right now, but there was this huge mental hospital right near town. It had a beautiful orchard, and Jimmy and I used to go up there and steal apples and run from the guards. It was close to our houses, and we used to go in the first building and down through this tunnel on our way to school, unscrewing the light bulbs as we went. In many ways I was just an ordinary kid. We used to go there in the summer and climb trees and watch the people. There was this one old man who used to mow the lawn and talk to the mower. We used to giggle, but he never saw us. Now, I'm embarrassed that I did a thing like that, but we were just kids. The patients weren't allowed to make friends with the people who weren't patients. We were told to stay away a couple of times, but that didn't bother us. Some of the patients made more sense than the grown-ups we had to hang around with.

Things were different at home, because my mother didn't work most of the time. Quite a few times my father was out of work, too. I didn't have very much of a relationship with my family then. My mother and father never rode herd on me. I never had rules, like being in at such and such a time. Around the time of junior high, my father just said, "You're old enough now. Let us know where you are." I mean, if I did something way out of line, he would let me know about it, but a lot was left up to my own judgment. He would correct my judgment at times, but it was my judgment—one of the things he taught me was to be responsible for myself. I just was kind of like a boarder there. My sister by that time was old enough to do the housework and take on other household responsibilities, which left me out. Denise was born around then, and Harmony took care of the baby. I had to be a little boy—not a little boy—I had to be a man by that time.

Most of the time we were in Vermont we were poor, but we never gave the impression to the outside of being poor. We always gave the impression of being lower middle class, but we were outright poor. We were even on welfare a few times, but we always ate good. You can really eat good on surplus food if you know what you're doing. My mother was always a good, immaculate housekeeper, even though there were the kids running around. We were on and off welfare. My father would have good jobs, and then he wouldn't have any. He could learn a job 10 times faster than anybody else, but instead of being recognized and being promoted, he had to wait because of the seniority system. It used to frustrate him, and he would quit. He had one job where he worked his way up from a sweeper to night plant manager. They wanted to promote him into sales, and then they found out he didn't have a high school diploma and they didn't, so he quit. He was there about six months. He had about five different jobs the four years we lived there.

I remember people were good to us when we were in real bad financial trouble. They brought food and stuff over. This black guy that my father knew, who raised dogs, came over a week before Christmas and brought a turkey and all the goodies for his Christmas present to the family. I have met some really great people in my time. That is why I close my mind when I find a bad person. People really have to rub my nose in it before I see the bad. That's why I am so gullible—because the people I grew up with were really nice.

In spite of the money situation, it was nice. We usually went on picnics on Sundays. Most of the childhood that I like to remember was in Watershire—

the summers, especially with the mountains and the quarries. I liked riding through the woods on my bicycle and swimming with Jimmy. I was never around my grandparents that much. I felt close to my grandfather, and there were times when we would go out walking in the woods across timberland that he owned. He was a very calm person, and nothing blew his mind. If anything bothered him, he would take a walk.

When I was in Vermont, I went to Rickland Junior High School which was a progressive school run by a state teachers' college in cooperation with the city. Other universities were in on it too, and it was really great. Like, I had to take shop, but I didn't mind it because part of the shop was shop math. I liked the way they taught things. They had courses in logic and in psychology. The teachers were fantastic. We got into good discussions and took up computer languages in math. I got to understand math real well, but I never could do the drudge work. The courses really opened my head to school. My grades were good there, and I liked it.

It was my own positive school experience. The people were more open than in any school I had been in. I felt close to this one teacher who was my math teacher. He would sit up on top of his desk like Buddha—with his legs crossed—and throw erasers at the students that were sleeping. The way he taught was the same way you would learn in college. There was dialogue, rather than just going over multiplication tables and things like that. It was really interesting. Some of the English was even good. We would listen to music, and then they asked you to write a composition about it.

One thing that I did at the school was play soccer. Three foreign students that were part of an exchange program played along with us, which made it interesting. We weren't in a league or anything like that—it was more-or-less a group of people getting together after school. I really liked soccer, but it's been so long now that I don't even think I could dribble. I didn't like sports, except for that and swimming.

I used to swim in junior high school and was getting pretty good. I even swam competitively in the free style and under water. I could go double the length of an Olympic pool under water. I swam in city competitions, but never outside of it. I even won some ribbons. I don't know if I still have them or not. I was a good swimmer. I learned almost before I could walk.

After I had been swimming for awhile I saw a sign in the swimming pool saying that they were going to hold precision swimming classes for anybody who was interested. At the first meeting about 30 girls showed up, and me. I started taking lessons, and they began putting a team together. I was good, just as good as the girls, as a matter of fact, better than most. I made the first team, until they went for exhibition, and then they put somebody else in my place. They told me that the team had to be all girls to compete. That bothered me. I kind of dropped it and went on my merry way. Boys aren't sup-posed to be free-form swimmers.

During the time I was in junior high I withdrew and wasn't anybody's friend except Jimmy's. I didn't go to parties, or anything like that. As a matter of fact, I have never been to a birthday party that I can remember. I had never been to a regular party until after I got out of the VA Hospital.

I took up the bad habit of smoking in junior high. I was just horsing around with cigarettes, learning to inhale. I told my father that I wanted to smoke, and he also found a pack, which made it obvious. He said, "Look, I don't mind if you smoke, but don't do it in front of me and buy your own." So I got a part-time job working at White Park. There was a big pond and there was skating, so I worked renting skates and selling food and hot chocolate.

Things started happening about the time I was beginning junior high. I re-member this one thing vividly. I was walking past the hospital on my way from school, and I had these real peculiar sensations in my breast. After that I had them for about two months, and then I started to get real heavy on top. It just hit me: "Jesus, my breasts are developing. What the hell is going on?" I desperately wanted it to continue, but then I didn't want to be made fun of and become a freak. Right after that started happening I was starting puberty, and hair was starting to come out around my genital area. When changing for gym, I noticed that I was different from any of the other boys. I was depressed, but I was glad at the same time. I was developing a female hair pattern instead of a male pubic pattern. There was also no hair on my arms, or legs, and none on my chest, or other parts of me. Some of the kids started shaving, and I wasn't anywhere near shaving. I started getting very self-conscious about my body and would wear my gym clothes underneath my street clothes to school so that I wouldn't have to dress in front of everybody. They used to mock me because of the size of my genital area, which was a little bit ab-normal on the small side. Too much was adding up in my head, and I was get-ting uptight, but I was kind of glad about it. I didn't want to develop the characteristics of a man. I didn't want to have anything to do with shaving. You know how some kids practice shaving when they are little? I never did.

This was a definite time of a swing in my life. I started to become aware of boys sexually, too. The girls started dressing differently than they did before—they started becoming more feminine. I felt like going that way too, and all of a sudden I felt that I had so much to cover up. It was like a mad dash mentally to keep covering things up. I remember standing out in front of the school with groups of kids. I would want to stand over with the girls and to get in with what was going on with them—to talk about things—but I couldn't. They wouldn't let me join them, because they considered me a boy and someone to take them out on dates. I didn't want to be in with the guys, because I knew I didn't have anything in common with them. I was looking on them sexually, and they were thinking of me as one of the boys. I was left hanging in the middle, and for a while I even swung away from Jimmy and stayed totally by myself.

It was at about this time we moved from School Street to Hanover Street, which wasn't too far away. During this time I was just hanging on for dear life. I used to go to bed and cry sometimes, because of wanting so much to say something to someone and not being able to. I knew that no one would accept me.

I remember the gym teacher used to make fun of me because I wasn't as strong as everybody else. And they would yell at me for wearing my clothes to school, but I just refused not to. There were times that I even broke down in tears. I didn't want to go out on the gym floor and play with the silly basketballs, but they used to say, "Get out with the basketball." I wished they would have banned me from gym, but they didn't.

I knew about sex when I was in junior high. Jimmy and I used to look at dirty pictures, or at least what were called dirty pictures. They were retouched French photographs, with the photography being terrible. Jimmy's father had brought them back from World War II from France. There was a whole album of them, and Jimmy gave me a couple of books to take home. He said that his father wouldn't miss them. I took them home and put them in my pillow case. My mother found them, and my father called me in and sat me down and said, "Your mother found these." He was lying in bed and I was sitting on the edge saying "Yep," expecting the worst. All he said was, "I think it is about time you read this book on sex." So he gave me this book and said, "If you have any questions, let me know. Don't think you know everything, because you don't. You're at the age when you are going to start experimenting. Use a little common sense. I have rubbers in the top drawer underneath my underwear. Just don't bring home a pregnant girl." That was the farthest thing from my mind. I hadn't even dated a girl, and he knew it. I did go out with a girl once while I was in junior high, and my parents paid for it. It was my first date. All I did was take her to the movies and back. I was more interested in the movie than I was in her.

I just didn't want anything to do with girls romantically. I wanted the girls as friends, but they didn't want me as a friend so I was just totally hung up right in the middle. I didn't want to get sexually involved with boys, but I wanted them to recognize me for what I was—a girl. I had these feelings, and I knew they weren't right. I didn't think of them as homosexual feelings. It just didn't cross my mind that I was a homosexual. I never really considered that until I was in the Navy.

I dressed in girls' clothes as much as I could during this time, but that wasn't too often. I did in my own room with my sister's clothes, and when I got older with my mother's. I wore them just to see how I would look, and I associated clothing with sexuality. I used to get mad because I didn't have long hair and because I couldn't wear makeup when the other girls started to. I used to get upset because I couldn't go to school as myself. My voice started to change—get deeper—which used to bother me. It was a very weird time in my life. I wanted to be around Jimmy, but I was afraid to tell him. It used to upset me when he used to talk about girls that he went out on dates with. I was feeling jealous, because I couldn't be the girl. It was traumatic, and I cried quite a bit. I was jealous because he was going out with a girl and wouldn't recognize me—that I was a girl too. Even though I felt like a girl, I wasn't built like one and it bothered me. It was like being two separate people, one that was inside me trapped and the eternal one that I couldn't change. My mind said that I was one thing, and my body said that I was another. I was torn—on the one hand I was trying to keep up the front, and on the other hand I wanted to satisfy my inner needs.

Generally, life got less and less happy for me in Watershire. It used to frustrate me when I would see girls in the school doing all the things that I wanted to do, like going to cooking class. When I got older, I used to get more and more embarrassed having to dress in the boys' room. I wanted to talk about it, but I knew people would get mad at me.

When I was with the boys, I used to make up wild stories about my sexual encounters, and stuff like that. This was in the last part of junior high—the ninth grade. I would say that out of 10 kids perhaps one had had some kind of sexual experience, but 8 out of the 10 would say that they had. I lied and told them about mine. I did that during high school too. I just made up stories as I went along.

I had what society would consider homosexual relations once during this time. I kind of fooled around with Jimmy, but that wasn't anything like rela- tions. The one time was right before I left Watershire, and I was forced into it by a guy I knew and my family knew very well. One day he picked me up on the way to school and told me to skip that day. He had a car and was out of school. So I went along with it—everything to amaze a 15 year old. He forced me into it after we got all the way into the country. He told me that I either did it or get out. I had oral sex with him, but I couldn't take it—I just didn't like it. Basically, I was forced into it. He held the first time over me and said that he would tell my parents what I did if I didn't do it again. This happened for two or three other times, and finally I got wise and thought, "Well, if he tells my parents, he is going to get in more trouble than I am," which I told him. He didn't bother me after that, but I haven't had oral sex since then.

I came out of puberty hurt and angry—angry at society and angry at myself—and not understanding myself. I couldn't understand why I had these feelings, and why I thought the things I thought, and why I couldn't control my feelings. On top of it all, Jimmy started going with my sister right before we left Vermont. That really upset me. He was always kind of attached to her, and that used to frustrate me to no end. As a matter of fact, I caught them making out, which really pissed me off.

CHAPTER

5

High School

It was toward the end of the ninth grade that we moved to Central City. Moving was kind of a spur-of-the-moment thing. My father was out of work and thought there were more opportunities there. It was like getting away to get a new start. The whole idea of coming to Central came overnight. A good friend of the family who had moved there came back to Vermont and visited my father and talked to him. The next morning we packed a truck and moved. I didn't even get a chance to say goodbye to Jimmy. When we got to Central, we had no place to live or anything, so we stayed with someone for a week until we found a house to rent. It was the spring, and there was only two months left of junior high school.

The first year in Central my father worked for the Salvation Army driving a truck. He made fairly good money. There were men who the Salvation Army was trying to rehabilitate—they kind of worked for my father. They were paid according to how much stuff they brought back to the shop—so much a pound for papers, so much for a refrigerator, dresses, and so on. My father was always a good hustler, so we had a livable salary coming in, at least.

The first school I went to in Central was Maner Junior High. Like most kids, I called it a jail. I ran into a lot of snags in school. One thing was I wasn't used to living in large cities with such large ethnic populations. We had blacks in Vermont, but they weren't like the blacks I ran into here. Like there was Billy Beacon's father in Watershire, who owned the biggest rug cleaning

53

business in town. There were tough Italians in Central too. They tried to hit me up for protection, but I refused to pay. There was this one gang that used to hit everybody up; the majority of them were Italian. It was one of the first times I stood up for myself. They came up to me asking for money, and I just walked away. It caught them off guard, because they thought I would run or stand there and fight. This one kid ran and jumped on my back. He hit me so hard and he was so heavy that I bent right over. He didn't have a tight hold on my neck, so he went right over the top of me and landed on his back in the middle of the street. It must have looked good, because nobody bothered me after that. I didn't make any friends but took a job selling newspapers downtown on a street corner for awhile. I stayed home most of the time, or went around on my own.

After that I went to Brian High, which kind of dates me. In my year it was all greasers—kids with their hair swept back, wearing pegged jeans and leather jackets with chains. The big thing was to go outside for a cigarette and lean against the building with one foot on the wall, like Marlon Brando. The way I felt about that school is that it should have burnt down a long time ago. It was built around 1800, and it should have been condemned along with the attitude of most of the people that worked there.

When I moved to Central, I had never had algebra, because in Vermont my school was in the zone for modern math so they taught the equivalent of algebra, but it wasn't called that. When I got to Central, I asked to be put in an algebra class. There was two months left to the year—two months before I would complete the ninth grade. They wouldn't let me into it because it wasn't on my record, and they put me in business math instead. I had never had business math in my life and I didn't want to take it, but they insisted. So I took it.

Come the start of the tenth grade they wanted to put me in advanced business math. They told me that I had done so well last year that I should be in it this year. In Central, at that time, you had to buy your own school books, so I refused to buy the book. I figured that if they wanted me to be in business so bad they could buy them. I told them that I had had all these advanced math courses in Vermont, but it wouldn't sink in. It was outside their system, therefore they couldn't follow it; they didn't have the time to check. Sitting in the vice principal's office got to be a habit with me after awhile. Every time I showed up in business math without my book, they would send me down to the office, and he would lecture me on buying books.

The people in the school used to get very upset with me being feminine. They never said anything outright, but I could tell by the reaction I was getting, especially with the vice principal. For example, just for looks' sake I asked a girl to go to a dance with me once. I wanted to go to a high school dance, because I had never gone. This was in the tenth grade, and I asked a senior. I liked her—she was a nice kid. Our lockers were right next to each other. Of course she turned me down. I knew she would, but I didn't feel like going with the dimwits that were in my class. Somehow it got back to my teacher and the vice principal. One day when I was in his office, he mentioned to me that he had heard that I asked a girl out for a date. He said it very jokingly—like, "Isn't that funny you asking someone out?" I said to myself, "Fuck you, buddy," and just ignored him. I tried to ignore him and most of my teachers most of the time.

Actually, girls like to be around me, and a few actually asked me out. I guess it was because I didn't threaten them sexually. There was one girl that wasn't actually my girlfriend, but it looked that way. The whole relationship was for looks more than anything—if I had a girl to be around, the others would think I was normal and not bother me. I used to go over this girl's house about three times a week and never get home until one or two in the morning. That really looked good to the guys in the neighborhood. All I would do was sit there and play canasta with her and her mother—her mother liked me because I was a good influence on her daughter. People thought we were going steady, but we weren't. I don't know if her mother suspected that I was different. Looking back on it now, I think that perhaps she might have known.

This girl wasn't even going to Brian High. I met her when she came to see someone who lived in the neighborhood. I enjoyed her company. I really liked people, but I was staying totally away from boys if I could help it. I was very unhappy playing role games. I was tired of trying to be the big he-man. I felt then that I wanted them to accept me as a female, and I knew they couldn't or wouldn't and that used to make me very unhappy, so I just used to stay away from them.

School, that was really something. Like biology—I'd ask questions and you weren't supposed to ask questions. This one instructor, Mr. Ackerman, died, and this teacher right out of college took over. I didn't like her. She'd be explaining the different species, and I would ask things like, "How do you categorize the species that come in between major species, like the platypus?" She would get all frustrated and say I shouldn't ask irrelevant questions. It was basically lectures, and if you opened your mouth you got in trouble. I was one of these people that always questioned everything, so I got in trouble.

The only course I used to be great in was social studies. We had this teacher who was great, but he used to get into trouble for how he taught. He was controversial because he had tapes of the Senate hearings on prisoners of war in the Korean conflict and why they went to China afterwards. They were turncoats; we had two weeks of discussion on the turncoat controversy. It was really great listening to that—we got along swell. I used to stay after class all the time and talk to him. He didn't mind anybody being inquisitive. Most of the others just put you down.

School was a real bummer. It totally turned me off. After being in such a progressive and open school in Vermont, all of a sudden I was faced with a very strict procedure. I developed a running feud with that biology teacher. I never handed in my biology experiments. I was getting 50's in biology, and she was happy about that. The only homework we had was the experiments, so just before the state exam she said to me, "You can't take the exam unless you hand in your experiments." She didn't realize that I had them all done, and that I just didn't hand them in. I said, "Okay." The tests were the next day or the day after. I gave them to her, all 15 of them, neatly typed, with full-page drawings—the whole bit. I sat down and took the exam and got 96 on it. That totally pissed her off; boy, was she mad. If I wanted to, I could do stuff. I happen to be very stubborn when I am angry. I was frustrated with the school, and the only way I knew how to get my aggressions out was by doing things like that.

Most of the teachers were set in their ways of thinking, you know, "You think my way or don't think at all"—it was like programming a bunch of animals. That is the way I still think of it. I felt I had to disagree. That's part of education, and these people didn't seem to feel so. When a teacher told me something, I would ask them to prove it. If they couldn't, then I wouldn't accept the thing. Most of the times they just blew up.

After awhile I said, "The hell with it." It was getting so frustrating. After my second week in high school, I didn't crack a book. I stayed totally out of all sports and copped out of gym whenever possible. I also skipped a lot of classes; I was a habitual skipper, matter of fact.

I had one interview with a school counselor. He was supposed to see all the students and determine their educational goals. He thought because I was doing so well in business math and that my mechanic aptitude, as shown on a test he gave me, was so good that I would be a good truck driver. The first thing he asked me was what my father did, and I told him, a truck driver. He decided that I should be a truck driver. I told him I wanted to take the college prep course, and he told me there was no need to go to college. He actually talked me out of going to college. It was totally absurd. It's like they were trying to program me for something I didn't want to be. They didn't understand me, in the first place. Nobody bothered to sit down and ask me what I had before or what I wanted or what I knew. They gave me two tests, sat down with me for 15 minutes, and told me what I was going to be and what I was going to take, and that was it. I guess that's all they can do when each kid gets allotted 15 minutes. When I started to argue with him, he actually told me my 15 minutes were up. I told him to get fucked, and I was sent to the principal's office.

I spent more time in the principal's office and skipping than I did in class. According to my schedule, I was supposed to go to business math every day. But when I would show up, my teacher would look up and say, "Fry, do you have your book?" and I would say, "Nope." She would send me down to the principal's office and the vice principal would say, "Do you have your book today? Did you buy it yet?" I would say, "Nope," and he would tell me to sit down. I would take out a book and ignore everybody. That is the way I spent my business math classes, sitting in the principal's office. They got frustrated with me. They used to send letters to my parents, but they never came to school. They were both working, and they didn't get home until 5:30 so they couldn't make it.

I failed gym in high school, because of so many absences, for one thing. I used to wear my clothes under my street clothes. The school was so old it didn't have showers, so I didn't have to dress and undress in front of anyone, but I still didn't like it. They had a football team, and things like that, but I ignored everything to do with sports. The time I spent in school was mainly at the library. I would sit there and read. The librarian and I got along well. I would have her order special books from the city library. I read psychology textbooks, but I also got into science fiction. I spent a lot of time daydreaming about being a girl—wishing I could be myself, wishing I could be allowed to be myself to the fullest in other ways, too. In most classes I felt restrained. I lost interest in almost everything.

I used to bring my lunch to school and sit with the girls. After lunch I would go out for a cigarette. People used to get uptight about me eating with the girls. They didn't talk to me very much—kind of ignored me. It was better than sitting with the guys though—I would much rather be ignored than harrassed.

It was right after I moved to Central that I first went out and bought women's clothes and wore them. I had worn clothes before, but I had taken them from my mother or sister and put them on and then put them back. These were my own. I kept them hidden down in the basement of our house. There was one bedroom that I was supposed to share with my brother, and another for my sisters. To be alone, I fixed up a room down in the cellar, which made it a lot better. I kind of partitioned off a section. That's where I slept and wore the clothes when nobody else was in the house.

There wasn't really a decision on my part to do it when it happened the first time. It was more a question of when I would do it rather than if I would do it. It's like something that was always there. It was a drive in me wanting to express myself that led me to it. It's like a compulsion. It's a compulsion to be yourself, which was expressed in my dressing.

I must have been 16 when I first did it. I mostly bought underclothes, because they were the most feminine. I would dress downstairs and look at

myself in the mirror. It made me feel good to see myself like that, but I was always filled with guilt and fear of getting caught. I wore the underpants in
public, but I didn't buy them to do that. It wasn't until after I got them that I
thought of them as being the only things I could wear without people
knowing. Even though I knew they couldn't be seen, I felt very self-conscious.
I felt people could look straight through me. It took a hell of a lot of nerve for
me to do that. I was so into hiding everything about me that even doing something like that was just too much for me to handle. So you can imagine what it
took to totally give up my masculine way of life.

During this period I remember experimenting buying different-sized bras.
It blew my mind because I found one to fit me, and little boys weren't supposed to fill out bras. I never wore bras under my normal street clothes,
though. I tried once or twice to put a shirt over one, but everything showed so
I figured there was no way to wear it outside. It was summer, and I would
have looked pretty ridiculous walking downtown in a heavy jacket.

I dressed at home often. Let's put it this way, I dressed as often as I could.
"Could" meant that every member of the family had to be out of the house,
and I had to be sure that they weren't coming right back. I was supercareful
about it. I never got anywhere near getting caught.

My father would drop back to the house if his route was in the neighborhood, so I had to watch for him. He would stop for a drink of water or a beer.
My mother was more regular, so I didn't have to worry about her. My mother
would write me excuses for not going to school so I could stay at home a lot,
which gave me a chance to do it. Mostly, when I stayed home I watched TV
and read.

At the end of the tenth grade I finished all my subjects and passed them except english and gym. I had to repeat the english. I went to summer school
and found it very enjoyable, for the simple reason that the teacher they had
was nice. She would have us do things like write poetry. She told me that my
poetry was really fantastic. I wrote this one poem about Vermont that I took
home to my mother—she thought it was great. The teacher gave me some real
positive feedback on it. She told me that she didn't like it personally but it was
a very good poem. I got an "A" on the poem.

I remember having a fight right before I started the eleventh grade; it was
the summer. Kids knew I wouldn't fight them, so they used to tease me. This
one kid got me up in the park and started calling me names and pushing me.
He had these three girls with him that he was trying to impress. I don't remember specifically what he said, but he started shoving me and pushing. I
usually didn't fight back, but I was quite a bit heavier than him so I did. I
grabbed him and dumped him on the ground and sat on him and hit him in
the mouth. He kind of mellowed and started telling me that what I had done

was unfair. He said we were supposed to box. That's how naive I was. I listened to him and got up, and he left off and belted me in the mouth and I went off crying, running down the hill at McCarthy Park.

Finally, the eleventh grade rolled around, and it wasn't much different from the tenth, including the math. It was the end of September when the principal called me into his office and said, "If you don't buy books next week, I am going to throw you out of school." I said, "You can't throw me out, because you can take this goddamn school and shove it up your ass." I walked out and quit. That's exactly what I told him, too.

The principal thought I was a wise guy. As a matter of fact, he used to say to me, "What are you? A wise guy?" I wasn't a wise guy. I just wanted to get a decent education.

CHAPTER

6

At War With the Navy

I joined the Navy Reserves the day after my seventeenth birthday, July 5, 1962, the summer before I left school. As I told you, my mother and father had been in the Navy, so I was keeping up the tradition. I mentioned to my father that I was thinking about doing it, and he picked it up as a very positive thing and drove me over to sign me up. I didn't tell him that I really wasn't sure that I wanted to. I was very ambivalent about the whole situation, but I figured it would give me some prestige in the neighborhood; maybe it would make a man out of me. I hoped that people wouldn't tease me as much if they saw me in uniform. I went to reserve meetings that summer, but felt very out of place and very awkward.

After I quit school, I sat around the house for a week before I got around to telling my father what had happened. He was pissed off and right away started harping on me to get a job or to do something. It was my father's idea that I call the reserves and ask to go on active duty. I was apprehensive about that, but there wasn't really all that much else to do, so I called them. I was told to go down to the regular recruiter, and if I was accepted by them they would discharge me from the reserves. They did accept me, and I also got a battery of tests. These were aptitude tests which I passed really high. I said to them, " I don't want to be just an ordinary sailor. I'd like to get in nuclear engineering if I could." The Navy was becoming very nuclear at the time, and it sounded like something that I might be interested in. Nuclear engineering technician—it sounded great. They said, "Sure," and I joined.

I'm not sure how I passed the physical. The only thing I could figure out was that they weren't looking for things like this, and, anyway, it wasn't superobvious at this stage. I was fat—190 pounds. I was developed in the chest for a guy, but it could be written off as fat. It was like you couldn't tell where the rolls of fat left off and my chest started.

So off to war—my war with the Navy—let's put it that way. My father was very proud of me, and before I left he took me out to get me drunk for the first time. We went to a little bar on the north side. I was only 17 at the time, but the bartender was the only one who knew it and he was a friend of my father's. The men who went there were all ex-20-year soldiers, sailors, and recruiting sergeants who were on duty in Syracuse. My father dragged me in and said, "Yeah, my son's going into the service." He was really tickled pink. One of the guys said, "Do you want a drink?" I said, "Yes, a beer please." I had had beer before and liked it. He said, "No, not that shit. Have some Old Grandad." I took it, and when he asked what I wanted for a chaser I said, "I don't want any chaser." I was really feeling good. I belted down nine of those things and couldn't walk. My mother was so pissed off because my father had taken me out and gotten me drunk.

The next day he was supposed to take me to the train. I didn't have any money to my name, so he was going to borrow some to give me to take. He got up too late to get the money, but he saw me to the station. I saw tears in his eyes. I never had seen that fellow cry before. It was really someting. I was a big boy now. He cried even though he wanted me to be in the Navy.

The Navy and I got along pretty well. I was in boot camp at the Midwest Naval Training Center. They had ranks in boot camp like commander, lieutenant, and petty officer. I actually thought they might make me a petty officer because I was a reservist before I went in, but they never did. I guess they felt that I would not be a good leader of men. I thought I had the ability to do it, and I wanted to. Boot camp wasn't all that bad. You don't have the physical regimentation in the Navy that you do in the Army. No obstacle courses and stuff like that. You did have to run everywhere, and you did a lot of marching. I happen to be superuncordinated, so I was put at the tail end of my company all the time. I was still pretty heavy.

It seemed like I was always being chewed out for being the most uncoordinated member of the whole group. I didn't know my right hand from my left when I went in, and I can't say I got all that much better. We had the manual of arms, which I still can't do well. It took me quite a while to get that. I was always being put on extra duty for messing up some place along the line. I used to have to go and do special drill, which was mainly pushups, so when I got to chow in the evening it was the tail end of the food.

There was quite a bit of unhappiness in the Navy, even though I liked it. The unhappiness was related to my feelings about being a female and the fact that I was made fun of for being femine looking. The Navy was supposed to make a man out of me, but it made me nervous to be with all those men. At this point I thought I had no choice; either I adjusted to being a man, or there wasn't anything else. Up until I went to the VA I didn't know there were alternatives. The way I feel now, there is no way I could live as a man and not be totally neurotic or psychotic, but at that point I was trying to play that role.

The men in the Navy treated me like a "fairy." I think almost every company has their "fairy;" the one that people take things out on. The whole service was making me uptight. You see, you couldn't be around females for one thing, and at this point, even though I knew I couldn't be a female, I much preferred female company. The swearing got to me, too. They were constantly swearing. I didn't like them talking about all the girls they had screwed, and stuff like that. I knew most of it wasn't true—all of the bragging. I couldn't bring myself to brag about something that wasn't true. I was branded as a "queer" and a "cherry" and everything like that. They would make comments like, "Don't drop the soap when he's in the shower." I got fun poked at me constantly. They didn't come right out and say, "You look feminine," or anything like that. If you're a guy and you look feminine, you're automatically considered "queer." You are not feminine looking, but a "queer." Nobody inquired—it was just taken for granted that I was a "queer."

That one expression, "Don't drop the soap," stayed with me all through the service. People used to goose me wherever I went, too. After awhile I was just a ball of nerves. I didn't know what was coming off. I had never hung around homosexuals; I didn't know how to react to these circumstances. I was neither a man nor a woman of the world, so I didn't know what was coming off. As a matter of fact, half the time I didn't even know what their jokes meant, which was embarrassing. I had never had this brought up to me so obviously before. I'd always stayed away from people, and now all of a sudden I was into living with a bunch of people that I just couldn't handle.

There were times when I would really long to be on the outside and be a female. This would happen on Sunday when I read the papers and saw advertisements with women in them. It was like the sense of wanting to be a female became sharper because of the loss of opportunity to be with them, if that makes sense. There was no opportunity to dress as a woman at camp, either. You have locker searches all the time.

The Navy is big on making you the cleanest person possible. I remember not wanting to take showers with everybody else because of being self-conscious. I used to go by myself—wait until everybody else was through. Most of the men took their showers when they got up in the morning. I used to take mine before I went to bed.

While in boot camp, I went to see a psychiatrist at the suggestion of my company commander. I don't know what brought me to his attention, but I was getting ridden a lot, and I was considered an oddball generally. One time I told him that I was getting uptight with all the regimentation. I didn't know what to tell the psychiatrist. Everybody in boot camp bitches about rules and regulations and all that. That was getting to me, but not half as much as the other stuff. I saw him for about 15 minutes or a half-hour and told him the rules were bothering me. I certainly wasn't going to tell him that I thought I was a female. I'd get bounced out of the service so fast it wouldn't be funny; and it wouldn't be an honorable discharge, but a homosexual discharge which is the worst kind. When I told him I didn't like all the regulations, he said, "Well, even outside there is regimentation—you have to stop for stoplights, don't you? There are rules and regulations everywhere you go. There is no getting away from them." That was his mentality. I couldn't bring myself to tell him more. He never made a diagnosis, and he never put it in my record that I saw him. There was no reason to see a psychiatrist—that's what he told my company commander. I had had psychological tests before I went in the service, and I also had some before I went into the submarines, which we will get to. They didn't want any nuts on those boats. Passing those tests were never any problem for me, which is another reason the commander was told I was all right.

Funny thing happened when I was at boot camp. I had a gun droppped on my head. That's a very interesting story. One of the times when we were drilling early in the morning we went back to the barracks, only we were having inspection, which meant we couldn't go inside. We all sat on the staircase and leaned our guns against the bannister. I was on the first floor. I had had double duty that night. I sat the midnight to four watch. Usually it is split in half, 12 to 2 and 2 to 4, but I had messed up the day before so I had to do both duties. I was tired, so I laid down, put my coat under my head, pulled my watch cap over my face, and started to go to sleep. Some idiot on the third deck, they were three stories high, had his gun laying up against the bannister, and as he stretched his legs he pushed the bottom out and it went down the stairwell and hit me right smack in the forehead. I immediately screamed and blacked out. Everybody thought I was faking. When I came to, I couldn't move. I could hear everybody going on, though. I remember somebody said, "Princess is fucking around again."

All of a sudden the blood started caking through my watch cap, and they got fairly upset. They went in and got the company commander. He came in and pulled up my watch cap and went outside and threw up. I was hit right between the eyes. There are a lot of blood vessels there, and of course it was bleeding profusely. There was blood coming out of my ears, nose, and mouth, but it had pooled inside my eyes and it looked like both my eyeballs had burst, which is why he had thrown up. Most of the men just took off. They called the ambulance, and the ambulance driver slapped me on the face and said, "Are you all right?" and washed it off and made me stand up and walked me to the ambulance, which was totally asinine.

They pulled up in front of the infirmary—didn't even take me in. I walked in on my own, and they drove off. There was this chief sitting there, and he said, "My God, what the fuck happened to you?" No paper or anything did I have with me, and I could hardly talk. I told him what happened and he called the duty doctor. He took a look at me and stitched my forehead up and sent me back on duty. No x-rays, no nothing. I was lucky; the doctor had just gotten through his residency as a plastic surgeon, and he did a beautiful job sewing me up. You can hardly see the scar now. He took something like 20 stitches or more on my forehead. They did a damn good job fixing me up, but the thing that pissed me off is that in any head injury they take a head x-ray. They didn't—not even a neurological examination to find out if I had a concussion or anything. From my reaction afterwards I did have a concussion. He said, "Go back to the barracks and lay down." I went back to the barracks, and I couldn't even walk; I couldn't walk a straight line. I fell over twice.

I went back and laid down. One of the chiefs came through and chewed me out for staying in bed. I told him the doctor said to. He said he didn't give a fuck what the doctor said—"Go back to your class." So back to my class I went—come to find out everybody thought I'd died. They were fairly glad to see me. After that accident I didn't have to march at all, because I couldn't. For awhile I couldn't focus, and that is when I started having seizures. I'd be walking along, and all of a sudden I'd black right out. To this day they keep telling me that the seizures are psychosmatic. It's really funny—I never had the seizures before that; I had them afterwards.

Toward the end of boot camp, around the twentieth of December, we went home for Xmas—15-day leave for Christmas. I shocked the hell out of my mother coming in. My eyes also started to cross after that and I couldn't see, so they gave me glasses and they put a patch over one eye so it would strengthen the other eye. I had this big bandage on my head. My mother had never seen me in glasses. It was something. A patch on my eye and this big bandage, and she comes to the front door and I said, "Hi." They were amazed at my haircut, too. It was a regular boot camp haircut, about one-eighth inch long.

I looked totally ridiculous, but I felt kind of proud because I was in uniform and I thought people were looking up to me for the first time. It was kind of an ego trip—I was very much on an ego trip. Other people responded to that trip, which was really nice. They did things for me; they showed me some respect. I felt very proud that I had gone through all the bullshit and passed. I felt good that time home. I felt that perhaps I could succeed as a man. I didn't see any other course. I never thought of the Navy in terms of whether I could or couldn't make it as a male—it was always in terms of "I have to make it." Even though I was having this feeling, I still was having fantasies and nightmares about my gender.

So people were responding to me as a person in uniform, and it made me feel good. All of a sudden they were showing me some respect, and that bullshit. It made me feel more accepted—that was my whole trip, trying to be accepted. I never could quite make it.

I heard jokes about stuff in the Navy and told some when I was home. My mother got shook-up because I was swearing like a trooper. "Fuck" was every other word at boot camp. I came home trying not to swear a lot. I didn't like to, but you had to do it in camp, otherwise you'd get knocked around. If you deviate from what they considered normal, you were in trouble. At home I made one mistake. We were all at the dinner table and I said, "Pass the fuckin' butter." My mother just about died. My father gave me a glance as if to say "Don't do that.". My parents gave me an ID bracelet watch that Christmas.

I went back to boot camp and graduated. Nobody from home came to graduation. I would have liked somebody—I mean after putting up with all that bullshit for 12 weeks and finally getting through. It was near Chicago. I would have liked for them to come, but I was a realist and knew they couldn't.

I was glad boot camp was over with. I felt I had completed something—like graduation from high school or college. There was a feeling of completion—even if you don't enjoy something like high school you still are glad at the end of it.

I went to Hawaii from there. You can pick your assignment after boot camp, more or less. If you want to go to school, you have some choice where you go, that is, if you have a high school diploma which I didn't have. You can pick the ocean you want to be on, anyway. I remember flying out of Chicago, heading toward Hawaii, leaning back and dreaming about being a female. I was a member of the United States Navy.

Hawaii was beautiful. It was very relaxed, very warm and sunshiny, and very easy going. The duty I had was nice. It was at the motion picture exchange. I had to inspect and rewind films. When they show films on ships, they don't rewind them like you do at school. We did that. We inspected them by hand, too. My hours were regular—nine to five.

Every eight days I had duty, which meant I had to sleep at the motion picture exchange, which was kind of nice because we had two refrigerators and a hot plate for our use. We did a lot of scrounging and supplied ourselves with a whole kitchen. If someone wanted a special movie, we would get it for them.

In exchange, they would get us stuff like a big whole baloney or fresh bread. I actually liked to have duty. Some of the men asked me to take it for them, and I did. Some even paid me. You could stay up as late as you wanted. You could at your own barracks, too, but there you didn't have to contend with anybody else. Also, I had 5000 movies I could watch. I used to show myself five and six movies a night. I would lay down on the couch and relax, and set the changer for automatic and use three projectors. All you had to do was push a button to click from one to the other. We had first-run films, too. I would be by myself on duty most of the time. I'd go out and make myself a sandwich and put my feet up. I liked being alone—away from the men.

I worked with the same people that I roomed with in Hawaii, which was tough because you could never get away from them. I lived in a four-man room with bunk beds. We arranged the rooms the way we wanted, so we had the big high lockers between the beds which were kind of catty-cornered. It's hard to explain, but we fixed it so you had a tiny alcove to yourself, kind of. At least you had some privacy, but not very much.

I went to Waikiki and tried to learn how to surf. Wiped myself right off a coral reef one time and almost got killed. I was very self-conscious in a bathing suit, so I didn't go swimming that much. We had a pool on the base, and you really didn't have to leave if you didn't want to, but I used to go on the island almost every weekend. When I was off base, I more or less walked around by myself. I used to sign up for guided tours and stuff, seeing that we got them for nothing.

I left boot camp thinking I had myself pretty much under control about hiding my wishes to be a female. About a week after I was out I began wondering if I could be a success in keeping up the mask. Dreaming of being a female became my constant fantasy. It was less so in boot camp, because I didn't have time. You were either sleeping or trying to get to a place where you could sleep. You were so much involved in getting through that you didn't have time to even fantasize about anything, except on Sundays when you read the papers. After I got to Hawaii I realized that nothing had changed. I hadn't beat the problem. I wasn't friendly with the others. They rode me, too. I ignored the way the others acted as much as I could and tried to pay no attention to what they said about me being "queer" and other things.

I dreamt a lot about being a female. When I was on duty in the motion picture exchange, watching the movies, I related to the female more than to the male actors. I mean, as you watch movies you put yourself in the actor's place. Well, I was always putting myself in the female's place. It became very noticeable in my own head.

While in Hawaii I went through a short period, two or three days, wondering whether I was a homosexual or not. I had two or three of these periods when I was in the service. The femininity was starting to bother me—my dreams and the films—and I started asking myself if I was a homosexual or not. I just came to the attitude—"No I'm not." I didn't have any sexual relationships in the Navy up to this point. I wasn't so much fascinated with men, I mean, physically attracted to them. I was wanting to be a female, to be a woman, not so much to go to bed with a man, although that was a part of it. It's not so much wanting sexual relations as it is wanting social relations. I don't think of sex that much even now. The hormone treatments I'm taking cut back my appetite. I don't really get horny, or anything like that. The thing that goes through my head now and started then was, "Why can't people treat me as what I am—a woman? Why do I have to be something that I'm not?" In Hawaii I would, as I do now, get angry with people. This would be triggered by males talking about females in front of me. I really start hurting when that happens. I'd say, "Why can't they treat me that way. I'm the same." It was like a slap in the face. I wanted people to respond to me as a female, so I could respond to them as I wanted.

I was only in Hawaii for about two and one-half months when this kind of like a psychic thing happened to me. I had this strange feeling that I had to go home on a certain date. I applied for my high school equivalency test and passed. I did rather well on it—up in the ninetieth percentile. With that under my belt I applied for diesel mechanic school. You see, after I got in the service they told me there was no such thing as a nuclear power technician as such. That was the reason I joined. It was in boot camp when I found that out. I broke right down and cried. My hopes and dreams went—poof—right out of the window. Diesel school was the closest thing to it, so I applied. When you change duty stations you get a 15-day leave, so that's how I got home.

I left Hawaii and got home at 2:00 a.m. My mother was going to have a gall bladder operation at 10:00. Really psychic—freaked me out. We got to the hospital just in time to see my mother being prepared for the operation. She was surprised to see me. Nobody wanted to say anything about her going—they didn't want me to worry, so nobody wrote about it. I don't remember too much about that leave.

One thing that I did was to go over to Brian High. My old class was still in school, and I had my diploma. It pissed them off. I showed a couple of teachers my diploma from the University of Hawaii—a couple of the ones that told me I couldn't make it. I remember showing them a picture I had had taken of me in Hawaii, too. I still carry it around with me. If you ever saw it and could see me now, it would blow your mind; me in uniform and everything. I had something printed on the back of the picture—a saying. I used to think about it when times got rough. It comes from Alcoholics Anonymous. "God, grant me the serenity to accept the things I cannot change, the courage to change the things I can, and the wisdom to know the difference." I knew that I couldn't change then, but it's very appropriate now when I am changing. What is possible has changed.

I don't know why I carry the picture with me now. There is a lot of sentimental value to it. My mother has a big 8 × 12 of it at home with parts painted in—Hawaii green in the background. It's really funny. I don't think of it as really me. I think of it as another person that I like very much, but who is no longer around. There are a lot of qualities that he had that I happened to have liked and admired. It's funny—you become a split personality. I don't have any other pictures of myself in the Navy. I didn't like to have pictures taken.

The diesel school was in Erieville, Michigan—that's where I had my boot camp, too. The school was good; it was a challenge and I came out ninth in a class of 30. I was good at the book part of it, but the practical application, I was lousy. I used to blow everybody's mind with how clumsy I was. I still can't even handle a wrench. We learned a lot of stuff—mostly it was in a classroom. We learned about diesels, how they worked, gasoline engines, transmissions, generators, electronics, hydraulics, air conditioning, refrigeration, turbines, and that's about it.

I slept a lot there. I was tired all the time; I didn't talk to the others, and I just stayed totally to myself. Some of the others would ask me questions about the work, but I never felt part of the class. After class I just ate dinner, walked around the bay, went to the library, read for awhile, and then went back to the barracks and went to sleep. I never did my homework. It was easier to stay away from people there than it was in Hawaii. I didn't even try to make it with them.

I kept thinking about being a woman. I wanted to wear women's clothes like I had before, because I associated dressing like a woman with being a woman. While I was there I did buy a pair of underpants. I stashed them under a bush and kept them only two days. I worried about getting caught, so I kept them about five miles from the base. I went and got them twice and walked into the woods, where I changed. I felt very self-conscious. I walked around, but I ran right back and changed. I thought that I might get caught, so I ripped them up and threw them away.

One day in 1963, while I was becoming a diesel engineering mechanic, I got a weekend pass and went to Milwaukee by myself. I went to the USO club and then went to a place and had a few drinks, which is unusual for me. I was feeling the drinks and was more daring that I usually am. I walked around the streets. At that time I was usually very covert about my feminine feelings, very uptight about buying clothes or anything. The stores were open, and I wanted to buy a bathing suit because I wanted to go swimming. I got it in my head that I had to buy a girl's bathing suit. I was compulsive about it. I wanted female clothes and a female bathing suit. If I had them, I could look at myself in the mirror and see a female instead of seeing a male. I kept fighting off the impulse—I knew I had to be a man. I finally got myself together enough to say, "No—there is no way to do it. That would be supercool." If anybody finds out, you're going to get booted right out of the service—an undesirable discharge—and everything else thrown at you. I said to myself, "There is no way in hell that you can be a girl."

It made me feel extremely guilty to dress and to want to dress. I said to myself, "You know you can't be a girl, so why go through all this?" In my head this guilt and the fear of being caught were synonomous. The whole idea of it was very dirty in my mind, and bad, and therefore I was a bad person. Society felt the same way, so that it was bad according to society and bad according to me.

I walked back and forth outside the bathing suit store three or four times and then walked around the corner to get away from temptation. There was a tattoo parlor there. I said to myself, "I'll fix it so I'll never be able to wear a woman's bathing suit." I went in, sat down, pointed to a tatoo, and said, "I want this one." It looked just like my father's. Talk about being patriotic; it was an eagle and an anchor about four inches high and two inches wide, and I told him to put it on my upper right arm.

At first I was kind of glad about the tattoo, because I felt that I could never be a female. After awhile I started degrading the tattoo, especially when I got out of the service in 1964. At first it made me feel more acceptable in some respects. It was taking a step in forcing myself to be something and to get approval from others. It more or less reinforced my masculinity. In the barracks they thought it was great—a beautiful tattoo. It was really good looking; one of the best I've ever seen, as a matter of fact. It was perfectly clear, and all the colors were bright. He did a beautiful job on it. It was a hell of a compliment to him having to have it taken off.

After diesel school I went to submarine school in Newson, Massachusetts. I was going to become a submariner. I had this thing that if I was going to do something I was going to do the best. I thought submarines were the best. I also liked the idea of the submarines because I'm very uncomfortable in large, open places. I'm more comfortable in closed, confined places. I was really tickled pink when I was accepted. Going into the submarines was also my way of getting into nuclear power school. You see, I found out that if you get into a regular submarine program like I was in, and then you're in the subs for six months, you can ask to be transferred to nuclear subs. You could then apply for nuclear power school, which is really something. They send you to school for two years—Bainbridge, Maryland, and North Dakota. You get the equivalent of a college education for two years. They take you as a high school graduate and take you all the way almost the the equivalent of a four-year science major. I never made it past three months submarine duty, though.

I went through the submarine school. I enjoyed the school—it was something I really liked—being part of an elite. I enjoyed being respected. I also liked being able to work to my full capacity. As a matter of fact, there were things there at the school that were very hard to do. I wanted to be really good, and so I gave it my all.

I got out of the submarine school and was assigned to a river boat at the home base. It was the submarine USS Fish SS 123. Submarines were always called boats. She was converted from a fleet type to a guppie class. Remember the old war movies with subs, with the guns and all that? She was that before she was converted. All the upper decks were taken right off, and she was cut in half and a new bow added. She was a good boat. We did some cruising and diving off Newson. We also used to take new students out.

I was there about three months. You normally lived in the barracks; you didn't stay on the boat, unless you had duty. On weekends I was going off on leaves. I told you that while I was in Hawaii I began thinking that maybe I was a homosexual—well, this happened a few other times. Once was when I was home on a 15-day leave. It was during the state fair time, and there was a guy who I went to work for at the fair to make some extra money. The guy ran the rides. He was gay, and I didn't know it. He propositioned me, and I took him up on it but I couldn't do it. I went with him, but I couldn't do it. It just totally turned me off. The whole experience turned me off. I just couldn't take it, because he was relating to me as a guy. It is the same anytime I tried to have sex with anybody—I couldn't do it. I wanted to be related to as a female. It wasn't that I was afraid of being gay. As a matter of fact, I remember saying to myself, "Jesus Christ, I wish I was gay. It would be a hell of a lot easier." But I just knew I wasn't. It's like you know what sex you are; I know I'm a woman.

Thinking I was a homosexual never lasted very long. Maybe it was more of a wish than a thought, now that I think back on it. In the Navy I knew people who were totally homosexuals, but I stayed away from them. I didn't want to be associated with them. I was having enough trouble convincing people that I wasn't homosexual without hanging around with people who were known to be.

I have only had one homosexual relationship that was slightly fulfilling. That was when I was in the submarines. That one encounter lasted for some time, in fact. It wasn't quite homosexual. The guy was a homosexual—I guess a bi-sexual—and he thought of me as a female and treated me as such. That's the only way I can possibly go to bed with a person and enjoy it. Well, anyway, he picked me up around Providence while I was hitchiking. He owned his own home. He invited me to his place for coffee. I said, "What the hell—yes." So I went for coffee, and he propositioned me. I opened up to him a little and told him a little about myself—that I felt like a female, not a male.

It was the first person I ever told. I saw him for approximately three weekends and then stayed totally away from him after one experience.

He treated me differently. It's hard to explain. He treated me as a female. He was the first person to ever do that. It's more or less how a person accepts you. It's like something you know. You know people accept you as a male, even though you don't think about it. He opened doors for me, and things, but it was more than that. I had sexual relations with him twice. I had weekend passes, so I stayed at his house. I could be myself. I dressed as a female. I bought the clothes in a store in Providence. It was the first time in front of anyone. I had bought clothes before this, a couple of times, in Newson, but I was going through what you might call the purging stage. I would rip them up and throw them out to try to force myself to stay as a male.

I usually avoided talking about what I'm saying to you now, especially with psychiatrists. People misinterpret what this was about. According to society, if you perform a homosexual act, you're a homosexual. They don't take into account how you perform that act—as a male or as a female, or where your head is at. That's the easiest way to put it—they don't take into account what you're thinking about when you do it. Like the only way I could think of having sexual relations with a guy is as a female. The only way I could do it would be to let him know how I felt and how I wanted to be treated. Like this guy in Providence—he treated me as a female. I didn't think of what I was doing as a homosexual, but you probably will.

The third time I went down to see him all the clothes that I had kept there were all moved around. I asked him what happened, and he made a very big joke about it. He said, "Oh, I had some friends over and we were masquerading." I actually got sick and told him to bug off. He was actually masquerading with other homosexuals in my clothes. Then it kind of hit me—totally turned my stomach. I just couldn't dream of something like that. It angered me—it repulsed me. I kind of got the hint that something like that was coming, so I shouldn't have been so surprised. The second time I saw him he had changed some. He referred to me as being gay and referred to me as "he" a couple of times. The first time he always called me a woman's name. I didn't want to be involved with him anymore. Then this thing happened, and it blew my mind. I was going to tell him we could write and I didn't want to be involved, but after this happened I didn't even want to see him. I was looking for somebody to support me. Somebody I could more or less lean on and confide in when times got rough I could have stayed in that relationship if it was the way it was the first time. I might have even gotten out of the Navy. I knew I could have, anytime, by just telling them about what I was feeling.

That affair, although disastrous in ways, made me feel even more that I wanted to live as a woman. About a month after that, close to the end of my stay in Newson, I bought some clothes and got on a train and went to New York City for a weekend. While I was in New York, I went down into the street dressed as a woman. It was just something that I wanted to do. It was the first time ever in public.

I didn't really plan it when I first started, but like after I got going, I planned. Some time during the week I decided to buy some clothes. I knew I had a weekend pass coming up, and I thought about going to New York. Friday I got off work about noon. They let us off early. I went to town and went into different shops fairly easily. I didn't pace up and down or anything. I was nervous and uptight, but I didn't want to be so self-conscious as to walk up and down in front of the stores. I gave the people in the store the spiel that I was buying something for my sister or my mother. I didn't buy all the things in one store—it was about three different ones. I had a wig, too. I got it through a mail order before the Providence thing. It was the only item I took with me when I left that guy. When I ordered it, I had it sent to a post office box in Newson. I'd seen the advertisement in the back of a men's catalogue. I remember the place I bought it from—Fredericks of Hollywood. I think the magazine was *Stag,* or something like that. They are always floating around the Navy bases. The ad read, "Buy something for your girl friend," that kind of thing. When I bought it, I had the plan of dressing in the back of my mind. I didn't dare try it on until the weekend in Providence. I kept it in a locker in the train station.

I took the train to New York and got a hotel room at the Warrenton—kind of a middle-class place. I went to the hotel room, dressed, and sat around for awhile. This trip to New York wasn't any big thing to me. It's not anything very important in my life, because nothing really happened. When I got to the hotel, I sat in my room quite a long time. As a matter of fact, I hardly left. I got to New York around 8:30 at night, got to the hotel about 9:00, and didn't leave the room until about 1:00. I dressed and just sat around watching TV. I couldn't bring myself to go out. Finally, I walked out and went to the elevator. I .didn't meet any people. I walked across the lobby and just walked outside the door onto the street and said, "Damn," out loud, like I had forgotten something. I was so petrified I turned around and went back into the hotel room and changed. When I got back to my room, I was so glad to close the door behind me. The sweat was just rolling off me. I just couldn't fathom doing it—it was really weird. I was just too frightened; I couldn't do it. I went back to Newson and left the clothes and the wig at the hotel.

While in the submarines we went off for cruises. Some really funny things happened on those cruises. One thing was I dropped a banana cream pie on my chief's head. They put me on as mess cook because I was a good cook. It was like KP, only there was a little more to it. I learned to cook at home the

Navy way, so I could help out a lot. I was a good mess cook, except for a couple of screw-ups. I was coming down the aft battery hatch, bringing pies on a big metal sheet. I was on a ladder balancing the tray on my head kind of, and holding my back against the tube. The chief was walking under me, and the pie came right down and hit him on top of the head. He called me every name in the book—he really had a fit. I was standing there laughing—I couldn't help it. Nobody else was laughing, but they did afterwards. Another time I was coming down the aft battery hatch, and it was winter time. I grabbed hold of a hatch to shut it. In order to shut it you had to put one hand on the rim and grab the wheel with the other hand. This was because it was spring-loaded. I was trying to pull the hatch shut, and my feet were full of ice. They slipped off the rung, so I slipped with one hand hanging onto the rim. I was just hanging there. I started to scream, and what else could you do but let go. I dropped and landed on an officer. They were very upset with me—very upset. After that I was considered very clumsy, which I was. I was totally uncoordinated. I'm about the most uncoordinated person going. This is why I can't even dance. They transferred me to the engine room; they figured I couldn't harm anybody there.

Shortly after I went to New York we went on a long cruise. It was called Operation Springboard, which meant we went to Puerto Rico and played war games. Other ships threw grenades at us in the water, and you could feel the concussion like depth charges. It was like simulating war. We also were testing new armaments.

On the way down we went through a hurricane. I was totally seasick all the way. I think 4 people on the boat out of 98 weren't seasick. The waves were breaking so high that they had to take people off the watch. We couldn't submerge, it was so bad. All I did was lay down on my four-hour watch in the engine room; every so often I would move my head and look at the meters and make sure they were registering, and then turn my head to the side and throw up.

After awhile the storm went away, and we got to Puerto Rico. We stayed for about five days. They gave us barracks at the Navy base, and we went out during the day and came in and slept in the barracks at night. When we were down there, the guys found out that I had never been to bed with a woman. I just looked like a person that had never been to bed with a woman, and they kept riding me about it. They didn't know for sure, but I never told them "no" so they got sure. They started talking about making me a man of the world. One night they took me to this bar called the Topside Club. They had all these girls around. They would come up to you and say something like, "five and two" or "five and three", which meant five dollars for her and three dollars for the room. Most of them couldn't speak English. The guys called one girl over and said that I was a "cherry". They wanted to fix her up with a "cherry" they told her. She was thrilled about that. One of the guys who spoke Spanish was telling her this. She took me in tow and took me out to this hotel. There was this big fat guy at the desk on the second floor with an old lady behind him. I had to pay her the two dollars. We went to the room, and all that was there was a bed and a dresser and a urinal. It was very dirty, very crummy. She proceeded to introduce me to a few facts of life—it was an interesting experience and one that I will never forget. I didn't want to go through with it, but then again I knew that if I didn't she would say something to my friends and I might not get my dolphins. I would be ridden something fierce. So I was in kind of a very hard position. So I did what was expected of me. When I was undressed she joked quite a bit—teased me about being feminine looking and having a small penis. Even though I wanted to be feminine, it still hurt me to hear that because I was still trying to be a man. The guys in the Navy still kidded when I was in the shower, too, which hurt me. I continued to take showers at times they weren't there.

Everyone was pretty drunk that night. After I went back to the bar they asked me how it went and that kind of stuff. I played the part of the bragger. They were a little ridiculous. They didn't understand.

I went back to the prostitute once on my own. Even though she made fun of me, I was curious because of the fact that it had been my first time and I didn't know whether my not getting enjoyment was just because it was the first time or what. Even though I had physiological relief, I gained no psychological pleasure from it. I found that it was true the second time, too, and I gave it up more or less as a lost cause.

When I was on the cruise, I was what they call a nonqualified. That is, the lowest form of life on a sub. It is lower than someone who doesn't have their dolphins yet. A pair of dolphins is worn on the left breast pocket. You get those after you have been on a boat. If you don't get them within six months, you are taken out of submarines. The way you get them is you have to learn every pipe, every wire, what it goes to, what it is for, what the voltage is, in the whole boat. This means that an officer takes you from one end of the boat to the other and you just walk through, and if he says, "How do you load the torpedo and shoot it?" you show him what you do, and if he says, "There is water coming through the pipe. How do you shut it off?" you tell him how to shut it off. You go through each department of the boat, and if you pass you get your dolphins. Also, the rest of the people on the boat have to agree. There is a big ceremony afterwards. As a matter of fact, you get thrown in the drink.

I really wanted to get those dolphins. When you get in a position like that, you can't say no when the guys want you to do something—you have to say yes. If you say no, they are going to make life so miserable for you. Even though I thought it might help, going with that prostitute didn't give me any more prestige. After that I mostly stayed by myself.

On the cruise we also stayed on this one small island for awhile—San Croix. We were the first Navy Ship to pull in there since World War II. There was a cruiser and our sub. It was a very beautiful island—the water was a very deep blue. It was only about 12 miles long and 3 miles wide. Just a beautiful, slow, tropic island—nobody rushes you anywhere. Not any tourists—peaceful. I really liked it. I liked walking underneath the palm trees. I'd like to go back there someday. Something happened while I was there. I was on liberty and all of a sudden somebody came and got me. They said, "The OD (officer of the day) is really pissed off at you." I said, "What did I do? I didn't do anything." He said, "You better get back to the boat." I thought they were joking, but I went back to the boat anyhow. I thought they were just riding me like they always did. I got back to find out that I was in trouble for doing something, or for not doing something. To this day I don't know what I did or didn't do. I was restricted, but I didn't know what the hell for. We went back to Puerto Rico for two or three more days and then left for Newson.

When I got back, I turned in my request to get off the boat. I just couldn't take it anymore. I was very paranoid. Everybody was riding me. I can't remember any specifics, but I was being ignored and looked down upon. People were making shitty comments to me, and stuff. My head couldn't take it, so I said, "Fuck it, it just isn't worth it."

When I left the boat, I felt that I had failed. I wanted to get the dolphins, and I thought about not being able to get them. I also wondered why I couldn't get along with people; why people were hating me. Why did I bother them so much? I never have figured that out. It bothered me considerably and still does. I just couldn't understand the mentality. I was useless. Why do people have to ride someone who is different?

I was playing a role in a game and knew it. It was a very unreal role, a sailor, and a very unreal game to me. I think that, if I was more successful in the role, I might have been able to cope with it better. If they didn't ride me so much and if I got some support, I might have felt more comfortable. I don't know if I would have gotten my dolphins or not—that's kind of up in the air. I was almost forced to leave. There's one reason I kept jumping from duty station to duty station. As soon as people started knowing me, they started riding me and I had to leave. People's first impression of me was okay. I could hold the masculine image. But after they spent some time with me it was almost like I couldn't hold up the front very well. It was shabby, and people could see right through it. That's when the remarks about "queer" and things started coming out. I could play the role of a male superficially, but I didn't have the masculine personality to go along with it to be able to relate to people the way they wanted me to.

I was always pretty quiet; not boisterous or anything. I used to say, "Excuse me," like "Excuse me, Tom, I have to get the wrench," instead of, "Move over, you stupid bastard," which is what the rest of them would say. Me being quiet and polite was like putting the topping on the cake. It really finished me in their eyes. You just weren't supposed to be polite. I'm not just joking. In their society I just wasn't polite and in their own they were, but I just couldn't relate to the way they did things. They used to bug me out—when they talked about girls, especially. Everytime they did it made me shocked and angry, and I had to leave.

They kept goosing me, too, which scared the shit out of me and made me yell. I would try to keep my mouth shut when that happened, but I couldn't. Whenever I was around the guys, I used to tense right up. I would try not to trigger their joking, but by tensing up I would trigger things. I used to blush about everything. When they talked about girls, I used to turn bright red. I think all and all I was very hard for them to figure out. It was very hard for me to figure out.

My style of handling this was running; going deeper inside myself. I just couldn't handle it. Like I said before, until I went in the Navy I was never around people much. I didn't know how to react. I fell back on what I did in the past, which was retreat physically, and if I couldn't retreat that way, I retreated inside myself.

From some of the things I said you might think that I played up being the clown. This is not the case. I remember I used to break out in tears when the kidding got bad. Of course, the tears made things even worse—they had something else to kid about. I remember once I was looking for a place to lie down. I didn't have a permanent bunk, so I went forward and into the torpedo room. There was an empty bunk, and I asked if anyone had it. They didn't answer me, so I climbed in. I didn't undo the flash cover; I just laid on the top. This Third Class Petty Officer came in, a Polish guy, and told me to get the fuck out of his bed. He didn't want any "goddamn queers" in his bunk. Those were his words: "I don't want any fucking queers in the torpedo room." He chewed me out like he owned it. Come to find out, it was his berth. But nobody had told me. They were just standing around laughing. Like, by not saying anything, not saying it was his berth, they were letting me in for it. I just burst out crying and walked away. There are very few places where you can get away from anybody in a submarine. Every time I saw him after that he gave me those looks.

I got very little support from the guys on the ship, but one time when I was in Puerto Rico one of my tormentors said something that was kind of supportive. There was one group of people that kind of were my tormentors; the bulk of the others were totally indifferent. They never did anything one way or the other. I was walking through San Juan, and one of the guys in the clique who bugged me less than the others saw me. He was really drunk—drunk on his ass leaning against a doorway. He called me over and said, "Friend, I don't like what they are doing to you, but try to stick it out." He was so drunk when he said it that I didn't approach him about it when he was sober because I don't think he would have remembered. If he did, he probably wouldn't want to say anything about it. I was always a good Samaritan, and I took him down and put him in a cab so he could get back to the base. It made me feel good that he had said that. After awhile I started developing feelings. Like, I was wondering if all that was happening around me—the tormenting, the joking— wasn't just all in my head. After he said that I knew that it wasn't just in my head. The things that I was receiving were real. I got off the boat as soon as we got into port.

As soon as we got to Newson, the next day, I went to a—I forgot his actual rank—clerk, I think, and I told him I wanted to get off the boat and wanted to be released. Submarine duty is totally voluntary. I went before the captain, and he asked me why I wanted to get off. I said, "I just don't like sub- marines." I didn't want to squeal. That would have make things worse. I didn't want to say anything. I just wanted off. So I was transferred to the Naval Operations Base where I worked as a cleaner for about two weeks until I got my new duty station. Funny thing, though—I left the boat as a qualified submariner. It was in my records. I didn't find that out until I read them when they discharged me.

So I just cleaned up offices for two weeks. I stayed to myself and started to flip out. In a situation like that, a person in my position starts saying to himself, "Am I wrong? Am I sick? Or, is everybody else sick? Everybody else can't be sick, therefore, I must be sick." I started doubting my own sanity. I started wondering what was actually happening. I never really doubted my sanity until this point, but I was pretty shook-up.

I was transferred then to a submarine tender and made a mess cook again. There were at least places you could get lost. It was a big ship, so I could al- ways go to a different part where nobody knew me. I also went on leave in Moreshead, weekends. That's where we were stationed. I didn't dress at all— just went in. But after awhile they started bugging me again.

While I was on the Star I started having more and more seizures. Before that I had seizures, but they didn't happen very often and only lasted a second. Now I was getting them three and four times a week, and they lasted some time. When I felt them coming on, I would try to lie down. Nobody noticed for awhile. When people did notice, I got very embarrassed.

One night out in the galley I was dishing out food, and the next thing I knew I was lying up on a table on the sick bay. I had passed out, and they carried me up there. There wasn't anything obvious. My blood pressure was about normal, and I wasn't having full-blown seizures, a grand mal or anything like that. At first they thought it was hyperventilation. The doctor told me to try ventilation. The next time I got dizzy I was supposed to get my head in a paper bag. I did that once, but I still passed out. I didn't know anything about seizures. I didn't know what was coming off. They told me that seizures could be triggered from psychological factors. The more tensions you have, the more readily you have seizures. Nobody thought that they could be organic—caused by my blow to the head. They thought they were psychological. They told me that, and I believed them. I was starting to doubt my sanity, anyway. I didn't know what was coming off, and I wanted help, anyway. I didn't know what to do and where to get it. Help with coping with the Navy, with people, with the seizures—I wanted help with all these things. I wanted to find out what the hell was going on. I talked to the doctor two or three times. He even kept me in sick bay for three days once. I didn't know until later that it was for psychiatric observation, not for the seizures directly. I knew I couldn't tell him that I was a female. I knew I would automatically be considered nuts. I knew that since I was a kid. You don't tell anybody that. But I wanted to find out what was going on. When he recommended that I see a psychiatrist, I was happy. Even though I knew in the back of my mind that the whole seizure thing was not psychological, it would give me a chance to talk to a psychiatrist, I thought.

The doctor sent me to a psychiatrist over on shore—to the station there. I walked all the way over, because I couldn't get a bus. I said to the clerk, "I would like to make an appointment to see the doctor. I was sent over by the *Star.*" The clerk looked up and said, "Okay," and handed me a form and told me to fill it out and bring it back and then he'd make an appointment for me. I looked at the form and walked out the door. It really pissed me off. I wanted to talk to somebody then, not four weeks from then or something like that, after I filled out the form. I looked at the form. It had such nice diddies on there such as, "Do you love your mother? Do you love your father?"—all multiple choice. That there was no place even to write down your own comments; pissed me off. I ripped it up and said to myself, "Fuck it. They can take their psychiatrists and shove them up their ass." I walked over to the *Star* and didn't even go tell the doctor that I had gone.

I didn't rip the form up in front of the clerk. I never saw the psychiatrist. After that I didn't see the boat physician for quite a few days. Finally, one day I was down in the galley and somebody said, "The doctor wants to see you," and I went up to the sick bay and saw him. He said, "I'm transferring you over to the Navy hospital—go pack your gear." I didn't know what was coming off. I went down and packed my gear and went to the end of the dock, where I waited for the bus. The doctor didn't tell me anything—just to catch the bus and go to an office over at the hospital. I thought maybe finally he was going to look into my seizures. I thought maybe I was going to get a neurological examination or something. I got over to the Navy hospital. I gave them my papers and waited. After a long time someone came up to me and said, "Fry, come with me." I said, "Where am I going?" They said, "Neuropsychiatry Unit II." I thought that it was neurology. When we got there, "clank"—the doors shut after me and were locked. I freaked out. I just really got cold inside and though, "Oh, my God—what did I get myself into?" It was the locked psychiatric ward of the Naval Hospital. The nuthouse—the thought of being in it seemed like a nightmare. I said to myself, "Maybe I'm totally nuts." Such a place blew my mind.

They took me to the nurses' station. There is this Lieutenant Commander who is a nurse. She was sitting there. She said, "All right, sit down. What's wrong?" I said, "I don't know what the hell is wrong with me. I just keep passing out. I thought I was going to a neurologist and I'm in a nut ward." She said, "Give me all your sharp instruments and your aerosol cans." They take everything from you. They had taken my duffle bag already. All I had was my ditty kit. Then she sat and talked with me for a few minutes and said, "You don't belong here. We'll put you in the open ward." I was really relieved.

I sat around, and on the third day I saw a psychiatrist for the first time. I spent a half-hour with him and didn't see him again. He asked me things like, "Do you like boys?"—and stuff like that. It seemed almost like his questions were off the printed form. The whole thing was pretty ridiculous. He finally came up with, "Do you want out of the service?" When I first went in I thought that I might make a career of it, but I wanted out so I said, "Yes." I was in the ward for about two weeks. Nobody from the staff talked to me after that psychiatrist. I didn't know my diagnosis or anything. I finally cornered the doctor in the hall, and I pushed him into telling me my diagnosis. He said finally that I looked like a schizoid personality. He made the diagnosis on the basis of the half-hour he saw me and the records from the *Star*. He didn't give me any tests or anything while I was there. That was the reason I was discharged. A schizoid personality. Schizoid personality is a catch-all term that doesn't mean too much. It just means that they don't know what is wrong. My major hang-up was that I was introverted and depressed. I was not severely depressed or anything, but extremely introverted. I didn't talk to anyone. I imagine they thought I was more depressed than I was.

I didn't tell them what was really on my mind. When they asked me if I liked girls, I said, "Yes." "Do you like boys?" "No." When they asked me if I had ever had sexual relations with boys I said, "No." "With girls?" I said, "Yes." If I would have said I had relations with boys or I liked boys or that I felt like a woman, I would have been dishonorably discharged instead of medically discharged.

When they asked me what was bothering me, I said nothing. He said, "Why are you here if nothing's bothering you?" I told him I was sent here. Every hospital that I had ever been to asks why you are there. When I went to Central State Hospital, they asked me, "Why are you here?" How can they be so idiotic? They force you to go, and then they ask you why are you there. They are actually asking you what's bothering you, but it's a weird way of going about it, but that's about par for the course.

The patients and the lower staff were very nice. They were very uncrazy— very congenial. Nobody bothered me there. It was the only place in the Navy that nobody bothered me. I used to sit around and play chess. The facilities weren't anything. There wasn't even a day room—just beds around the walls and tables in the middle—that was all. I felt a little ill at ease at first because I was a nut, but then I began taking advantage of it. If anybody wanted to talk, I told them I was crazy and don't bother me. That's when I took on a philosophy about being nuts, or a way of looking at being nuts. It's not so bad being nuts because nobody bothers you if you tell them you're crazy. You get away with anything. You can totally be yourself if you tell everybody you're crazy, because they expect you to be. They don't expect you to play their silly games.

I had to go before a board which consisted of a couple of officers and a psychiatrist. I walked in, sat down, and someone said, "Is this a formal request for discharge?" I said, "Yes, sir," and they discharged me. It only lasted a few minutes. The Navy can't discharge you medically without your permission. I was given a form to sign, and I was out of the Navy. I was glad to get rid of the Navy in ways. Everyone, after being in awhile, would like to get out early, so I was glad. On the other hand, I didn't know what I was doing and how things would go. I got out with an honorable discharge for medical reasons, but it was psychiatric medical. There is a code number on my papers which tells anyone who knows what to look for that it was psychiatric. I am glad that I got out just a plain nut and not a homosexual nut. Even though I knew I wasn't a homosexual, if they ever knew how I felt they would consider me one.

So I went into the Navy October 9, 1962, and got out June 4, 1964, a little less than two full years. I took a bus home. They gave me $50. I didn't call my parents. I walked home about three in the morning, opened the door and walked in. I went to the bedroom door and knocked. My father said, "What the fuck are you doing here?" I said, "I'm discharged." He said, "Why?" I said, "Medical."

As rough as the Navy was, I don't regret my time in the service. I regret some of the things that happened; some of the things could have been better. I was seeing a little of what the world was like. I was on my own for the first time, away from my mother and father. Ha—if I could go back as a Wave, I might, but they don't take transsexual Waves. I learned a helluva lot. Even the bad times I learned—now it is helping me to be with people. I was finding out that I could make it on my own, even though I couldn't get along with people. It was very much a learning experience. I learned what I wasn't—let's put it that way.

7

Jobs, Marriage, and Other Headaches

I told my parents that my reason for leaving the Navy was a medical discharge. I didn't tell them it was psychiatric until a couple of weeks later. I just said I was having troubles and tried to talk around it. I stayed home without a job for six months. I didn't look up anyone or contact anyone; just moped around the house. That period is kind of foggy. I was getting unemployment insurance, but my father kept riding me to get a job; I remember that quite clearly.

I decided to put in a request to the VA for a veteran's pension, because of the blow on the head. I kept getting these bad headaches that went down my back and stayed about a week. I went to the hospital. They checked me out and said there was nothing wrong with me, and gave me zero percent disability. Zero disability is at least admitting on their part that something happened to me. I told them I was having blackout spells, and they asked a psychiatrist to see me. It pissed me off. I only talked to him for 15 minutes, but they were seeing everything in terms of me being crazy, because of what it said on my discharge. I have finally given up trying to get compensation out of the government. I have filed off and on since 1963, approximately five times. Four times for the blow on the head and once for psychiatric reasons. They have now recorded my seizures on an EEG, which proves that they are real and not just psychosomatic, but I still haven't been able to collect. They still link it to my cross-gender problems. They wouldn't give me compensation for my psychiatric problems, because they say I went in with them. I didn't even say that my psychiatric problems were caused by the Navy; I just said that the Navy aggravated them. I was giving them the benefit of the doubt, since I don't consider the transsexual thing as my disability. I think my emotional problems are related to it, and the Navy aggravated that. They even turned me down on that. They turned me down on everything, which aggravates me to no end. The only thing I could do now is get a lawyer and fight it, but they know more about the red tape than I do.

One thing I did do during that first six months back was apply to the Peace Corps. They said that you didn't need a college education to apply, and I always was a hell of an improvisor, which I though they were looking for. I took all the tests and everything, and they sent back for references, and all that bullshit. They must have found out I was in the Navy, that I got out on a mental disability. They give routine security checks, so it had to show up. So, that's the reason I didn't get in. But also, my father refused to write a recommendation when they asked him to. I asked him why not, and he told me, "I think more of the country than—sending you over to represent us." That is one thing I will never forgive my father for. The least he could do was lie for me, or at least give me a good reference. Even if it weren't for the Navy discharge, any person reading my records would say, "Wow, if this person's father won't vouch for him, who the hell needs him?" They sent me a letter saying— what the hell can I say about the letter? It was like a recruitment letter for Vista.

During this period I was feeling very messed up and confused. I threw temper tantrums around the house and did things like that. I would get pissed off at something and heave my glasses against the wall. It was always at home, never outside, and I never threw anyone else's things. I was really uptight that I couldn't be myself. I was conscious of what I was doing. I had feelings of rejection and anger. I would get angry and let my anger build up, and finally something would happen and I would just blow.

My first job was at the Hotel Royal. It was part-time nights as an elevator operator. I did that for a couple of weeks, and then the hotel changed owners and they did away with the operators so I lost my job. One thing happened while I was working there that I remember. There was a gay bar right down the street from the hotel. It was called the Zebra Room. I used to get out of work about three in the morning, and one night I stopped in to get a cup of coffee. I had never gone there before and wasn't looking for anything but a cup of coffee. There weren't any other places open that time of night, except the

White Tower which was five blocks away. Gay people won't bother you if you just tell them to bug off. If you mind your own business, nobody bothers you. If you hang around constantly, that's different. Well, I was sitting down having my coffee when these two huge guys come in and sit one on either side of me. One leans over and says, "You look like a nice kid, what are you doing here—you ought to go home." I said, "You're right." No sooner did I get out the door when the cops came to raid the place. I don't know why they were so nice to me, but all I know is that it really shook me up—the thought of the raid. I could have been picked up—it was that close.

After the elevator job I waited around for a couple of weeks and then went down to the state employment service. I thought a lot about what kind of job I wanted and decided that I wanted to be a nurse. I don't know how I first heard of the program, but I have always liked medicine and related fields. I didn't think that I could get a college degree then, and I wanted something that I could make a decent living at. I figured I could make a lot of money as a male nurse because there weren't that many, and I thought that the program would have mostly women in it, among whom I would feel comfortable. Of course, the fact that it was a feminine occupation entered into my mind. I figured I would go though the nurse's aid training and then apply for nursing school, but it didn't work out that way.

The employment office was very nice when I told them what program I wanted. I was tested by a counselor, and he told me that I would make a very good nurse. They didn't discriminate against me until I got into the class. The first day in the course one of the instructors started with, "Well, it looks like we have a male with us." That was the reaction I got from the teachers. Two instructors were fairly young, but they were really assholes, or at least one was, the other I didn't get to know all that well.

Every time they showed a movie with a nude woman in it or gave instructions on how to take care of a woman, like how to bathe a woman, I had to leave the room. Any time they showed pictures of babies being born I had to leave the room. Any time they showed pictures about feminine cleanliness I had to leave the room. I was leaving the room more often than I was in the class. The staff was really angry at me because I was the only male in the class and I was fouling up the way they usually did things.

All the girls in the course were called aides, but they called me an orderly. We took our classes at North High, but I couldn't practice bed bathing and I had to leave the room when the others were practicing it. It really got me angry. I never gave a bed bath until I actually got in a hospital, and then they got mad at me because I didn't know how to do it. The students practiced on each other in class. I got practiced on a lot—about four a day. They wanted a male to practice on. They had the place set up like a hospital room with two beds in it. When I got my bath, nobody was supposed to be in the other bed. The moment they were through I was supposed to jump out of the bed and go out into the hall and wait for them to get through giving each other baths. I couldn't practice on anybody, but they practiced on me. The instructors were so totally uptight about sex that it was crazy.

There were practice placements where you had half-year placements. There were two that you were supposed to alternate to and from. One was the maternity ward at St. Michael's Hospital and the other was the infectious disease ward at City Hospital. I was told that I couldn't go to the maternity ward because I was a male.

They sent me up to City Hospital and assigned me to only two patients, both of whom were men. There was hardly nothing to do. They wouldn't let me take care of female patients, and I wasn't even allowed in their rooms. It wasn't very manly, but in all my spare time I used to go down to the kids' ward and read to them. They really liked me down there reading to them, but my supervisor didn't think I should be doing that. I enjoyed playing with the kids. They behaved for me. I've got a childlike personality. They liked my work on the placement, except for one old nurse. They like having trainees there because it was free help.

The straw that broke the camel's back was one day I went downstairs with two other nurses and we were told that in between taking care of our patients we were supposed to go downstairs and familiarize ourselves with some machines. I was down with them alone, looking at and studying the equipment. Our instructor got very upset that I was alone with two females. She said that if I could not behave in an acceptable manner she would have to throw me out of class. Me, of all people, supposedly making advances at two girls. I told her what to do with her training course. I talked with the girls at lunch a couple of times. The instructor that I thought was a bitch they couldn't stand either, and they thought I was getting a lousy deal.

One of the trainees got a job at the VA, and I met her up there when I was there. We were talking, and she said that one of the instructors got fired. I asked her "How come?" and she said, "You're the one that should know. She gave you such a hard time because you were a man." I guess they found out about her, but a little too late for me.

About a month after the nurse's training I was looking through the classified when I saw an ad saying something about wanting hard-working men and women to go cross-country. I found out it was a traveling salesman job selling magazines door to door. I'm a pretty good talker, but I'm not a very good liar and that's what they wanted you to do. You were supposed to go tell the people whose doors we knocked on that we were neighborhood kids out to win a contest. They could help us win by buying subscriptions from us.

They had it down to a science. They told us little things to do that were supposed to promote sales. Like, we were suppose to run to the houses, so everybody would think you had fantastic news to tell them if they were looking out the window. They gave you a script to memorize. I forgot the actual spiel now, but they had it broken down in easy-to-memorize sections. It was against my principles—all that lying. That's all the script was, a pack of lies, but they taught it to me. I start turning red from my head to the tip of my toes and get shook-up when I lie. I did it for awhile, though. The men who ran the show thought I should be selling more than anybody, because I was so young looking that everyone would belive I was a neighborhood kid. Because I was feminine I looked about 13 or 14, while I was really 19. I did as well as anybody.

They recruited people in Central City to fill out their crew and started cross-country, going west. There were about four cars and five people in each car. The driver was the head of the team, and he would take you to an area and each one of the crews would work a block.

We stayed in motels along the way, usually three or four to a room. The way it was told to us was that they would pay for food and lodging and the income was free and clear. Once we got on the road I found out that they kept track of the expenses and then deducted them from our pay, which no one ever received anyway because our expenses were more than the profits. All we ate was cheeseburgers, French fries, and soda. The crew was a funny bunch. Most of them were from Los Angeles. I kept to my usual self, and they didn't bother me and I didn't bother them. They must have thought that I was weird, but I didn't let it bother me. I went as far as Minneapolis and finally told my boss to go fuck himself. All the time with them I never got paid, and I got tired of cheeseburgers. He was pissed but I didn't owe him anything, even though he tried to say I did.

I hitchhiked from Minneapolis to Central City and met some really nice people in my travels. I was totally broke, and some really beautiful people actually bought me cigarettes and food and stuff on the way. I got to St. Louis, and I had to get to the other side of the Mississippi, only there was a 25¢ toll and I was completely broke. I stood at the entrance to the bridge for awhile and then started walking away. This old gentleman stopped me and said, "Are you having troubles? It looks like you want to get to the other side." I said, "Yes, I do. But I'm broke." He took out his wallet and gave me two bucks. People that picked me up hitch-hiking actually bought me dinner. The people were really great. You can find some beautiful people around. It strengthened my faith in humans. It gives you some hope.

After the magazines I didn't get a job for awhile. There was always a rest period between jobs. My father used to get very angry with me because I kept telling him: "Look, I'm not going to become a laborer." He would say, "Oh, one of these guys that wants to start at the top." I would say, "No, I just won't do laboring." It was a feminine thing. I didn't want masculine jobs. The feminine thing was bothering me—I didn't know what to do about it.

When I applied for jobs I pushed together my periods of employment so it didn't look like I was unemployed so long in between jobs. I would put down that I ended one job a month later than I actually did, and say I started the new one a month earlier. If you don't do that they wonder what you were doing unemployed so long.

I worked at Marks Decorating, which is a company that decorates for businesses and places like that. I mainly cut drapes for a project they had for the Medical Center. I was underpaid, but it wasn't that bad a place to work. Most of the places where I worked I stayed pretty much to myself, except on the traveling job where I had to eat with everybody else. I stayed on the job two months or so. I left mainly because of the lousy pay, and I was getting bored. I was still living at home then. After Marks I worked for Omega Industries as a shipper, receiver, and material handler.

I had a lot of jobs during this period, and I always felt very paranoid and very nervous when I went for interviews. Most of the time I wasn't all that nervous because I didn't really want the jobs for the simple reason that I didn't want to do masculine work. I felt that they would know that I was odd if I applied for women's work. I knew they thought I was odd anyway. I knew I was odd. The only question that entered into it was what type of odd would they take me for. I was pretty much paranoid all the time, so being paranoid while going for an interview didn't shake me up all that much.

I guess I kind of worried what labels they would put on me. I didn't want them to know I thought I was a female, seeing that I was still trying to be a male. I was still trying to force myself into being a male, even though I had flunked out of the Navy. That is the way I looked at it—I had flunked out of the Navy and hadn't succeeded in my attempt to be a man, but I was still trying.

Speaking of trying to be a man, something happened while I was working at Mark's that was another attempt at my acting like a man. My father was working at Omega Industries. One day I decided not to go to work, which I did every so often because the work was so boring. My father decided the same thing, so we both started off to work but started back to the house after we knew Mom was out. So we bumped into each other up by Lorenzo's Bar on the north side. I don't drink, to this day, but we decided to go in and have one or two. We were sitting at the bar talking to the bartender, whom my father knew, and my father started getting under the weather. At about 1:00 in the afternoon this girl came into the bar and my father said to me, "See that girl;

she's a prostitute." I said, "Yeah, that's great." My father said, "You want me to fix you up with her?" He kind of caught me off guard, and I said, "No, I don't think so." He kind of rode me a little, and I finally said, "Yes," but I didn't have any money. I was trying to get out of it. It so happened that she gave credit to people who knew the bartender. I said, "Well there is no place to take her. Mother is home, and I don't think she would appreciate me bringing a prostitute home with me."

I was trying to get out of it, but at the same time I had this desire to show my father that I was a he-man, not to myself but to my father. He said I could take the car, an old clunker with no muffler. He told me to go to the Easy Wash parking lot, because there was no one working there that time of day. He said, "Nobody will bother you." I said, "I don't have a driver's license." He was drunk, so he didn't care. I went out, and she went with me. I was so nervous that I didn't know what I was doing. I started up the block, and she says to me, "You just hit a car that was parked on the side." I said, "You're crazy," and proceeded to the car wash. Took quite a bit to do it, but I did do it. I knew she would be reporting back to my father. I made up this fantasy in my head where she was the man and I was the woman. It was the only way I could make it. So back to Lorenzos. She went back in to look for more customers. She only charged $5.00. My father asked if I had any trouble with the car, and I said no.

We went home that night and were watching TV when we heard a knock at the door, and who was it but the police. They asked my father if he owned a blue jacket, and he said "No, but my son does." Come to find out the owner of the car I hit got our license number and turned me in. They got me for driving without a license. My father said wasn't there some way we could settle it out of court. "My son was just changing the car from one side of the street to the other." My father hired this good lawyer who charged $300. We waited three months for the trial, because he wanted to wait until the right judge came up, and then wound up with a $50 fine and a suspended sentence. The judge told my father that he didn't think he was a very good influence on me. The prostitute thing wasn't anything important. The prostitute in San Juan, the prostitute in Central City, and my wife are it. I don't consider those heterosexual relationships, by the way. I consider them homosexual relationships.

Just as in the service, I thought that the people that I worked with thought I was gay. I withdrew, didn't make any comments to anybody, just did my job, and that was it. I guess I never was really successful at playing the male. I make a very lousy man. I would try, but after awhile people could see through me. My act would finally start breaking down and they would put two and two together and come up with five—thinking I was gay. It was true in the Navy and throughout my whole life—everyone assumed I was gay. It made me angry. I hated gay people, even though I never really knew a real gay person. I thought they were all like drag queens, and it turned my stomach to think people thought of me like that.

For about a year I worked at Omega industries as a shipper and receiver, then as a steelworker operating the Plantagraph burner. I learned the job, and they put me on the night crew, practically running it by myself. You cut metal on it, and the burning metal comes off it, and you can easily burn holes in your pants. I bought a pair of pants a week and burnt them out one after the other.

One night after I had been there awhile the guys there started razzing me. I don't know why, because they didn't even talk to me before this. I remember this one night—they were standing around in a group, and I kind of went over to get a light or ask someone something. At that point I was trying to join in, or something. All of a sudden it was like the whole group turned on me. I found myself in a position where I didn't know what to do. They were teasing me about my femininity, and then they started teasing me about the holes in my pants. "Hey, why don't you get some decent clothes," and stuff like that. They were all older steelworkers—rednecks. I was kind of in a circle surrounded by them. Somebody grabbed the pocket on my pants where there was a hole and ripped it off, and then somebody grabbed into a hole in my pants leg and started ripping. As he did that, somebody grabbed on my shoulder and everybody was laughing and joking. They wound up ripping my pants right off me. By this time I was hysterical—I didn't know what they were up to. I cried. I didn't know how to cope. I ran out and left. One thing you might think I would have learned is that you don't cry in front of a bunch of guys. But I cried—when I get shook-up I cry, and I can't stop it. I think it's very human to cry—not feminine. My only emotional relief sometimes was crying, but that was judged feminine so I couldn't even get away with my only outlet. Once a psychiatrist at the VA said that if more men cried there would be fewer people in mental hospitals. After this I actually stopped crying. I couldn't cry for awhile. The people at the VA asked me why I didn't cry. I guess I stopped because I didn't want people to laugh at me and think I was feminine. When I was at the VA, instead of crying I used to hit my head and my fist against the wall.

I didn't go back to Omega the next day—I called in sick. I went back the day after and felt very uptight. Everybody was acting funny, like somebody—the boss—had climbed down on them. After that I left there. That incident did it. I didn't get along with my boss either. He was an incompetent bastard, and I told him so. One day he gave me an order for 24 round 12-inch circles. After I cut them and gave them to him, he said he wanted 24 12-inch squares. That material is too expensive to make those kinds of mistakes. He told me it was my fault—I still had the order form but he wouldn't look at it. That's how obstinate he was. For my mind he was just a dumb Polack.

While I was working at Omega I stayed home from work one day, and I was looking through the paper kind of looking for another job. I figured doing that I would have a good excuse for my father, cause he would always come home and say, "Why the hell aren't you at work?" I saw this ad: "IBM wants computer technicians and missile technicians." I said to myself, "That sounds great," and I called the number. The company representatives were staying in one of those nice hotels out by the airport, so I went out there to talk to them. They had this big suite of rooms, and all this bullshit. They gave me these tests and then told me that I did real well. I filled out the employment form, and they asked me things like what I was good at in the service, what did I study in diesel school, and that kind of stuff. They told me, "Don't call us, we'll call you," so I figured nothing was going to come of it. About three months later I got a telegram. My mother calls me at work, and she says: "You've got a telegram here—do you want me to open it and read it?" I said, "Of course." It said, "Call Cape Canaveral collect" and gave the IBM office and extension number. I called, and they told me that they had reviewed my materials and thought that I would be good in the field and they wanted me to come down for a personal interview. They wanted to know if I could take a couple of days off. I told them yes and they told me to go to the IBM office in Central City and pick up a check for $375 to fly down on such and such a day. They had a hotel room for me, and the whole bit. Really the big treatment.

So I saw all the people down there including the director of personnel, and he told me what the job would be and what it would pay; between $10,000 and $12,000. They were nice; gave me the red carpet treatment. This was when the Apollo program was just starting, and Gemini, too. Gemini had just gotten off the ground, and they wanted people to work on the Gemini and later the Apollo. IBM had made the instrument package right behind the command module, and the hydraulic and pneumatic systems. I told them that I was very interested in the hydraulics. He said, "Great," and "Don't call us, we'll call you." They even offered me housing down there. You see, some of the experience I had in the Navy is hard to find. The same techniques that I learned for submarines apply to spacecraft.

I got a letter back from them saying "sorry." It made reference to the government and security, and they couldn't accept me. It didn't come right out and say specifically that I failed the security clearance because of my mentally ill discharge, but that is the only thing I could figure out that would be the cause. You can't get security clearance, from what I understand, if you have any kind of a discharge except an honorable one.

I really would have liked that job. I think I would have stayed too. A damn good job with good money. At that point I didn't know about operations, but even if I had I would have taken the job and I could have saved up a considerable amount of money and made quite a name for myself professionally. If you make a good enough name for yourself professionally, nobody cares whether or not you are a male or a female. I imagine those things can be handled a lot easier when you have money. It wouldn't have been boring either, and I always had an interest in science fiction.

Toward the end of the time I was working at Omega I decided to get my own apartment so that I could have some privacy. Up to this point I hadn't been dressing much, because I was afraid of getting caught at home. So I got this small place and bought a few things and used to dress in my apartment. I just practiced. I was too scared to go out on the street. I would just put them on and sit about and look in the mirror and dream about being a woman. The tatoo really started bothering me at this point, seeing that it was so obvious when I dressed. I liked to dress, but I felt guilty about it. I felt it was wrong, but I knew dressing wasn't all of it. I knew I wasn't a female. I knew I couldn't be a female. I felt trapped. There was only one way out, and that was to continue to force myself to be a male. I went through phases of ripping up all the female things I bought. I'd go to the closet and throw them out, and then try to be a man and not dress. Then I'd go out shopping again. It gets expensive. I did that about three times.

After I quit Omega I hung around for a month or so and then decided that it was time to become employed again. This time I thought that I would just walk down Regent Street and inquire at the various stores. One of the first places on the street is Wall's, so I thought I would go in there and maybe get a sweeper's job, or something like that. I went and saw the manager and told him how I had been in the Navy, and he said, "Well you should make a good restaurant manager." So I joined. There looked like possibilities of advancement. I did on-the-job training at the Central City store, and then the district manager came around and said, "I've got a position open for you in Lakeview," which is a small city 40 miles north of Central City. I was sent up there as an assistant manager. I gave up my apartment and moved there. I was there for about a week when my boss took off on vacation, leaving me with the whole operation to take care of. Everything went fine in terms of keeping up the sales, and what have you, but I had this personality conflict with the head waitress that got pretty heavy. She had the only set of keys and was put in charge of opening up. She wouldn't let me have them, so I had to wait around all the time to have the place opened and closed.

She resented me for taking over. I worked from seven in the morning until eleven at night, seven days a week. I got $65 a week. Because I was getting paid by the week, I didn't have to punch a time card, so nobody kept tract of my time. I figured out that if they were paying me by the minimum wage, by the hour, they would owe me more than $500 dollars. When by boss got back I tried to get on a per-hour rate, but he wouldn't let me. He had me down on my hands and knees scrubbing floors, in addition to everything else. I don't mind scrubbing floors, but I was supposed to be the assistant manager, and I was supposed to have the respect of the other employees. I was just getting fucked over royally.

I liked the job and was doing well. Under different circumstances I would have done alright. He kept me busy and I like keeping my mind occupied. I learned all about the books, ordering food, cooking, and other such things. I didn't worry about my gender feelings, being so wrapped up in my work. I stayed in a furnished room and just got home late at night exhausted and went right to bed.

The employees were nice, and I even went out swimming with them a few times. I still had my tatoo then, but I felt much more relaxed than before. I just knew that I wanted to be a girl and didn't let too much else bother me. I thought of writing the head office, but I knew that all that would mean is trouble. My boss would have me keep the job, but he would take it out on me for complaining. I stayed on the job about one month, and then quit.

I went back to Central City and moved in with my parents. I liked the cooking part of my work, and thought I would get into Manpower training again, only this time in the cooking program. I hung around for a couple of weeks and then went down to the state employment service.

The cooking course was good. I got along with everybody really beautifully there, and nobody rode me. I could cook what I felt like and got to cook as well as some of the teachers after a while. I got into some good raps with the counselors there too. After they got to know me, they got angry with me for not going on to college. There were quite a few males in the program. Sexwise it was about half and half. I hardly missed any of the sessions. The staff liked me. There was one guy down there with a short crew-cut who was the remedial reading teacher. When I first went in to see him, he asked what I had read lately. I told him that I had just finished *Exodux* and mentioned some other books. He said, "Well I guess you don't need remedial reading." He gave me an arithmetic test, and I scored high. He gave me a spelling test, and I flunked terribly. We started talking, and all the sessions I had with him all we did was sit around and talk philosophy and things. I enjoyed it.

Some time around this time of my life I began getting strong pains in my stomach. I went to the VA to have it checked out. They never did give me a diagnosis, which is about par for them. They didn't tell me what it was (I think it was prostrate or kidney problems). While I was there, this young doctor became interested in me. I hadn't said anything to anybody at this point about me wanting to be a female, but this guy examining me recognized female characteristics. It was his own idea. I was just laying there on the bed, and before I knew it he had his professor over looking at me and eight medical students, too. They were poking me and feeling my breasts and measuring me. He called in another doctor to look me over, too. I hadn't told anybody about me wanting to be a female, and there they were examining me thinking there was something feminine about me. Physically, I have small genitalia, secondary female pubic pattern, very soft hair, little facial hair, and no hair on any other parts of my body. Just one of those things wouldn't have meant anything, but all together they meant something. I also had full hips and infantile breast development. This young doctor wanted me to go before one of those case conferences, which means you go to an auditorium and stand before all of these medical students and doctors while they look at you and discuss you. And you're naked—right. I agreed to do it without stopping to think. I just about passed out thinking about it later. I couldn't walk in front of an audience, let alone walk in front of an audience naked. They never discussed what they had found or what I was feeling. Up to this time I had never discussed it with anyone.

I was taken to the place where the conference was held, and I was sitting outside the door. A medical student walked in, so the door was open so I could see in. There were these seats and all these people in a semicircle around this stage and podium. I said, "To hell with this." I just started crying—it just started hitting me. Here I had never told anybody about my feelings, and now there were doctors looking into it, and I was really scared. I knew what they were looking at. I wasn't positive that they thought I had feminine characteristics, because they never discussed anything with me. I was kidded all through the service and in junior high school about my development, and it just added up. So I broke right down and ran back to my room and laid on my bed crying. I just started freaking out emotionally. I felt so bad that I decided to go and talk to my own doctor. I remember knocking on his door still crying and asking if I could see him. He said "Come in." I sat down and said, "you know, the endocrinologist wanted to see me because of me having female characteristics?" He said, "Yes." I said, "Well, I couldn't go before all those people, I was too shook-up." He said, "Do you want to tell me about it?" I said, "Yes, I've always thought I was a female, not a male. He said, "Well, the best thing you can do is go to the psychiatric clinic to take care of a problem like that." That's all he said. Didn't say anything about the physiological part of it. I just sat there a few minutes and left. I was angry. I didn't think it was a psychiatric problem, but after doctors kept telling me I had a psychiatric problem, I began to think I did. It developed itself into a psychiatric problem. I feel that if I had been treated in the beginning, say in 1965, with hormones and the like, it would have never developed into a psychiatric problem. By wanting to be female and having to fight society and everybody else, it became a psychiatric problem.

I wanted medical help, but no one would give it to me. This doctor I told was nice enough and seemed to know his business. You start doubting your sanity when a guy like that says, "You're like this so you've got to be nuts." When I was younger I never went to a doctor to tell them. I knew what their reaction would be—you're nuts—you need a shrink.

The funny thing is that the minute I told my doctor about wanting to be a female, he acted like he never heard it or had forgot it. I was like totally pushed underneath the covers and not dealt with. So were my stomach pains. Kind of like, "Forget it, and perhaps it will go away." I guess they didn't think it was a serious problem, or that it was and they didn't want to aggravate it. They probably thought that whatever was bothering me was a psychiatric problem—it was in my head, not in my body. So I left the hospital after being there for about a week. That was the first time I had ever told a doctor about it, and it was put on my records. I don't know exactly how it was put there, but the next time I went to the hospital they knew. After that the VA was cold and indifferent to me. It pissed me off that they put it in my records. I only told it to this doctor because I was upset—not for public knowledge.

In the cooking program itself I got into baking. Even though the girls did most of the baking, it was baking that I really enjoyed. I asked one of the teachers to teach me how to decorate the cakes, and she told me that there was a special program in baking that taught that in it. I transferred into that program. There was one week to complete the cooking, but technically I completed it.

The program was over at the Moon Bakery over on the west side. There was a really good, sharp baker who was teaching the course, named Ben Cohen. He had lots of good, old, Jewish recipes—cheesecake that would melt in your mouth. I was really good at cake decorating. As a matter of fact, that was my first love. I could make orchids on top of the cakes. It would take me a day, but when they were finished they looked like real orchids sitting on top of the cake.

I had stopped living by myself while in cooking school and had moved back in with my parents. Joan, a girl that I was seeing, lived out in Mechanicsville near my folks and used to drive me back and forth. I was successful putting up a good front. I had my girl who was picking me up after class, and I was holding back acting feminine. I was actually quite successful in the baking school. Mr. Cohen liked me because I was good at decorating. There were only six in the course, and he didn't like women, so I was sort of the fair-haired teacher's pet. I stopped going to the school. I can't remember why. With all the other jobs there was always a clear "why," but for some reason I just stopped. I don't know if it had anything to do with me having strong feelings of wanting to be a woman and being self-conscious, or what. I stayed in until one week before it was completed and never actually got a diploma.

I called Cohen and asked him if he could fix me up with a job, and he told me to go down to the Hotel Central and there would be a job waiting for me. I went down, and the head chef gave me a job as the cold meat chef, which was making sandwiches, fruit salad, and that kind of stuff. It was supposed to in-volve as much decorating as it did food preparation. The chef was a maniac—one of those tempermental Frenchmen who would pick up a knife when he got angry and start swinging it around. He got pissed at me a couple of times for no good reason. I don't think he liked me because I was feminine.

The money wasn't good, so I quit. I really didn't quit, I just didn't show up again, and I eventually called them and told them I wouldn't be back.

You might wonder why I had so many jobs in this short period of time. I think it was a large part of me not feeling comfortable around people after I got to know them, but I think part of the reason for leaving is the way people reacted to me. Even though I was trying not to be feminine, I was, and that turns people off. A lot of people don't know how to respond to feminine men. I got under people's skins because they couldn't figure me out and didn't know how to respond to me. If people can't put a label on you, they get confused. It is like just before I made the switch to dressing and living as a female, people were confused in that they couldn't tell if I was a man or a woman, so they didn't know whether to address me as "he" or "she." People wouldn't talk to me because they didn't know whether to say "he" or "she." They didn't want to be embarrassed by calling me the wrong thing. People have to know what you are. You walk down the street and the first thing you do when you see a person is to say to yourself, "That's a male. That's a female. That's an older person;" You categorize in your mind. One of the first things you do is to de-termine the sex—if you can't do that, it blows the whole system up. They don't even know where to start with you.

I went to the VA for a short stay in 1967. What happened was that I found out, by taking the wrong one, that I'm allergic to certain drugs. One of the drugs is scopolamine, which is found in over-the counter tranquilizers like Nytol, and those things. I was nervous, so one night I took a couple of those pills and freaked out totally. I was actually tripping off that stuff, that's how violent the reaction was. What happened during the three days after I took them was really weird. I was at home, and my mother came home and found that I had filled the bathtub with cocoa and water and had taken out all the light bulbs in the house and piled books in the middle of the floor. I sat there trying to butter my cigarette lighter and eat it. I was really out of it. This was before I got married or anything. When my mother saw me, she thought that I had had a total nervous breakdown, so she called my father, who rushed home. He drove his car through the fence he was so excited. My mother called my brother, who was asleep upstairs, and had him run across the street and call the sheriff. The sheriff came but said there was nothing they could do because I wasn't endangering the public. They finally talked me into going to the VA, convincing me that there was something wrong with my stomach.

When the admitting doctor saw me, he wouldn't admit me at first because I wasn't acting weird then. I just sat there. I could act very rational and answer all the questions, but the block between my conscious and my subconscious kind of wasn't there. I was coherent, but if somebody mentioned a lamp or some other object, I'd relay everything that ever happened to me about lamps in my whole life. It was phenomenal. After this doctor wouldn't admit me, my father demanded that I see a psychiatrist; There was one on duty, and they called him. When he arrived, I was staring at him and he asked what was wrong with me. I said, "A firefly is crawling across your glasses." That was it. I got admitted. I remember now that there were a lot of fireflies running across his glasses, but it was logical because he had on horn-rimmed glasses and they reflected light across the top of the bow as he moved his head, making it look like fireflies crawling.

I was in the hospital three days that time. It is normal for a drug to remain in your system that long. The staff actually thought I was tripping, but after they found out about my allergic reaction, they gave me a mess of drugs to make me sleep, and when I woke up I was O.K.

Before I went home, one of the doctors who looked at my chart saw an entry on my record about me wanting to be a female. He called me in for a conference and said, "It's in your records here that you have feelings of wanting to be a female." I said, "I know," but I actually didn't know. I had no idea that the doctor the year before had put that in. It pissed me off. I think it's unethical. He didn't do anything for me—I told him in confidence and there he went and put it in my records for everybody's knowledge. I asked this doctor directly whether or not I could get into a psychiatric clinic for help with the problem. He said he would try to get me in the out-patient clinic, but there wasn't any room at the time, so he said, "Why don't you call back in a month?" I told myself "The hell with it. I'm not even going to bother." A year later I ended up as a resident patient on the locked ward.

The next job and the last before going to VA psychiatric for a long stay was at Marshall Scientific Supply Company.

I was a shipper-receiver and had lots of responsibility, which I liked. I learned to handle chemicals, some of which were very valuable, like this special shipment of platinum I packed and was worth maybe $20,000. I liked the work, but I was beginning to break—right before going to the hospital.

While I was there I bought some beautifying cream, that I read about in a magazine, that contained estrogen which I had read somewhere was a hormone related to female secondary sex characteristics. I also did some reading in medical journals about the effects of estrogen. It is related to breast development. I bought the stuff and centrifuged it at the company laboratory, which caused all the oil to go to the bottom and left a thin layer of waterlike stuff at the top. The water was what I saved, because it contained the estrogen. I took that and mixed it in orange juice and drank it. I tried to get as much information as possible about medications and things that might be related to my difficulties, because I knew that I could never go to a doctor for help. I didn't really know what I was doing. I didn't really think anything would happen by drinking that stuff, but it was kind of a desperate attempt to do something to satisfy my feelings of wanting to be a woman, which were getting stronger. Come to find out, when I went to New York City and started seeing Dr. Campbell, you can't take estrogens internally because your body just eats them right up. He just laughed. The most it did for me was to give me diarrhea.

Even though I felt that I wanted to be a woman and the doctors at the VA had recognized me physiologically as having characteristics of a woman, I had no place to go for help. I still had great fantasies that somebody was inventing a machine that would put a woman's body in the place of mine. I was pessimistic about the medical profession. I didn't trust them. I just saw them as a bunch of bastards who didn't give a damn as long as you conformed to what society said you should be. I was a-21-year-old male, so I acted like one and got married. My wife tried to help me as much as possible, but it overpowered her. It was too much for her. I don't blame her at all—she knew about me and what was going on before we got married. I couldn't have gotten married any other way. I didn't see any alternatives but to try to live as society says a man should. I went into the Navy to play the role, and got married to play the role, but it just didn't work.

I met my wife, Joan, in a drugstore across the street from the apartment. I was in Manpower cooking school at the time. I was basically very lonely and didn't have anyone to talk to. I didn't have any friends at all and was probably the only person that when I made out applications for a job I had to make up some of the names for references. I just used to go to work and come home. I would go over to see my parents, but we weren't getting along at the time and I hadn't confided in them. I didn't know any of the people at work. As a matter of fact, I didn't know the names of the people around me. I needed someone to respond to my emotional needs and someone whose needs I could respond to. I wanted a male, but since my name was John I had to marry a female. The homosexual route just wasn't for me.

I was 22 and she was 24 when we got married. The courtship was kind of brief. We never went out. I used to go over to her house and she would visit mine. Mostly, I went to hers. She lived with her three sisters, and I used to go over there for dinner and to watch TV. They were nice. They didn't know anything about what was going on with me until I was in the hospital and we were getting the separation. Joan and I used to go out driving, too—she had a car. I was superstraight at the time. I used to wear sports shirts and slacks— tried to be a big dresser playing the role.

Her mother was dead and so was her father, so she had kind of a tough life. My family kind of adopted her more or less after we started going together. She even moved in after a while. She was more of a Fry than I was.

She was a little afraid of men, and she had some feelings of insecurity—you might call it an inferiority complex. She had been let down by boys before, and after her father died she was the oldest so she more or less had to stay at home and raise the family.

We were driving one day in the car, and she said, "Guess what?" I'm pregnant." I said, "Oh, that's nice." It kind of hit me like a ton of bricks. I said to myself, "Me, capable of that"—it blew my mind. Here I was frowning on masculinity and here was something that was the most blatant masculine thing possible. You would think that it would make me feel more like a man and more able to be a man, but it didn't work that way. I remember when we told my parents. We were sitting there on the porch, and I said, "Guess what? Joan's pregnant!" They liked Joan, so they just had to think about it; my father was happy about it—especially when we were making plans for the wedding. I was being a man.

We got married because of the baby, but not really, because we had talked about it before it happened. The baby kind of speeded the plans up. We would have gotten married even if it wasn't for the baby, I think. That was because I was at a point where I needed someone, someone to be close to, someone to love. And by this time I didn't give a damn whether it was a male or female. I just needed someone. She was about in the same boat.

It was a Catholic wedding, since Joan is Catholic. I almost overslept the day of it. I wore a dark suit. I was going to wear my blue blazer and blue slacks— I used to dress that way all the time. Flannel slacks and white ties or white turtle necks. I was a very sharp dresser, but I was told that I had to wear a suit, which I did. I forgot what my wife was wearing. We had mass, and there were her relatives and my mother and father and sisters and younger brother.

I was really very straight then. No folk mass or anything. I wasn't the hippy freak like I am now. I never let my hair down, so to speak, until after I got out of the VA. I was too conservative in the way I thought and the way I dressed.

Our agreement when we married was that we would try it. We both tried as hard as we could to get me to conform, but I started becoming a total wreck. The more pregnant my wife got, the more sick I got. Morning sickness and the whole bit. I knew what was happening to me psychologically—I was starting to relate to myself like I was having the baby and was getting terribly confused in my head. I was getting low when I finally said, "The hell with this."

I thought that I should be having the baby. I looked on Joan as the masculine part of the twosome. She had a better job than I had; she made more money; she was more domineering. Not that she wasn't feminine, but our relationship was different from a traditional one. This was before liberation, and yet our roles at home were very interchangeable. Nobody played the husband or the wife. She worked at an insurance company and still does. She is an underwriter now—worked her way up from a stenographer. She is very bright. Sometimes I would clean the house, sometimes she would, and the same with about everything. A real liberated couple. We lived together for three months before I went into the hospital.

As I said before, you might think that having a child would make me feel more like a man and make me feel good, but it actually built up self-loathing in me. Looking back on it now, I see that over the years of my childhood, adolescence—that whole bit—I build up kind of a mask around myself, a mask of masculinity. I kept building and building on the mask, and by the time I got married I thought it was impregnable, but when Joan began getting larger, it began to crack. I took a lot of time to rid myself of that mask, even after I left the VA. It's even harder for me to imagine now than it was then—that I had fathered a baby.

8

Entering the Psychiatric Ward

In February of 1968 I had the breakdown. I don't know if I would call it that, but that's the term they lump the kind of thing I went through under. I just reached the point where I had to do something about it. I just couldn't hack it any more. My wife being pregnant is what drove it home. I kept fantasizing that I was the one who was pregnant, and when I confronted it that I wasn't, that's when it happened. When I went to the hospital, it was like being the opposite of psychotic. The psychotic usually goes to the hospital to get his fantasy taken away. I went to have my reality taken away.

I knew that it was time for me to enter a hospital. I thought it would be best. I walked into the admitting office and said, "I want to be admitted." They asked the reason, and I said, "Psychiatric." They called the psychiatrist on duty down, and I talked to him and told him my problem, and they admitted me there and then. I told him about my wife being pregnant. I told them about my feelings toward my wife and child, and I told him that I wanted to be a girl and it was just tearing me apart. "I can't function any more. I can't do anything." This was the first time I checked into a psychiatric ward on my own, and it was the only time that I was in the hospital for being a transsexual. The other times I went, they were for normal head hassles anybody could have—Joe Blow down the street—just emotional hang-ups.

I choose to go to the VA because it was a place I had been before. If I had had friends in the city who I could trust or a place I could go, I probably would not have gone there, but I didn't. The only place I thought of was the VA. I had heard of City Psychiatric Hospital, but I heard some scare stories. Some friend of the family knew someone who went there and they gave him electric shock and the doctors didn't care for him right. (I'm still afraid of shock therapy, because I don't think the people who give it know what it does. It does more damage than good.) Also, I didn't want to go to City Psychiatric because once you go there it's on your record that you were in a nuthouse. If you go to the VA, it doesn't mean you're a nut necessarily, because it is a general hospital, too, not just psychiatric. Any application or form that asks you if you have ever been a mental institution, you can answer "no."

I also knew that they took your driver's license if you went to a state hospital (City's run by the state), and I didn't feel like going through all that bullshit of trying to get it back. I ended up getting it taken away, anyway, but I didn't know I would. The state somehow found out I was in. Nobody at the VA would send them a letter saying I was alright. They can issue all kinds of letters saying what's wrong with you, but not what's right with you. I lost my license in 1968, and I can't get it back. It's ludicrous. That's one reason I want to move out of the state.

When I went to the VA this time, they had me tagged. Schizo was on my medical records. That is one thing about nuts, anybody can add a diagnosis, but nobody takes any away.

I had been in the VA hospital for about two weeks and I hadn't seen a doctor—I hadn't seen anybody. I was very afraid and nothing was happening. I was still hiding my transsexualism. The only person I had told was the person who admitted me. For some reason, it never dawned on me that they had put it in my records, and all someone had to do was look them up and they could see what I had told him. I started talking to this attendant and was building up my courage to open up to him, and he came right out and said, "It must be rough thinking you are a girl." That was like a slap in the face. They knew. Then, I realized that everybody knew. During the first few weeks there, I was fairly alright—you know—I was shook-up, yes, but not that bad. Then I found out that everybody knew, and it shook me up very bad. I had feelings that the attendants and everybody else were making fun of me. The floor went right out from under me. I almost went totally catatonic. I didn't want to talk to anybody. I felt that everyone was talking about me, and they probably were too. It just never dawned on me that everybody reads the patients' charts but the patients. I decided to kill myself. I was very depressed at other times in my life and I was depressed when I went to the hospital, but I had never considered suicide before. It was hard to do on the ward, but I smoked a pipe and there was a piece of metal in there that I could use. I unscrewed the bowl and took the grate out and started grinding away at my wrist. I was sitting in the day room. I kept working away at it, and the blood started getting all over everything; but I hadn't hit a main vessel, which was frustrating. Here I was grinding away for about 30 minutes, and I hadn't hit anything. It was pretty damn deep, too. Nobody noticed what I was doing. There was blood all over the place, but it wasn't spurting.

After I had grated myself for so long I was tired, so I hid the grate, pulled my sleeve down over my wrist, and went to the nurses' station and asked for a bandage. I was going to wash it off and put the bandage on it and try some other time. They saw the blood dripping off my fingers and panicked. They sewed me up, and everything. I still have the scars.

I don't know if it was a serious suicide attempt, or what. I just felt like ending it all. There was no hope. I was thinking, "I'm dirty-no-good—there is no way to get peace—I will never be able to be a whole person—everybody is talking about me." I felt that I would be made fun of for the rest of my life, the way everybody makes fun of sexual deviants. I think the suicide attempt was more like a cry for help, when I look at it now. But when I was doing it, I was thinking about it like it was suicide but was not too serious about it. It's hard to explain. I was ashamed about being a transsexual, and that's why I hadn't told anyone in the first place. I thought everybody was just looking down on me, and it wasn't worth the fight. It just really was sickening.

After that they put me on "special" for the week. Special means that they have someone sit by you 24 hours a day. They sit with you at night, and if you go to the bathroom they wait right beside you. It's so you don't hurt yourself. Actually, the VA was pretty good about it. You go to a state hospital like Central, and they strip you, drug you, and lock you up in a seclusion cell if you try anything.

After this I got to talk to a psychiatrist. I hadn't seen one since I was admitted to the hospital.

I continued seeing myself as having no life in the future, no reason to live. Here I was, I thought, a female—my mind said I was—and yet biologically I was a male. I had to pretend to be something I wasn't and even at that everybody thought of me as being perverted and every other term going. There was no way for me. I had tried to change. I tried in the service to become more masculine, and by marriage I had hoped to do the same, but none of it worked. I didn't want to change me, but I was desperate to change. I was hoping that perhaps it would go away. It never went away. I couldn't stand to live like a male any longer, especially after I found out people knew about it.

I didn't know what my diagnosis was at the time. I wasn't friendly enough with the staff to find out, but later on I was—schizoid personality, homosexual with cross-gender identity conflict. Since I wanted to be a woman, I had to be a homosexual in their eyes.

The future looked like it was going to be more of the past. It was very, very bleak. I didn't see any hope at all. I withdrew—even stopped eating. It wasn't a conscious attempt to starve myself. I just lost reason to do anything. I was introverted before, but now I became almost totally that way. I just laid in bed and dreamed. When I wasn't fully sleeping, I was in a half-dream state. They gave me drugs to get me out of it, and after about a month I got out—but it wasn't the drugs. It was one nurse's specific attention that did it.

It was a nurse named Jane, a young nurse—very nice, a real trippy personality. Happy-go-lucky kind of person. She used to come by and sit and talk to me. She just talked, and by her talking I found myself getting wrapped up in her and opening up more about myself. I began to trust her. During this time the only times I got up were to go to the bathroom or get coffee or to see Dr. Lowe. It started out with her just talking to me about things going on in the ward and how my wife was. That bothered me a little, "How is your wife?"—because she was pregnant. I didn't feel guilty or anything about her being pregnant. All my bad feelings were concerned with me. Joan knew what she was in for when she married me.

Well, anyway, I became more open. I started talking and eventually joking around with the people on the ward. I told them about what was wrong with me—not "wrong with me," but where my head was and what I was trying to figure out. I made some friends. Two of them are back in different VAs.

The first period at the VA I didn't know the term "transsexual." I didn't have the word to put on me, but I knew I was a transsexual even through junior high and high school—some in grade school. I had never heard the term, so therefore I couldn't say I was a transsexual, but I was a female trapped in a male's body, and that's what a transsexual is—so I can say that I thought of myself as a transsexual. What I did know is what other people thought about people like myself from hearing jokes, and so on, all my life. I was ashamed, and basically that's why I was so depressed.

I was admitted to the central VA seventh floor which is the locked psychiatric ward with about 60 to 70 patients. It was dull and drab with dormitorylike sleeping rooms and two day rooms. Some of the psychiatrists were good, and some were not so good. The first doctor I had was all right. Dr. Lowe spent some time talking to me, asking about my past, and then he asked me what I wanted out of life. At the time I didn't know the details about sex change operations—I had kind of heard of them, but I didn't feel that it was possible for me. I talked to Lowe for a considerable length of time. He was about the only person I talked to, and we finally came up with three alternatives for my treatment. The first was intensive psychotherapy, the second was male hormone shots and intensive psychotherapy, and the third was female hormone shots and psychotherapy as a prerequisite to possible surgery. He told me to think about the alternatives carefully, and I did for a week or more. And then I told him that I decided on the female shots and psychotherapy. He said fine, and then they had a case conference on me. All hospitals do case conferences. It's a very horrifying experience. They call you into this large room, and you have everything from student nurses to the heads of units sitting around looking at you and talking to you. They are trying to do a diagnosis, all of them together, and then they ask you to leave and they talk about you. They had four or five psychiatrists from outside the hospital in on my conference. We talked awhile, and then they asked me about what I had decided about my treatment, and I told them what I had told Dr. Lowe; female hormones and psychotherapy to see how it works.

I left, and after the conference—a day after—Dr. Lowe came in to tell me that they had decided at the conference that they wouldn't give me female hormones and what they would give me was intensive psychotherapy. They just turned the thing around on me. Why did they ask me in the first place if I didn't have a choice? They wouldn't even tell me where to go to get what I wanted.

I know that Lowe was all for it, and so were the other younger doctors, but there were two against me, and they were the older doctors with more pull. The older doctors prefer walking the middle of the road, not doing anything that would get them or the hospital in trouble. One doctor's comment on my whole situation was, "If someone wanted to be an umbrella, would you try to make him an umbrella?" That was his theory on the whole thing. There were some others at the conference who wanted to try aversion therapy, shock therapy, and other things. They had all the big shots down there. Dr. Nero, Dr. Rietz, Dr. Barr, Dr. Nickel. Dr. Nickel is the psychologist who came onto my side. He was kind of against me at first, but he changed. The way I looked at the doctors and the other staff members was that they were either for me or against me. It ends up that you have people on your side and people against you, and then a whole mess of unknowns kind of floating around. It's good to find out who is on your side and who isn't. Jane, on the nursing staff, passed the word on to me about what physician felt what way. She'd say, "Don't freak out while this physician is on duty—just stay clear of him when he is OD, otherwise you'll end up in seclusion—they are out to get you." So I had to learn to play a kind of cat-and-mouse game, but there were a few doctors there that were really cool.

Lowe was on my side, but he was only a resident. The chiefs of service have most of the say about who gets what treatment. The doctors had to report to them and get their approval. Nine times out of ten the doctor who had the final say has never seen you. They may only know you from a tape recorder, and that's what they base their judgment on.

I was very angry and very frustrated about the conference. I couldn't see any sense in it. I think they thought that Lowe went out of bounds by even suggesting alternatives to me. I felt frustrated and angry. You're fighting all these people, and you know you're right. At the time I didn't know that much about psychiatry—the ins and outs of it. They snow you with fancy words that don't mean anything. They play word games with you, and you end up getting the shaft every time.

I saw Dr. Lowe for I don't know how many months. I talked about my feelings, my childhood, and basically what I felt about things. All the time that I was with him I still never got clear about the "white line." The white line is the professional term for the boundary line between the therapist and the patient. He seemed to want me to open up to him as you would to a friend, and yet he didn't want to be a friend—it was confusing. You couldn't be a friend and a therapist at the same time he told me. The confusion stayed with me for a long time, and it upset me quite a bit. But I liked him as a person. As a matter of fact, sometimes he would come down and shoot pool and sit around and talk with the patients. That's the only time I ever got him to answer any questions. He used to do it with all his patients. He was the only doctor in the hospital who did that. He wasn't afraid of walking down the corridor and meeting his patients. He'd go looking for them. Probably, another doctor would have confused me more than Lowe did, because I wouldn't have liked him.

The whole thing was that I didn't know what therapy was, and I didn't know how to go about it. I didn't know what you were supposed to do—there wasn't any couch. You know how always there is a couch? You see it in cartoons, with this bearded shrink sitting back, or something like that. That's not the way it was. I didn't know the difference between therapy and analysis and didn't know the different techniques of therapy—directive and nondirective. I didn't know what to expect as the end result, and I didn't know how I was going to achieve it. I took a long time, over a year, to learn about therapy. I learned through trial and error.

So I started seeing Lowe three to four times a week, an hour at a time. Having that much therapy is really unusual. We just sat and talked, and I don't think we got any place. He asked leading questions, and they didn't give me any answers. It wasn't a back-and-forth conversation like I thought it might be. I did all of the talking, as a matter of fact. He was taping most of my sessions, which made me very nervous. He finally took the tape recorder out. Any psychiatrist I have ever talked with has always put me on tape. They say something like, "I have a recorder—I know you won't mind," or they say nothing and just do it. What can you say? If you tell them you mind, they think you're hostile. I didn't tell Dr. Lowe that I was nervous about the recorder; I was too afraid of him. He finally left.

About three months after I was in the hospital, it was a Wednesday and I was in the middle of a group therapy or student government meeting, there was a call at the nurses' station. Dr. Lowe came out and called me. He said, "Mr. Fry, I want to talk to you. Your wife is in the delivery room right now. She just had a baby boy." I freaked out, I said, "Why didn't you tell me before this?" He said, "I didn't want to worry you." She got on phone from the recovery room so she could talk to me. I just said, "Hi," and then talked to the doctor.

I was kind of pissed. I had told them that when they found out that my wife was in the hospital I wanted to be told. "Wake me up day or night," but they didn't. I was very uptight about the baby. I was worried about it and her especially, with me in the hospital and not being able to help her. I was totally restricted at the time. I couldn't leave the ward. They didn't tell me, but they had a logical reason, I guess. They said that they didn't want to upset me and there was nothing I could have done anyhow. That's what they told me. One of the things that I asked even before I was admitted was could I see my wife when she went to the hospital? They said, "Yes," but then after she got there they started saying, "No." They finally took me over after she had been there for five days. I did want to see my son, even though I didn't like the idea that I was his father. I was still related to the child, and he meant a lot to me. I loved Joan very much, and I still do. Besides marrying her to play the role, I also loved her and that entered into it. People can love each other no matter what their sex is.

I finally got permission to see the baby, and two doctors took me over. Dr. Lowe and Dr. Manis both walked me over. They were afraid I might get super upset and freak out. I remember Dr. Lowe—a typical psychiatrist—saw the baby and said, "What a beautiful head." It was really something. I felt confused. The doctors were right when they said it would upset me. After the birth, that's all that I used to talk about, all that Dr. Lowe would let me talk about in the sessions was my feelings towards the baby and my wife.

After I found out I called my father and told him to come up and bring a box of cigars. I figured I would play the role and pass out cigars, and that kind of bull shit. My father never came. He was out getting drunk. He was just tickled pink. She was living with my father at that time, and he had taken her to the hospital, which I didn't know.

I haven't seen Joan for awhile. When she comes over to see my folks when I'm there, I go upstairs. I didn't want to upset her or anything. I was afraid of seeing her, and her seeing me. I don't think she could relate to me as Jane, and that would bother me, and her, too. She still thinks of me as Johnnie. I think that she thinks of me as having an incurable illness. She knew before we got married.

After Joan got out of the hospital she got her own apartment, and my social worker was trying to get me to go back with her, and that bullshit. I went to her apartment on a few weekends, but I couldn't follow through on it. It was such a big strain. I knew what I was, and I knew it just wasn't any good, my being with Joan. We talked about it and came to the decision that we should get a separation, which we did. Now she is working on the divorce, but that costs money and divorce proceedings take about six months. I could start them, but during the proceedings I couldn't take any other court action, like having my name changed.

While at the VA I did a lot of testing of people. Some of the suicide attempts were more like gestures to test people to see if they would respond to me. I couldn't believe that people could want to be friends, so I would put them in a position where they had to respond to me either positively or negatively. I used to see everything completely in black and white. This came out a lot in my psychotherapy with Dr. Meed, who was my psychiatrist after Dr. Lowe—that I see things totally one way or the other. I become very stubborn about it, and then when I do change my mind, I change it all the way. I don't think I was testing the first time I cut my wrists with the pipe grate—I hadn't started that yet. But like, at the hospital, I would take a mess of pills, and then let somebody know to see how they would react. There was one time when I drank some liniment which has poison in it, and I went and told the doctor on duty about it. She shoved ipecac down me, making me throw up. I can't say that I was consciously trying to get attention or test, but that was the underlying reason. It was like saying, "Are you my friend or aren't you?" Do you really like me?" People couldn't say, "I like you," and have me believe it. They had to do something to show it, and by helping me through some trial or tribulation they were showing me. It's kind of immature, but sometimes when you are ill that is the only way you can relate. Sometimes, there is no other way of doing it when you're ill the way I was this particular time.

I would say "psychologically messed up" instead of "ill," because I don't like the term "ill." I liked "mind fucked," but it doesn't go over with all people. When you are emotionally just plain wrung out, the only way that is left is simple immature action—you fall back on it because you don't have anything else. Sometimes I use the word "sick," because you are sick as far as society is concerned. I don't like to use it because of the connotations it has. Mental illness has a bad connotation. When I say I'm ill or messed up, I mean that I am confused or angry or hurt or at a point where my emotions are just all tucked up inside me. When society uses the term, they use it differently. I use it when I feel, like, trapped inside and you are screaming to get out and you can't.

I was at a point on the seventh floor where I didn't trust any contact with people. I was extremely confused. I had 20 some years hiding inside myself, and as time went on I became more and more introverted. After a while you become emotionally introverted. The pressure builds up inside you, and it's like blowing up a balloon. You reach a point where the pressure gets to be too much. When it happens to people, they start acting out in ways that people think are bazaar, and instead of saying, "Wow, that person is really hurting," they say, "Wow, that person is really weird," "That person is really sick." But when they say "sick," they don't mean let's try to help him. "Sick" means, like, leper. Get the person away because it is contagious. I built up inside and I just couldn't reach out and express anything.

My emotions were what was messed up. Somebody might say something to me, and I would get mad and slam my fist against the door. I knew that things like that weren't sensible, but in a way they were, because it was a way of releasing all the pent-up stuff. That kind of behavior isn't acceptable, even though it was sensible to me. It wasn't sensible to others. I wasn't destructive in that I would destroy other people's things or hurt anyone. I turned my destruction inward. I was punishing myself.

A lot of times I was angry at the hospital, and I would take it out on myself, or angry at someone else and take it out on myself. A lot of my anger and things were not directly related to my transsexualism. I mean, it was like two things, one was the transsexualism and the other was the mental hang-ups associated with the transsexualism. They are two separate things which are very much related.

The Fish Bowl:
Life on the Ward

The staff was all right on seven, but there were things they did that made you feel paranoid. Like, they used to keep a card on you during each shift, and they gave the card to the next shift. On the card was everything the patient had done during the day. Those cards made you feel that you were being watched all the time. The other thing they did was to sit in this big glassed-in nurses' station that sticks out into the day room and look at you. When you were in the day room, you felt you were being watched. You would look up, and you knew they were talking about you. You felt like you were in a goldfish bowl with the people coming in and out to watch you flip around. Matter of fact, that's the expression patients used when they talked about the ward. One thing we used to do is to go sit on the tables right in front of them and just stare at them. That would shake them up for a while.

They had a couple of seclusion rooms on the seventh floor. They lock people in there when they don't know what to do with them. When I first got there, I bothered people for a while and then tried to set fires, and stuff like that. So I got put in seclusion. The seclusion cell is approximately 8 feet wide and 10 feet long, and it's got one big, hugh window with shatterproof glass that you can't see out of and, of course, with heavy screen over it. Some of the cells have beds in them, and others have just mattresses on the floor. The doors are about two inches thick and made out of wood covered with steel, with a small window about six inches by six inches so the staff can look in on you. There is no toilet or sink. The cells are off the main corridor, and there is a door separating them from the main area. If you want water, they can close the door off to the corridor and lock it, and then unlock your door and let you out. They let you out to have water and walk up and down a little bit, but they have three or four attendants there when they do that. I don't know if they did that with me when I first went in there or not. I don't know if I was there long enough. I don't remember that time all that clearly.

Most of the time they put you there for 24 or 48 hours, and you only get a plastic spoon to eat with and a plastic tray to eat from.

Seclusion was a big thing on the ward. Watching someone being put in was a break in the daily routine. It's the one time you got to see all the doctors together. You see the nurses and everybody else running around. Really fascinating—better than sitting and watching soap operas on the tube, which was about the extent of the recreation on the ward. Actually, you had a number of choices for recreation. You could watch soap operas on the TV set in the dayroom, or go to the other day room and watch soap operas there. You could also sleep or play pool. Those were the things you could do. Once a week they might go bowling or go on a trip, but I'm not one for bowling. I hate it.

I remember the time I was put in seclusion involuntarily. That evening they were trying to watch the fights, and I tried to drag the TV into the bathroom, which they didn't like—that was, the attendants and the patients. I also emptied all the trash in the middle of the day room floor, and when they asked me what I was going to do with it, I told them I was going to burn it. They got a very good list of what I did, and nobody let me forget it. The aides who were there then and who are still there now, who see me, bring it up and we talk about it. They don't bring it up meanly—if they knew it would bother me, they wouldn't. Some of the things that I used to do were funny.

One time I did something that wasn't funny, which finished me—got me dragged into isolation. I was walking down the corridor, and there was this little old man in one of the rooms. After the fights Rocky and Max Black, the aides on duty, were sitting in the day room trying to play chess. This old man had a bad heart, and I walked by his room. Did you ever see these doors that are in the hospital that are really thick and bang when they shut? Well, I grabbed ahold of this door and slung it shut with all my might. To the old man inside, it must have sounded like the inside of a kettledrum, because he jumped right out of bed and started yelling, "Get that son of a bitch out of here." I didn't know the guy in there had any heart problems. I just shut the door. Rocky and Max jumped, and Max said to Rocky, "That son of a bitch has got to go," and they started chasing me around. I had been bothering them all day when they were trying to play chess. So they ran up behind me and grabbed me backwards—that's so they could drag me off backwards—so I was constantly off balance, which is an easy way for them to do it. The person can't fight that way because they can't see and can't grab. I didn't resist—I just totally relaxed by body, and that way they couldn't get me easily. It took five aides to put me in seclusion. They didn't ask me to go, but just grabbed me after they got the nurse's permission. After I got down there, I was pissed off. They put me in one of the rooms with a bed and locked the door. I took the bed apart totally and piled the mattress up against the wall, and the springs too. I took one of the poles that connected the two ends of the bed and used it like a ramrod into the door and the peek window. It went right through the window. They got very shook-up over that and took me out and put me in a room with no bed. Can you imagine little old nonviolent me being that destructive, but I was pissed off and was just trying to get out.

It's funny. Most people hated seclusion—it was a punishment—but I liked it in ways. I have a fear of wide, open spaces. The smaller a room is the more cozy it is, and the more I like it. The open ward scared me. The closer I have things around me, the better. I'm the type of person that, when I was a kid, I used to like to crawl underneath couches, behind couches, inside rolled-up carpets, and that kind of stuff.

As a matter of fact, later when they moved me up to eight, I asked to be put in—that's when I got really shook-up. They let me go, too. I would close the door and just lay down there on the mattress and go to sleep.

Most of the patients kind of conspire with each other against the staff in a friendly way. We used to have this charge nurse who would come around. She would be in charge of the whole hospital for one shift, and she was really funny. She acted like an old battle axe until you got to know her, and then she had a heart of gold. There was about 12 of us in the hall this one day, sitting on the floor. She comes through and says, "What's going on here?" We were just sitting there rapping—having an impromptu group therapy session of our own. One guy comes out with, "We're packed up and waiting for the bus to go to Little Falls." Somebody else said, "It used to stop here." She started laughing, and then this doctor came by and gave us a real weird look. We did a few things like that. Broke the boredom.

To tell the truth, I liked a lot of the patients, but some of the people that were on the ward would act as flaky as hell when we went any place. And I didn't feel like being rated flaky, too. A couple of times student nurses asked me if I wanted to go for a walk with the other patients, and I refused to go for the simple fact that some of them would act flipped out. I get embarrassed very easily, and these guys made me feel self-conscious. Like, you would be walking up toward the hamburger place, and one of them would yell out across the street to a girl. Just what men do normally, but about three times as loud. I guess I didn't like to admit that I was a mental patient.

The attendants weren't supposed to talk about the doctors behind their backs to the patients, but they did. The attendants were closer to the patients in some ways than they were to the doctors. They were kind of like the go-betweens. Some of them you trusted, and some you didn't. They could help you out. Some of the nurses were helpful, but one or two of them were bitches. They could give them a really tough time. I'd shake them all up. Some of the nurses just couldn't hack the idea of a person who wanted to be a girl. They set out to try to cure me. They would try to talk to me—after a while I would tell them that they were full of shit. There was at least that kind of give and take with them. There wasn't any give and take with the doctors. The doctors had their minds made up—they were the doctors and we were the patients, and you were wrong and they were right. I think most of the attendants looked at the patients like, "I had better watch my step because I could be here, too. I'm just like them."

The way doctors look at you is that they are going to cure you by their theory come hell or high water, whether the theory is right or not. You make the patient fit the theory one way or the other. When you come to see that, it becomes a game. You shop around the hospital to find the program or the doctor whose theory fits you—instead of the other way around. You know that the doctors aren't going to change to fit you.

Most of the patients hated their doctors. It wasn't so much for what they did, but what they didn't do. The doctors were never around. They saw the patients much more often than they do in the state hospitals, but they only saw them about once a week. I was seeing mine much more, because I was a special case. Once a week wasn't enough for the patients I knew. They would keep an eye down the corridor to see if the doctors were coming in or not. They had to walk down the corridor to get to the nursing station. The patients, if they could catch them, would surround the doctors and ask them questions and request favors like passes and things. Some of the doctors learned, though. They would walk down the fire escape and open the door right across from the nurses' station and run across the hall so the patients couldn't grab them.

There were two doctors that weren't like that, though—Dr. Stein and Dr. Lowe. They would sit with the patients every once in a while and play cards and stuff, which was pretty cool. Very undoctorlike, but very successful. The others never socialized with the patients whatsoever. The only time they would talk to you was when you were in their office and they had the upper hand, when they were in control. They didn't like to be caught off guard.

Most doctors don't know anything about where to go to get the operation, and if they do, they don't tell you. When I was in the VA Hospital, nobody would give me information. One doctor, who I was working with, was in favor of hormone shots but was not allowed to tell me where to go for them or anything like that—even though it was best for me.

The patients have this patients' government, which is kind of a joke. I used it a couple of times, and so did some of the other patients, but mostly we would joke about it. This was especially true of the veterans coming back from Vietnam. They were the ones who started calling it "student" government. At the VA patient government is like milieu therapy—someone's pipedream that doesn't work in practice. It looks good on paper, and that's about all; it doesn't do anybody any good. They can't make any decisions. What they can do is ask the staff to do something, but the staff makes the decision. Sometimes people who had grievances against each other took them to it. What happens is that they discuss it and then come up with a decision, and then the staff carries it out. The patient could have just as easily gone to the staff in the first place and asked for the same thing—in 99 percent of the cases they would have decided the same way.

The patient government makes people more dependent on those on the ward instead of directly doing something about what's bothering them. Instead of patient government and milieu therapy helping people, it only helps them relate to each other and forget about the outside, which is the reverse of what it is supposed to be.

Everyone on the ward was supposed to serve on a committee. I was on the Grievance Committee, which was just basically one guy bitching about another. It is supposed to be a logical way of one patient airing his grievances against another. So, instead of the two patients talking it out to each other, they go running to the Grievance Committee which keeps them from having it out with each other. Say, someone steals cigarettes, or one patient is a compulsive thief. One thing you learn right off in the hospital, by the way, is to keep your belongings on you at all times. He steals from one patient who gets pissed off and complains to the Grievance Committee. On the Grievance Committee are four patients and one doctor. The staff already knew the guy is a compulsive thief and the guy knew he was doing it, and it had already been kind of settled by the attendants—they told everybody to keep their cigarettes put away. So the Grievance Committee met on it and sent its recommendation to Patient Government, which was read at the meeting. It went something like, "A person who we shall not name" (it was asinine because everybody knew who we were talking about) has been stealing cigarettes." Well, the thing went on, and ended with recommendations that everybody keep their cigarettes to themselves, which everybody knew already in the first place. It made you feel like a fool. You felt that you were being made fun of doing all that for nothing.

It was funny, some of the patients used to go up to each other and say, "What's your major maladjustment?" I got to know some good people there. You become dependent on each other for survival, because if you don't have somebody else to lean on, the impact of the hospital can swamp you and take over you within 24 hours. If you aren't psychotic when you get there, you're going to be. Sometimes the patients are the only ones a patient can talk to. Most of the staff doesn't give a damn. Getting help is talking to a doctor once a week, and sometimes that's in a group. If a hospital is going to help someone and not mess them up, you have to have access to staff and therapy all the time. I think that's the only way a hospital could work. Right now, there's no individuality. Everybody kind of moves at the pace of the slowest patient. The rules are for everybody, and so is the therapy, and what have you—and it really doesn't work. Like, in some places, they have the rule that no patients can carry matches. Now, there are a lot of people on the ward who could use matches without being dangerous—most likely all of them. But they make the rule of no matches for everyone, in case there is someone who shouldn't have them.

Funny thing in hospitals, for most patients the biggest event of the day is the staff meeting. The staff is gone nine-tenths of the day; that is, they are off the ward that amount of time, but they spend a lot of their time in meetings talking about the patients. Even though they don't know about the patients, because they don't spend any time with them, they meet behind closed doors without the patient there to decide his fate. The patient is automatically categorized by 15 staff members and a mess of students sitting around in a room smoking cigarettes and drinking coffee. At these staff meetings, everybody is trying to impress everybody else with their vocabularies. Well, anyway, all the patients know what's going on behind the door and wait for the outcomes. It's just another thing that breaks the monotony of the day. One thing that I should say is that patients are brought into staffings, but more as examples, specimens, than as people who are supposed to participate. I have been "presented" twice to a staffing at the VA, and once at the Medical Center.

One thing that hospitals are big on is rules. The rules in the VA were made up for *everybody*. Even though the psychiatric patients were different from the rest of the patients with physical illnesses, they were supposed to still follow the same rules, which is kind of ridiculous. We did get them to be lenient with some of the rules with us. Like, all the other wards had their TV sets turned off at 10:00 and everybody had to be in bed. On the psychiatric ward, they made it 11:15 after the news, and then on the weekends it could stay on until the first late-night movie was over. We didn't tell them when the first movie was over, so sometimes we saw the second one, too.

We had more goddamn visitors coming through the psychiatric ward than on any other floor—there were always people just walking through, which I think they should limit. They were always showing new aides, new janitors, secretaries, mothers-in-law of doctors, and everybody else, just plowing through constantly. That really turned me off. It made me feel like I was on display.

The patients that weren't on the psychiatric wards kind of discriminated against us (the psychiatric patients). You used to hear it in the elevators all the time. If you were in the elevator and they didn't know you were on the seventh or eighth floor, and somebody else go on who looked nuts, you would hear people comment about them after they got off. Stuff like, "There's a candidate for the seventh"—things like that. It used to burn me, and at the same time I felt like hiding in a hole in the floor. I don't know, people have such weird opinions of mental patients. Funniest thing was when the new student nurses would come on the ward; they would be so afraid. Some of the guys would stand by the door and jump out and yell "boo," to scare them. After a while they would relax. They got acclimated slowly. Just had to keep them away from the real flippy ones. You could always spot the student nurses that were scared, because they would always stand by the nurses' station, and when they came into the day room they would walk real fast and were real tense. After a while they would calm down and sit in a chair and just rap with you. Student nurses are a blessing in any mental institution. They are the only light there is in a state hospital like Central. They were the only people some people had to talk to.

If you had an off-the-ward pass, you could mix with the other patients in other parts of the hospital—go down to the canteen and things like that. I put my foot down about one thing. They have a set of blues, they call them. They are like superheavy lounging pajamas made out of blue cotton, with a blue jacket with "USVA" written on the left-hand vest pocket. These were what you were supposed to lounge in, but I refused to wear them. That was because only the mental patients got them, so everybody else knew what ward you were on. After a certain amount of time you are allowed to get your own clothes and wear them. But then again, if you had something with short sleeves, everybody could tell you were on the psychiatric ward by your plastic arm bracelet and the fact that you had on street clothes. They knew automatically that you were a nut. All the other patients wore pajamas.

I found a good way to handle the arm bracelet. I went down to OT and had them put snaps on it, so I could take it on and off when I wanted to. I kept it in my wallet when I was off the ward, and when I needed it I just snapped it back on. That way nobody knew you were a patient in the canteen. It was stupid that they were on permanently. After I started working outside the hospital, technically I was supposed to have on a bracelet, which was ridiculous.

We used to have these groups come in and take us out for parties and picnics. I remember this one time we went to a spaghetti party over on the north
side in the Italian neighborhood. The women's auxiliary of the American Le-
gion or the Veterans of Foreign War sponsored it. They came with this bus
and drove us over there to this room over a bar where the Post was. They
were these old ladies running around trying to make everybody happy, but
what they really do is make you feel like a horse's ass with all the games and
stuff they want you to play. They act like you're 14 years old. Instead of trying
to get you into a decent conversation, like coming up to you and saying,
"What do you think of Nixon?" they come up to you and say, "Let's play pin
the tail on the donkey," or "Do you want to sing some songs?"—stuff like
that.

Most of the people who went were psychiatric patients. I think there were
25 who went to the spaghetti thing, and everyone but three were from the psychiatric ward. All the attendants that would go would be psychiatric aides. So
they were trying to do something nice by inviting us all over for dinner—
"Help out the boys in the hospital"—but it ended up making you feel like a
jerk. There weren't hardly any other people there except for a few auxiliary
women and two or three men to help out. Those who weren't patients walked
around with name tags on and these straw hats, and said things like, "Boy,
are we going to have fun tonight." Most of the patients just sat there saying to
themselves, "I bet—where's the food." I just tried to ignore everybody. The
patients kind of joked about the whole thing behind their backs. They would
say things like, "My mother made better spaghetti than this, and she was
Irish."

We were taken on a couple of picnics that weren't much better. These were
given by the Cooties which is something like the female equivalent of the
Shriners. They were the real happy-go-lucky fun type—right. We did the
same thing for picnics—the bus would come and they would pile us in it and
drive us out to some place. I remember this one we went to, the minute we
started getting off the bus they got out the balloons and filled them full of
water and started a tossing game. When stuff like that started, I usually
walked away and headed towards the woods or someplace to be alone. Some of
them were very condescending. They would come up to you and say, "Where
are you going? Aw, come on and join us. We're having lots of fun." You'd
say, "Look, I don't feel like it," and they would say something like, "You're
the only one who hasn't had a turn." If you refused, they really got frustrated,
and then they would leave you alone.

We always had the same thing at the picnics, hotdogs and hamburgers, and
no beer. Once everyone that the attendants said was okay got one beer. That
was just ridiculous. I mean, after the picnic half of the group would go back

and sit around the Bellows (a local bar) and get drunk anyway. They used to say that because you were on medication you can't have beer, but then you have an off-the-grounds pass so you drink it anyway. They could have left it up to you. The people who went on the picnics—who arranged them—were veterans who liked to drink and normally would have drunk if we weren't there, but they didn't have any beer either. Most of the people who organized these things were the jolly-helper type—that's what I call them, or the "do-gooders" is what we called them. They want to bring sweetness and light into the world and also like to be the life of the party. The do-gooders ran the picnics. Everything was taken totally out of your hands. Even having fun in taken out of your hands. So you learn to make your own ways of having fun. I used to actually enjoy the picnics, because I could sit there and watch everybody and get my kicks. It was amusing to watch them play these silly games. Like in a circus or a zoo, like monkeys, with everybody bustling around with sack races. No sooner would a patient shake something off about one thing, then someone else would come up insisting that you eat your fifth hot dog. "Yoo-hoo, Mr. Fry, where are you going?" I enjoyed it in my own sarcastic way. Probably about one-fourth of the patients really enjoyed it—those were the ones who never went out—but the majority just went to get away from the boredom of the ward.

The trouble with these people who took us out was they weren't used to being around mental patients. They didn't realize that we are people and that we do other things besides sit around watching "Seasame Street." Their impressions of mental patients are people who sit around all day drooling and reading comic books.

I'm laughing at these people who were trying to be nice, but that's not very grateful, but the way they act toward you is that you are too stupid to know the difference. I kind of feel sorry for them. Their intentions were really good, and they were really trying with all the knowledge they had. They were doing well with the information they had, but the problem was the information they had about what mental patients are like and what they enjoy was wrong.

Once and a while some of the people realize that we aren't what they thought we were and that's nice, but most of them don't.

I remember these little old ladies that used to come up to the ward for bingo night. They had this cart that they would wheel in and say, all smiles, "Come on boys—bingo time." This one time I was just laying in my bed reading, and I said to one of them, "Get lost." She said, "Come on now—don't you want to win a prize?" Most of the prizes were canteen books (coupons for the canteen), which you could con someone out of anyway if you really wanted one. I said, "Look, I don't want to play bingo," and she said, "It will help take your mind off things." I said, "Look, I'm here to get my problems solved, and I'm solving my problems my way. You solve your problems your way." I actually told her that. I said, "If you can work out your tensions by playing bingo, then go right ahead—it doesn't work for me." She got very upset, and thought I wasn't very cooperative. I didn't think she was either.

We also had ladies come around for "birthday time," with cakes—right. They usually had a cart with four or five cakes with "Happy Birthday" written on them, and they would wheel them around to the different wards. There was always a couple of women—not just one. They would come onto the ward and smile and grin and say things like, "Who wants to celebrate their twenty-fourth birthday?" By the time you're 24, you don't need a cake. When they came on the wards, most of the time they couldn't find anybody. They would all be hiding someplace or sleeping. The head nurse didn't want patients sleeping in their rooms during the day, so you used to have to go find someplace to sleep, like the library or behind the gym curtains or behind a book in the day room or in the coffee room. There was this one guy who was 78 and had diabetes, and they brought him a cake. He gave it to his friends. Poor guy—here he was a diabetic so he couldn't eat the cake in the first place, and in the second place he didn't want to remember his birthday anyway. If they caught you on the ward when they brought the cake, they sang to you. My birthday is on July 4th, so I used to stay away from the ward between the 2nd and the 6th day so as to miss them. If they didn't find you, they left it in the nurses' station, and then everybody could have it with evening coffee, which was good.

The whole idea of bringing the cakes the way they did was ridiculous. I can see it for patients who maybe are confined to bed with some illness, who might enjoy it, but all the psychiatric patients on the seventh and eighth floors are running around. They want something to do, but not to play childish games. Who the hell wants to be reminded by a bunch of sweet, old ladies that you're considered a nut? The guys on the eighth floor were out most of the day anyway. During the day you could usually find at least half of the eighth floor over at the Bellows getting drunk, so they could face the night. If you were out, you would stop and buy some hamburgers or a piece of cake and some coffee, and all that kind of stuff. So what the hell—who needs having little, old ladies coming up to cheer you up? You've got your own ways of getting cheered up.

One thing about all the hospitals I have been in, and especially about the VA, was that everything just closed up on the weekend. You know how on the outside everybody looks forward to the weekend because there are things to do? Well the reverse is true in the hospitals. Nothing goes on in the psychiatric ward between 4:00 on Friday and 9:00 on Monday morning. There is no recreation, no OT, no nothing. The whole place just gets bolted up. That's the problem with the outings too. They are always during the week, when you really don't need them. During the week I would just as soon see my shrink and go to group therapy and be left alone, but during the weekend I could use some people from the outside to talk to. Even if I didn't want to go on the outing, you kind of had to, because if you didn't they would say that you're withdrawn and not being cooperative, which would be bad on your record.

I think the records they keep on you in the hospital are just typical of the way the medical profession operates. They keep everything a secret—like it wasn't you who the stuff is about. Once something gets on your record, it never gets changed. Someone can say you did something that you didn't, or make a mistake—it would never come off. I would like to look over my record, so that I can tell them what's prejudicial.

Once things like diagnosis get in there, you're marked. The minute I mentioned to a doctor that I felt that I was a female, it automatically was put in as a psychiatric problem. After that everything that was wrong was considered part of that. They didn't even have to look at me—it was all in the records. Like, as soon as that was on the records, they automatically treated the seizures as completed psychosomatic. Everybody forgot about the rifle that dropped on my head. I couldn't fight the government for the money, because I was considered a nut. Just recently, they took an EEG and it was recorded. Psychosomatic seizures don't get recorded on an EEG, so I finally got a private neurologist and he found that they were phototropic. Before 1965, the VA was treating my seizures, or at least looking for a clue to what was causing them. The minute they had me as a nut, they stopped looking for clues. It wasn't until I got on the eighth floor that they tried to do anything about them, and then this doctor decided to try seizure medication and got them under control. I filed for compensation before I went into the hospital, but it didn't go any place. I probably could get it if I waited long enough, but it is just the idea of so much red tape, and the government can tie you up for years—you're dead before you get anything out of them.

CHAPTER

10

The Good Doctor

In total, I was in intensive therapy for three years. As I said, my first therapist was Dr. Lowe. Most people don't get that kind of intensive care with a psychiatrist at the VA. I was weird enough to get it, at least that's why I thought I got it. Everybody saw me as a "case." It's like, "Look, Joe, we've got a real live one now. I only read about these things in books, now we've got one and it's really great." In some respects that was good, because I could take advantage of it and get what I wanted, but in other ways it was a hindrance. It didn't make me feel good to be so odd.

There is a big to-do about transsexualism and the role of psychotherapy. Psychotherapy, psychiatrists, and psychotherapists have tried to "cure" transsexuals, but very few people ever got "cured." As a matter of fact, no transsexual has ever been "cured" that I know of. It's only a boosting agent, if anything—it helps people through critical periods. Certain doctors kind of latched onto me, who thought they could cure me. You have to contend with *their* feelings. Actually, I had some good therapists—it was their supervisors who were a pain. The only real bastard was at the Medical Center.

Before Dr. Lowe left a female doctor came on the ward, Dr. Meed. One night I was all shook-up, I don't remember what it was all about, but I talked to her about it and I liked her. Our personalities seemed to get along nice. I don't think you can have therapy with just anybody. You have to get along with the person. So when Dr. Lowe was transferred, I told him that I would

123

like to have Dr. Meed, and he said he would talk to her about it and see if she would accept me as a patient. She did. Matter of fact, after she went to another hospital she kept me as an out-patient so that I could continue seeing her.

I was on the locked ward for approximately six months, and then I graduated to the eighth floor, with coming and going privileges. I was less depressed, and they thought that I could handle it.

Dr. Meed used to get me out of a lot of messes. When I got transferred from the seventh to the eighth floor, it was with the stipulation that I get a private room. When I got up there I was put in a four-person room, and I started freaking. I went down to see the head nurse, and she said, "Nobody gets special privileges up here." I called Dr. Meed, and she got Dr. Nickel and another doctor and they went up there and said, "Mr. Fry is to get a private room. Nobody else is to be in with him. I got my own room with a private shower and toilet. It was really considerate. I made up with the head nurse after that.

I stayed with Dr. Meed all through my stay at the VA and for approximately six months afterward. The total time with her was about three years. Dr. Meed being a female was easier for me to relate to. Males are threatened by me. Also, she was very empathic. I didn't have to go into all the details; she seemed to know what was going on without me telling her. Jokingly, I say I cured her. When I first met her, she was very somber and always dressed in dark clothes. After awhile, when she left the VA she was wearing prints and letting her hair down instead of keeping it in a bun. At the rate she was going, I would hate to see her now.

Dr. Meed was really nice. We got along good, and she liked me as a patient and I liked her as a doctor. I followed her around like a puppy dog when she changed hospitals. I was staying in the VA, but then I'd get out during the week and go see her, which was totally against precedent, by the way. By that time, I had three doctors. I had a doctor in the VA to write prescriptions, Dr. Meed, and Dr. Campbell. Sometimes it got confusing.

Soon after I got to the eighth floor I went through vocational testing and counseling. The idea was to get you involved in some training or work that you could do during the day, and get you so you would have something to do when you left. It was an open ward that you were only supposed to sleep on. I had three days of testing that was analyzed by two different counselors. They both gave me the same results. I was in the ninety-ninth percentile for abstract reasoning, nintieth percentile in spatial relations—in the 90's in all the abstract areas. In the more concrete things like spelling and arithmetic I was down below the 50's though. All the percentiles were based on *male* high school graduates. They all showed that I was good working with people and in abstract reasoning. I have this special gift of taking something abstract and making it so people can understand it. They gave me an IQ test, too. My IQ varies with what drugs I'm on—how doped up and they got me—or what my attitude is toward the people giving it or whether I am depressed or not. It varies anywhere from 130 up.

So they gave me all these tests and called me in for counseling. The things that they listed that I was best suited for were in this order: epistemologist, psychiatrist, brain surgeon, lawyer, and I can't remember the rest. This is what they told me the books said I was good for, based on the tests. I wound up going to beauty school more than a year later, but that was about how useful the information was. I wanted to be a psychologist. I still want to be a psychologist. From the list of occupations they read, psychology seemed to fit pretty close to what I might be good at. What they told me was that because of my psychiatric problems I could never work in the field of psychology, or any other field with people. They said that to me. They counseled me. They gave me all these tests, and called me in for counseling and told me that I couldn't be what they said I should be. Pissed me off. God, was I mad. It just seemed so totally unreasonable. They didn't advise me to do anything, just what not to do. I was a year on the eighth floor, just hanging around.

There was this one friend that I had on the eighth floor; that was Nancy. She was really nice, and we got along fine—one of the only women around. Many times I had to carry her home from the Bellows. The nurses used to get really upset, because I would carry her into her room and they didn't think I should. It didn't bother the doctors—not any of them—the ones that were for me or the ones that were against me. The ones that were against me being a transsexual thought that if I had anything to do with a girl it must mean that I was getting better, and the ones for me knew that I'd never do anything in the first place, so why fuss. The nurses got upset because I was breaking the rules.

The VA would only prescribe psychotherapy—no female hormones or anything. Dr. Meed didn't agree with VA policy and was critical of them, but what could she do as their employee? She gave me some support and was helpful in making me understand some of my guilt, but I didn't feel I was heading any place. It was the official VA policy to work to make a man out of me, and I clearly wasn't moving in that direction in my own head. One day I was walking around to the University area, which is adjacent to the hospital, and I happened to run across the Christine Jorgensen story in one of the newsstands. (Before this I looked in the library for articles about people with problems like mine. Articles I read were in medical texts dealing with people who had hormone difficulties.) I remember when I was a kid hearing about her—I remember the scandal, but it wasn't all that important to me then and I was pretty young. I was interested in it, but it just didn't quite click, the connection between us two. Well, anyway, I picked up the book and read it. She said in that book so many of the things that I had felt and was feeling that I couldn't help but identify with it. I didn't identify with it all that closely, because I thought that things that happened to her couldn't happen to me, things like the operation, because I was just an ordinary person. I thought of her as some kind of a movie star or something. But there was some hope in her story. More important to my life than the story was an article I read in the paper about the same time. It was about transsexuals and a doctor who treated them. I believe that the first time I saw the word "transsexual" was in the Christine Jorgensen story. I had always felt that my troubles were physiologically based, and the article in the paper expressed that point of view. Psychotherapy was getting me nowhere, and this doctor's approach seemed right on target. The doctor's name was R. Z. Campbell and he lived in New York City, so I went down to the VA library and looked for a Manhattan telephone directory. They had one, and I looked up his name. There was only one in the book with those initials.

I took a chance that it was he, and wrote a long letter. I took a long time writing, being very careful not to say anything which might make him think I wasn't sincere or wasn't eligible for his services. I tried to keep from getting excited, but this was my first hope in a long time. My letter read:

6432 Marrow Street
Central City
19 August, 1968

Dr. R. Z. Campbell, M.D
88 E. 64th Street
New York, New York

Dear Dr. Campbell:

Having found your name associated with articles on transsexualism, I am writing for your advice and/or help. I am not aware of any doctors in my area that could offer me help with this problem. Possibly you can refer me to someone if you can't or choose not to assist me.

I am a twenty-three year old white male. For the past seventeen years, I have been obsessed with the idea that I am more female than male. At present I find it impossible to identify myself as a male in a physical or emotional make-up, except for the most obvious male characteristics. Even in that regard I have a smooth skin, very little body hair, and find it necessary to shave only once a week.

I was recently advised to consult a psychiatrist after twice attempting self-mutilation and suicide, so I acquired admission to the Veterans Administration Hospital where I received some sixty sessions of psychotherapy and psychiatric treatment. My feelings haven't changed; I still crave to be feminine externally to fulfill what I feel internally. I can not resolve to accept my body as it is. My requests for hormone treatment, or other necessary procedures to effect my desired change, were denied. I was unable to receive advice as to where or whom to go to, as the subject was closed. It is by my own personal efforts that I discovered your name and examples of your experience in this phenomena.

I suffer from deep depression, and am unable to maintain steady employment, and feel inadequate in my forced role as a male. May I interject at this time that I have never engaged in homosexual activities, and my feelings are not that of a male for a male.

It was once suggested in good faith that I wear feminine clothing, but even this in the privacy of my home is not a relief; I realize it is a cover up and transvestism is not the solution I am seeking or can accept.

I carefully read your remarks in a recent article, and I now have a feeling of hope mixed with anticipation of freedom from this terrible dilemma.

I know this is an imposition on your valuable time and experience, but I know of no other course to follow. I cannot fathom going into a strange doctor's office for help, and it would only result in being referred to a psychiatrist . . . a dead end street for me.

No doubt, you are besieged by letters of this nature, but I pray you will not dismiss this as a crank letter, or a result of a temporary obsession. I can assure you that I am sincere, and to the best of knowledge, otherwise normal.

I will appreciate a reply either as an appointment for a personal consultation, or referral to a doctor in this vicinity that will give me specialized care for my situation.

Very truly yours,

John Fry

A lot was riding on that letter. Almost a month went by before I received a reply which said:

R. Z. Campbell, M.D.
8437 Madison Avenue.
c/o W. Rider, M.D.
New York, N.Y.
September 16, 1968

John Fry, Jr.
6432 Marrow St.
Central City

Dear Mr. Fry:

Your letter of September 9th, addressed to my old New York office, was finally forwarded to my home. I have no office in New York at present, and cannot see any patients just now. I shall probably have an office again early next year.

Dr. W. Rider takes care of my patients at the above address and you could make an appointment with him. He is fully familiar with your problem and, if necessary, could be in touch with me too.

You are evidently a transsexual who has had the same sad experience with the medical profession as so many others. You may find the book, *The Transsexual Phenomena* by Dr. Benjamin. (The Julian Press, 119 Fifth Avenue, New York, N. Y, 10003) helpful to explain the situation.

Please read the enclosed carefully and try to be patient. I feel confident that you will eventually find help and with it, a happier future. I will do all I can, and so would Dr. Rider.

Sincerely yours,

R. Z. Campbell, M.D.

RZC/va
Encl: # 41.

Hearing from him was the most important and the happiest moment of my life—I felt that I had found someone who understood my problem. The possibility of an operation was new to me, and at first a little frightening, but the fact that there were alternatives to my misery was encouraging. I wrote Dr. Rider, telling him about my hopes:

6432 Marrow Street
Central City
October 7, 1968

W. Rider, M.D.
8437 Madison Avenue
New York, New York

Dear Dr. Rider:

You were referred to me by Dr. Campbell, since he cannot see any patients at this time.

Since February 17, 1968, I have been undergoing intense psychotherapy for transsexualism and related personality conflicts. I have been exploring the different possibilities of finding a compromise, without resorting to the ultimate necessity of a conversion operation, even though this is what I desire. I am trying to find the answer in hormone treatments, to make me more feminine looking. If this does not satisfy my desires, then I will have the operation and I hope this will accomplish what I seek.

I realize the problems involved in the operation, and that it is not "guaranteed" and is not reversible. So I am dilligently trying to find an answer that is more acceptable to a very unsympathetic group of people, the medical profession.

Since this is not a decision to be made lightly, I have been trying to look outside my emotions and think with my brain. I think that the hormone treatments are a logical decision to make, since this is bound to help in some extent and I can perhaps then make a good decision concerning the operation. I wish to make an appointment with you since you are the only one to help me and perhaps answer some of my questions. If at all possible I would like to see you some time at the end of November. This is because of my financial condition.

I would appreciate any help you can give me.

Very truly yours,

John Fry

I shortly received word that I could see him, and an appointment was set. Although he wasn't the famous and prestigious Dr. Campbell, I was so glad to have somebody to see who was interested in my problem and who I didn't have to go into a long detailed explanation with about what was going on. If nothing else, I thought at least I could get some advice.. So I flew down to New York. The first visit was $50. I was surprised to find that Dr. Rider wasn't there, but Dr. Campbell was. So I got examined by him. I sat down, and he took a case history, and all this. He was kind of amazed that I was a patient in the VA on a weekend pass coming down to see him.

When I saw Dr. Campbell for the first time, that's when I chose a name. He said "What's your other name?" I said, "What other name?" He said, "All transsexuals have another name." I said, "I don't. He said, "Well you better find one quick," and I said, "OK, Jane." I knew what I wanted, but I never called myself that. I never had a specific name for myself. I never had a second personality that I kept locked up, say, with my clothes. I never dressed to change my personality, because I was what I was. I just never thought of a name. I always liked the name Jane ever since I was little—I don't know, I just liked the name. Jane, the nurse at the VA was helping me then, too, so that was probably part of it.

A funny thing happened there. He did a really weird physical on me, which involved measuring my bones with a caliper, and he used a tape measure more than a tailor does. Every part of my body was measured and the skin was felt, and all this looking for secondary sex characteristics. At one part of the examination I had to lay down on the table and put my feet in the stirrups, which I had never done before of course. It blew my mind so totally that after the examination I tried to get up and forgot to unhook one leg. I flipped over on the floor totally naked. I was so embarrassed, I just laid there and kind of broke up.

He didn't prescribe anything right then; he wanted test results. The key tests came back a month later. I think one was a CBC, blood count. The other involved a urine specimen. I was supposed to save up 24 hours of urine, so my nursing friends up at the VA got me VA sample bottles to save it in without the VA knowing it. I swiped a couple of their 24-hour bottles and sent it to a private lab. I was playing one against the other. It was the only way I could get anywhere.

I was very encouraged by Dr. Campbell. The only thing I can say is that he is a very beautiful human being. I can't use any other word to describe him. He is compassionate and understanding. He seems to understand things without your going into long details of what's going on. It is very unusual to find a doctor like that. Besides, he was very cautious. He didn't want to prescribe any hormones or anything until he got the results back from the tests. But right after the exam, while I was down there in his office, he told me that I definitely had secondary female characteristics.

The second trip to New York was to see Dr. Rider. He just gave me medication and information on operations, and we set up the next appointment. I flew to New York City and grabbed a cab to the doctor's office. After the appointment I grabbed a cab back to the airport and went back on the next flight. That way I wouldn't be in New York overnight, and I wouldn't have to explain anything to the VA. After a while all the patients, staff and everybody at the VA knew I was going, but nobody said anything. The VA officially couldn't acknowledge my trips, and technically all they were doing was writing me passes. It didn't make any difference to them where I went or who I saw, as long as they weren't officially a part of it.

I can't tell you what it meant to me to begin seeing Dr. Rider. Shortly after I started taking the hormones he prescribed I began noticing some changes in me. They were more psychological than I had imagined they would be. I was more at peace with myself—less anxious—less liable to get upset. My male sex drive was nil, and I was much happier; I had just a very good reaction to them—I felt good. My breast size increased a little, but not all that much, and my fat distribution changed. I kept going back to New York every month, and then they started me on shots of the same stuff. Then I went every couple of weeks.

In Dr. Rider's office he had something that was really cool. His bathroom, instead of saying "Men" or "Women" had a question mark. Dr. Rider and his wife ran group therapy sessions, if you'd consider them group therapy. So I went to three of those sessions which I thought were totally ridiculous. I met quite a few transsexuals there, and got a picture of a transsexual community; if that's what it was. One time I flew down to see Dr. Rider to get my shot, he mentioned that he had a group that met the first Sunday of every month and asked me if I was interested in coming. I told him that I would be at the next session.

The first time I went, there were about 25 people. I was excited to go, because I wanted to meet others who were going through the same things that I was. I thought that I could relate to them much easier than I could to someone who hadn't. It's kind of a hard thing to relate to–I guess you would agree.

When I got there, they were all sitting around in a circle. The doctor's wife led the group. At the time I thought she and her husband were very nice people. Something happened a couple of months afterward that made me very angry at him. Well anyway, his office was near Coney Island, about one block from the boardwalk; right in the slums. Dr. Rider had two offices; the one I went to was for his poor clients and his transsexuals. I never saw his good office, but the one I went to had a receptionist who was Puerto Rican and hardly spoke English. It was hard to get anything across to her. The office had benches around a wall. He was concentrating mostly on Medicaid and Medicare patients at the time. Knowing some of the transsexuals he dealt with, I know he wouldn't want to shake up too many of his regular clients by having them in the same office waiting room. In some ways I can't blame him, but in other ways I don't like discrimination. I didn't want to be categorized as such, but I almost expect it. You almost expect that you are going to be looked down upon—you just have to grin and bear it and try to get as much as you can out of the system. Anyway, his office was very scroungy and dirty. Kind of pissed me off, because I used to look very nice when I went down there. Since I was taking a plane, I used to get really dressed up.

It was really funny at the meeting; Dr. Rider's wife introduced me as "a guest visiting us from Central City." Like isn't that a nice thing. For awhile everyone thought I was a guest speaker, in that I was quite a "wheel" female, as they put it. That kind of blew my mind. They had to be reassured that I was just another nut like themselves. The meeting consisted of a lot of rapping back and forth and actually saying nothing.

It was kind of overwhelming. I was getting very bad feelings from almost everybody there. I started becoming moralistic. I thought of these people as freaks. In a lot of respects they weren't like me, and they made me upset because I had flown all the way from Central City to see them and to be in their group. My immediate impressions were—a bunch of guys impersonating females. I never have got over that feeling. They were very very catty—the feelings that I was getting. I've only been in gay bars two or three times. I was getting the same feelings from them as I would from a drag queen—kind of frowning on the other person.

They took a break halfway through the meeting. You couldn't smoke in his office, so I went downstairs and everybody was down there too. I was feeling totally freaked out of my mind. These girls were talking about using prosthetic devices, and how many men they had seduced the week before. The majority of them just hit you psychologically as a male dressed as a female. I just couldn't see what I could learn from them. The cattiness really came out downstairs. One of the people came up to me and asked me if my breasts were real. I said, "Of course, why?" It was like they almost said, "Prove it." It just freaked me out, since I'm not the type of a person to use falsies or false hips or anything like that. They wanted to know if my hair was my real hair. I used to get that quite a bit. They actually pulled my hair, and I got angry. "Ask me. If you don't believe me, forget it; that's your hang-up; but don't go pulling my hair; it's not that big a thing." It just hit me, because here these people thought I was doing something like that. I just couldn't understand it— why they thought that way. I was very—unsympathetic, as a matter of fact. I guess I was mostly threatened.

I was saying to myself, "People group me with these other people, and I don't like these other people." I'm looking down on them, so where do I fit in? What am I? All these questions were coming out of my head, and it was becoming very hard to handle. I just really couldn't face it. I got very angry with the doctor because I was asking, "Why did he categorize me as such—I am not this."

The group was not run like a regular group therapy session. It was totally informal. It was just a meeting more or less to get people together to swap ideas. It wasn't anything like a consciousness raising group either. The people in the consciousness raising groups normally know what is going on and are getting out feelings about certain things. They didn't like getting into their feelings about anything. We were talking about stuff such as: How do you buy a dress? How do you measure for clothes? How do you apply make up? Bragging a little bit, there was very little they could have told me.

It cost me $6 to go to the meeting. The people who were supposed to get shots got their shots there, but that was extra. A visit was about $15. This came out of my own pocket. Twenty-five people times $6. That's quite a lot of money for the doctor for a two-hour Sunday session. Nobody thought about the possibility of being ripped off, I don't think. For awhile I had it in the back of my mind that he was a rip-off, not just because of this group thing. I just thought he was in it to make the money, and no and's and if's, or but's about it. I wasn't knocking his making money since he has to live, but I thought he was making a little too much. I have no idea of how much I totally gave him—probably only about $150; but that doesn't include airfare, which was $50 round trip, and the taxicab fare from the airport to his office, which was $6 one way.

A lot of people at that time liked Dr. Rider. He is a very conscientious doctor in certain respects. He is providing a service and is well read on transsexuals. This group could provide very beneficial services. It just wasn't appropriate for me—that's why I stopped going.

Coming back on the plane from the first group session I was feeling very rejected, very hurt, very uptight, nervous, frustrated, and angry. I was feeling just about everything; but confused mostly. For a few minutes I thought that maybe I was just like them. But I said to myself, "No way"—I just couldn't relate to it. I thought that if I was raised in New York City things might have been different. I thought my environment would have been somewhat like those people at the doctor's office. I might have grown up expecting that that was my life-style. You either had to fit with that group, or you don't fit anywhere in a place like New York. In New York it is very hard to be an individual. When you are very lonely, where there are people like yourself you have to conform to the group standads.

When I got back from that trip to New York, I changed in my sister's apartment. She was out of town. Normally, when I had to go to New York, changing was an extra expense. I had to rent a motel room, change, take the flight, fly back, go change in the motel, take the key back, and get off to the VA. It was kind of funny. Dr. Rider and Dr. Campbell wanted me to live and work as a female. The VA didn't want me to dress as a female. I had to find someplace to switch personalities more or less—to switch roles. It was like taking off and putting on masks.

The motel was $12, the airfare was $50, $12 for cabs, the doctor cost $15, and the group session was $6, so that's about $94 a shot, not counting eating. I was paying that almost every two weeks. I was getting state disability which ran $230 a month, so that just about covered it, leaving enough for cigarettes. I went back and forth to New York for about four months.

The reason I stopped going was that Rider kept making promises about the operation at this one particular place. He did that all the time I was seeing him. I was still under therapy with Dr. Meed, and I used to talk to her about it. Finally, she got fed up and phoned him and found out that there weren't any programs there. He promised me an operation. He said that it would be under a research grant, so I wouldn't have to worry about the money. It was Memorial Hospital in New City, the place I was supposed to have it. There are lots of researchers teaching in the hospital, so it is very logical that they would do something like that. Come to find out he didn't know anybody there. He probably got some information through the grapevine that they were doing the operation and decided to send me up there. He might have been waiting to find out more facts. It was probably very innocent, but it hit me too hard. I don't like to play games with things like that.

After the thing with Dr. Rider I was pretty down. I resigned myself to not going down there again, but the only trouble was my hormone shots. I went looking for a doctor. I just wanted to have someone who would prescribe medication or give me hormone shots. I was looking for a young doctor, especially. People who are just out of school or in school are more open to things than older people. Takes more to shake them up.

One of the doctors I went to was semi-recommended by a friend. It's this person's family doctor. She didn't know that I would get the response that I did. As a matter of fact, she was very shocked. I called up and made an appointment, and they wanted to know why. I said I just wanted to talk to the doctor—personal problems. This first one I saw acted very much like the second. With both of them I opened by saying, "I have been seeing a psychiatrist, my major problem being that I am a transsexual in the process of undergoing—or of preparing for surgery. My psychiatrist knows what is going on, but cannot prescribe medication I need. I am looking for a physician to handle me medically, as far as taking hormones and such." The two of them almost sounded alike. They said that it was not within their ethics to do something like this, and that perhaps I should change psychiatrists. I should delve more into this whole problem psychologically. They were very nice about it, but very nicely telling me I was totally crackers and that they didn't want any part of it. Then they went into this ethics bit. I think their ethics are pretty shitty. They didn't even ask for a psychiatric recommendation. I mentioned who my psychiatrist was. They didn't know her, but they could easily have found out who she was by calling the Medical Center, since she was working there then. They could have found out a little bit, but they didn't try. In a way I guess I was threatening to them. I found that out later how I threaten people. I hadn't reached the point where I understood that yet. At least they were being somewhat sympathetic—at least they were listening to me, which was as much as I hoped for.

I saw a third doctor and started out about the same way. His response was just said outright—that I was a very sick person and he wouldn't jeopardize his practice by upsetting his patients with me. He started getting very angry. He looked like he didn't know what to do. He looked like he was going to get violent. He stood behind his desk, and I said, "I'd better leave," and got up and got out of the office as fast as I could.

None of the doctors even recommended anybody else. I was very upset for about a month. It took me that long to get up enough guts to find somebody else. I was on very poor terms with my family at this time, but we did talk. My mother and father and wife said that I should go see Dr. Moore. Dr. Moore is a typical Medicaid doctor. He had an office in his house with three or four nurses and works a production line, very little personal contact with patients. Anything to make a buck, a pretty mediocre doctor. He screwed my father up a couple of times. I don't know if it was a mistake with my father, or what. Well, anyway, my father didn't have anything good to say about him, but he said I ought to give him a try. "The most he could do is refuse you," he said.

By this time I was getting very down on doctors. I am still very turned off by them. For one of the most educated professions they have some of the biggest assholes I have ever seen in my whole life. I went to see Dr. Moore. I sat down and went on with my normal spiel. By this time I had like a sales pitch. He said, "So you're a transsexual, huh?" Well, that's good. I was just reading some articles on that." It just freaked me out. I didn't know what to say. He said that he was just reading Dr. Benjamin's book, the medical edition. It is about twice as big as the normal one. At least he had read something and knew a little bit about what he was doing. He was willing to take me on as a patient and was willing to give me the shots, plus prescribe pills. Actually, he didn't know that much about hormones and their effects. It is very tricky.

Giving too much hormones is worse than not giving enough. I knew more about hormone and therapy treatment than he did. I kept an eye out that he didn't give me too much or too little.

It was good to get back to the hormones again. Like I said, they had a direct action on me psychologically. My emotions used to flare up very violently, and all that stuff. I became much more calm. I had more control. I could hold my train of thought much longer. Before I used to skip around from subject to subject. It's almost like taking a bunch of tranquilizers; not really though, because it gets at what's wrong with you. I didn't get that much breast development, but I did get a little more hip development. Mostly I just lost weight. I weighed 190 pounds before I started, and within two or three months I dropped right down to about 130. It was fantastic.

The hormones made me feel more like a woman. Don't ask how that feels. That is one of the most difficult questions. I am emotional but in a different way. What is it like to feel like a woman? It's the idea of feeling feminine. It's really actually an emotion in itself almost. It's kind of hard to explain an emotion.

CHAPTER

11

Cracking Mask

After I had been to see Campbell the first time, I felt very uncomfortable dressing as a man. The new men's fashions were coming in, so I wore those and kind of dressed unisex and let my hair grow. The VA wouldn't put up with me dressing like a female on the wards, but I bought clothes. The patients wouldn't have minded—they knew my moods—but it shook the staff up.

On the eighth floor everyone knew my problem. While it bothered the staff, Jane, the one nurse who was real cool, was a good friend of mine. There was also a doctor that I got along with well, too, Dr. Stein. One day he said to me in kind of a flippant way, "I never met Jane." I said, "Oh, would you like to meet her?"

My own room at the VA was where I really started seriously practicing dressing and makeup and gestures and the rest. I didn't go out of my room though, except when I went down to New York. Well, anyway I told Dr. Stein to come up to my room in a half an hour to meet Jane. I went upstairs and dressed and put on my makeup. He came up, and we talked for about two hours. I heard that I blew his mind. He left after the talk and didn't say what he thought about the way I looked. People have kind of stereotypes in their heads about what a transsexual might look like. He didn't say much, but I know he did.

After he left I changed into my hospital garb, took off my makeup, and went downstairs to talk to Jane the nurse who was my friend. She said, "You blew

137

Tom's mind. You better go talk to him and straighten him out." So I went to him, and he said, "Here I expected to go up there and see a drag queen, and there I see a TVC." I said, "What's a TVC." He said, "A typical Vassar coed." I went right out of my tree. It was really a great boost for me to hear that.

I started buying clothes and building up a wardrobe. I did more of that later on when I was working at McCrory's as a maintenance man. I was saving my money and buying clothes. Although I had bought clothes before, I was still very paranoid about going shopping. I did what I had done before, stupid things like going up to the counter and saying "I would like to buy a present for my wife," or for my sister. Christmas time and Mother's Day it was easiest to say things like that, but then there was always birthdays. I could never try the clothes on, of course, which made it hard. I can tell my size pretty damn close now, but at first picking sizes was very hard to do. I had a Sears catalog, and they had sizes to match measurements, so I sent out and bought a tape measure. That's the way I found my size first. I never took anything back, I was too paranoid for that. If it didn't fit, I just threw it out. It was tough enough buying things without taking them back. It has only been lately that I have been able to go in the stores without being superself-conscious. I take clothes back now. I even get angry now if they try to mess over me.

Underclothes were especially hard to buy. I was just embarrassed. Normally, people don't give those things as gifts, so it makes it pretty hard. When I did buy something it wasn't anything practical. It had to be something swooshy, because that was the only thing people would give as gifts. I got around the problem of buying makeup by having a girl friend go out with me to the store. She would be doing the shopping technically, and I would kind of play like I was tagging along. I would look at the shades and say, "That's a pretty color," and she would buy it. I did that for awhile with underwear, too, but she left town. It was much safer. Shoes were almost impossible to buy. I had to go in and buy them myself, otherwise they would want to fit Nancy, who was the friend. She wore a different size than me. I used to tell the clerk that my sister wore the same size as I did, but it was very embarrassing. I really couldn't go out and buy clothes the way I wanted to. Those that I did buy I would try on in my room and put them away—like I was buying to build up a wardrobe, so that when I did get out I could change.

There was one funny episode about dressing when I was on the eighth floor that I ought to tell you about. It was Easter weekend of 1970, I think. Jane, the nurse that I kind of named myself after, was on duty. She used to go to bat for me all the time. This one time I was practicing putting on my makeup in my room. She came in and gave me a few hints about how to do it. After awhile she said, "Why don't you ever come to the ward like that?" I said, "You got to be shitting me!" She said, "Why don't you do it now? If you don't, you're never going to be able to." I said, "Yeah, you're right." There were only 9 patients there, out of the 30 who were normally on the ward. I knew all of them really well, and none of them were really flipped. They were pretty well together, so I knew that I wouldn't blow their minds. I knew what was wrong with most of these people. Lots of patients tell each other things about themselves that they don't tell their own doctors. Most of them knew about me anyway. Jane, the nurse, knew the patients, too.

So, I said at first, "No, you got to be kidding." So she left, and then I changed my mind about an hour later and said, "The hell with it." I went out on the ward dressed. I walked real fast with my eyes closed out into the corridor, and then walked past the door leading into the big day room and walked into the kitchen to get a cup of coffee. Four of the patients were sitting around the day room playing cards. Jane was in the day room, and she told me that one of them looked up and said, "There is a new female body up on the ward." Jane came out into the kitchen and said, "Oh, it's you. Really great." We sat there talking just like it was a normal thing. None of the patients wanted to bother me, so they came into the kitchen two at a time and sat down to look. One was reading the paper and kind of peeked around so he could get a good look. It was obvious what they were doing. It was funny—they didn't say anything bad. That was the first time that I presented myself to a group of people that knew me. Before I did things like I told you about with the doctor. I would use my own room and talk to people one at a time. The Easter thing didn't go over too well with some of the doctors when they heard about it, so I was told that I couldn't do it in public.

I remember this one time on the eighth floor this minister came to see me. Religion is really funny in a mental hospital. It seems like all the chaplains are always trying to convert you or something or other. When I first went in I put down Catholic as my religion, but the only person to ever visit me was a Protestant minister. He wanted to talk religion, so I talked religion. He said that I was making a sin against God by being and saying what I did. I kind of went along with him for awhile. Talking to him was like a break in the day. I only talked with him for an hour. He sat down and discussed my philosophy of religion. I eventually told him I was an agnostic and nobody would change my mind about it. He asked me why I was there, and I told him. This was right after I had found out about Dr. Campbell, so I had had a big boost. He tried to cut the operation down, but he wasn't very successful; as a matter of fact he raised my faith in it. He told me that the operation was a sin against God, and that we should learn to adjust ourselves to what we were born as. I told him to get lost. I told him that I didn't think we had too much in common and I didn't believe a word of what he was saying. Now, when I go into hospitals, I put down Quaker because nobody bothers you.

Some nights on the eighth floor I would stay up and type, but I also used to get into some heavy rap sessions with the staff. Late at night is the best time to get cured. When you are sitting up late at night and everybody has gone to bed, it is peaceful and quiet and you can sit down with an aide you like, or a nurse, and you can really rap and get things off your chest. You can gain more of those sessions than you can with your doctors at the hospitals in some ways. In those talks you could stand back and look at yourself.

Outside Dr. Meed's office I never talked to others what I talked about to her. I didn't discuss my past with other people, or my innermost feelings. I guess I did discuss my innermost feelings with some of the aides in relationship to what I wanted to be and what I was hoping to become. I discussed with them the trials and tribulations I was going through, but most of it only after I had related it once to Dr. Meed.

The eighth floor wasn't all that good for me. After New York fell though, I was really uptight. I was still very much afraid of dressing, and I didn't know who or what I was. This one night I asked the attendant if I could go down to the seventh floor which is the locked ward. He got me permission, and I was just walking up and down there by the seclusion rooms. Dr. Stein was there. He had his office right near the seclusion rooms. I stopped and talked to him. He said, "What's wrong?" I said, "I don't know, I'm just coming apart inside. I'm blossoming—like going through metamorphosis or something—I don't know, I don't understand it." I went down into one of the seclusion rooms and lay down there and started dreaming. Come to find out afterwards that Stein had come down to check on me and heard me talking and taped what I had said.

He told me about it afterwards, but it was just between him and I. I lay down on this bed in the room and just curled up in a little ball. I seemed to go to sleep, but I really didn't sleep because I was dreaming, but very extreme and vivid. I never experienced anything like it before. I was dreaming that I was in this great big room and there was this one big door and there was this pounding on it. "Let me in! Let me in!" I was yelling, with a supermasculine voice. I was very much afraid, and this went on for quite awhile. My fears kind of built up and built up, and finally I couldn't take it any more. I had to do something. I opened the door. It had a chain lock on it. This big character came in and tried to grab me. I jumped back. There was still pounding on the door, and finally the door broke in and there was a person standing there. He ran over to me and ripped my clothes off, and I was a female. He started to rape me, and I looked at him and he looked like me. When I looked at him he died.

When it was over with I woke up and was on the floor. I had bit my lip and bled all over the place. I never want to go through anything like that again. It was just tearing me apart. Like my inner self fighting against my outer self. I talked with the psychiatrist, and we agreed that it was probably symbolic of me destroying my masculine mask. Somehow that experience was like a turning point to me. It was before I had dressed on the ward. I was dressing in my room but was pretty uptight about it. It was after Campbell and between suicide attempts. It was so heavy and so much a part of what was happening inside me. This was just prior to me getting over my tattoo, and I was just superheavy at the time.

I said that it was a dream, but it was much more than that. I would say it was a hallucination. A hallucination is seeing and hearing something that is not there and thinking it is real. When that whole thing was going on, I thought it was real. It is something that happens while you're awake, and I actually don't think I was really sleeping, but I'm not sure. I had this urge to get away from people. Just to curl up and get away. After it was over I felt like the most drained person on the earth, but I also felt like a gigantic weight had been lifted off me.

Over the three years at the VA I had a series of these kind of scarey looks at my real self. But each time I went back to doubting myself. I went through periods of being high and then being low, but I think the lows got less low. Toward the end of my stay I didn't like to be reminded that I was a male. When someone did, it really hurt and upset me. I'm still like that now only it doesn't get me down as much.

One thing that used to hit home, and still does, is going to the bathroom. When you go to the bathroom you have to face it, and you do that a couple of times a day. There is no way to get out of being a male when you go to the bathroom.

Those things can really get to me, though. Like that guy on Grand Street whose clothing store I went into with a mini skirt on and he calls me "sir." That ruins my whole day. Mentioning my wife would get me upset too. If people said "spouse" it wouldn't bother me so much but "wife", that's something else. It gets confusing. You get to start feeling like a pingpong ball. It was hard for me to get straight who I was and get my mind settled down to it.

Now and then I would hit lows, but I would come back. After I got to the VA it was like going up a ladder. I would get shaky at each step, but I was heading toward the change and I was making progress. The closer I came emotionally and physically to being a woman, the more neglected I felt. That's where the depression entered in.

It was about this time at the VA that I used to go through these elaborate plans or rituals of castrating myself. Not removing my penis—but castrating myself. I figured that if I removed the source of my male hormones perhaps that things would speed up a little bit. I got surgical equipment catalogs and had the numbers of the equipment I wanted. I planned it for two solid weeks—that was all that was on my mind. That was just before I did the thing at Morehouse, which I will tell you about next. This all happened about two weeks after I heard about the guy in New York and the operation not being set. I still had some supply catalogs, and I picked up some anatomy tests; I knew what I wanted to do and just wanted to make sure I would do it right. Dr. Meed found out about my plans and talked me out of it. She said that I was going to kill myself doing it. I told her, "Well, I can't think of a better way to die. At least they can't bury me as a male." That was the main thing. It is always in the back of my mind, that one thing—if I die, are they going to stick John Fry on my headstone? I couldn't rest with that. Dr. Meed stopped the self-mutilation, as she called it, by talking to me.

I read about castration in the Benjamin book. I had thought about it way before the book, but if I hadn't read it I might not have thought about it then.

Each one of these things—the hallucinations, the castration, and then the suicide attempt were me trying to see who Jane was and being down because I couldn't be what I wanted to be.

After I had been on the eighth floor awhile I tried to commit suicide. I was serious. I used to have this thing about going out by myself at night. I would go to a spot on the university campus where you can overlook the city, get coffee at the Last Stop and just sit there and daydream about being a whole person, a female that is. That's the terminology I used for myself: "being a whole person." This one day I was totally bummed out. I don't know exactly why, what triggered it, or when it exactly occurred. It might have been after I found out about Rider screwing me, I think that was it. I was going through heavy psychotherapy at the time—three or four times a week. I was thinking about my tatoo then, too; it was somewhat the situation I was in, too. The hospital itself was heavy. I was going to doctors who wanted me to be a female—that is, they knew I was and said it was OK for me to be one, and yet I had to act like a male and was treated like a male. I was in a male ward in the veterans' hospital. People say, "I wouldn't mind, if I was a female, being on a male ward," but I did. It really bothered me. After I got up there I had my own private room, but it was rough. There was only one girl there—Nancy. I became closer to her. She used to cry on my shoulder, and I used to cry on hers. I was just very depressed, mainly about the frustration of wanting to be a woman. The first suicide attempts down on seven were because I felt ashamed of myself—dirty and bad. I was full of guilt and superself-conscious—very paranoid, too. I was even afraid to go out into the street. This time it was much more my own personal suffering of wanting to be a woman.

Well, anyway, I went up by the new physics building on campus. I sat where I usually sat on the railing on the far side, with my back up against the wall, staring out at the city lights. It was summertime, 1970.

I was on self-medication—Dilamtin and Mysoline—for seizures. I went out
and planned this. I got an Exacto knife and put all my pills in my pocket and
went to the take-out place and got a couple of large cokes. I sat there for
awhile looking out over the city, took all my pills, and started slashing my
wrists. I was messed up on the pills, and that added to the troubles of cutting
my wrists. I couldn't get the veins. The tendons in your wrists are really hard.
You don't cut them where you think you should, because of those tendons. It
almost takes a surgical blade to get them. You can see the scars on my wrists
from hacking on them. Actually, I've got four scars on each wrist. I never
knew I was doing it in the wrong place; I was just trying to get through the
damn vein. Cutting is a very bad way to commit suicide anyway. The cutting
was just to make sure. I knew the pills could do it. I figured I had enough pills
with me to do it easy—I had 100. I knew they were fairly potent, because
when they first started giving me them they used to give me only a half a tablet
and that zonked me right out. I figured if that happened to me on one-half,
100 would do it for sure.

After trying for awhile I finally said, "Fuck it—I'll go back to the hospital.
I can't even commit suicide right!" I was pretty messed up going back, even
though it was only a block away. I didn't realize that the pills hadn't taken
their full effect yet, because they were like a big blob in my stomach. If I
would have stayed there longer, it would have worked. Unless you really know
what the hell you're doing, it isn't easy to commit suicide. I've got the
knowledge now, so I could go like a bat. The only trouble is you get rescued
before you get enough knowledge. Some pills make your stomach upset, and
you're liable to throw them up.

I made it back to the hospital. By the time I got on the ward, the blood was
caked all over me. I looked shit-faced, too. I felt like an ass, to tell you the
truth—not even being able to commit suicide. I was really angry with the
people on the ward afterwards. It's typical their attitude: "If you really
wanted to commit suicide, you would have." Pissed me off, because I couldn't
have tried harder. You say to yourself, "Goddamit, next time I'll really show
you." I had a friend of mine take a whole shitload of sleeping pills and went to
a park, climbed under a bush, and took the pills. They were looking for her,
because they knew she had the pills. Somebody remembered that she liked
trees, so they went to all the parks. They passed by her twice, and then they
found her just in time. Then they turned around and said, "Well, if you really
wanted to kill yourself, you would have tried harder."

From the ward they sent me downstairs to a doctor. He was a really beautiful doctor. It was Dr. Stein—I got to know him real well after this. After
something like that you are superupset, and I was. Most of the time you get a
doctor and he sits you down in the office with him on one side of the desk and

you on the other and says, "Do you want to tell me about it?" I went into this doctor, and instead of stopping and cleaning me up—the blood—or anything else, this guy did the most beautiful thing I've ever seen in my life. I was crying. Instead of asking me anything, or saying, "Stop crying," all he did was hold me for a few minutes until I could calm down, and then sent me to get sewed up and to have my stomach pumped. He just held me—just really nice. Something you need—human contact—not being yelled and screamed at and made to feel how fucked up you are. He was really a beautiful person—I really love him for that. I really respect him. He was a resident—finishing up in another place right now.

After he held me, he put me in a wheelchair and took me as fast as possible to intensive care. I had passed out by then. I was there for three or four days. I was pitiful for awhile. The slashes were nothing, but it was the pills that did it. The doctor who was up in the intensive care when I arrived was pissed off that he had to work on me, because he said I ruined a good game of cards. That will give you an idea of the difference in doctors. They sent me back to the eighth floor after that, and took my pills away. They knew that it was a good attempt, but Dr. Meed wouldn't stand for me to be locked up on seven.

You hear things from the patient grapevine how other people have tried suicide, so you know of ways of doing it no matter what ward you're on. My doctor knew that. Patients talk about it. It's a phenomenal thing, no matter when you try or how you try—if you don't complete it, it's an attention-getting thing.

I saw two suicides at the VA. One guy jumped off the ninth story. The other one was a girl who jumped out the laundry room window. She didn't even bother to look. There was another building down below, so she went four stories and hit. She broke both her hips and did something to her neck. She was totally paralyzed and went totally out of her tree. She didn't die, so it was only the one while I was there.

I knew the guy. He was a patient who got discharged and was trying to get back in, and they had him upstairs examining him. They made him sit around the waiting room for a couple of hours while they were getting a doctor to see him. He walked up to the window and just jumped out. The girl was just very depressed—she had been in for only a week.

I did most of my writing around 1969, during this period. I wrote some poetry. I also spent a lot of time writing what I called "self-analysis," which was just writing about what I was feeling. I was dressing in my room, and I had seen Dr. Campbell before I started writing. All the writing is really feelings that I wasn't allowed to express or that I couldn't bring myself to express because of the situation I was under. I used to go down to the OT room, and there was a typewriter down there. I was only supposed to be down

there for two hours a day, but when I started writing I was down there from
nine in the morning until four in the afternoon, just writing and thinking it
out and using the typewriter. I was interested in learning how to touch type,
and I did that when I was down there, so I didn't have enough time to really
write. After awhile I went downtown to a typewriter place and rented one and
brought it back to the ward. I set it up in the day room and used to type into
the night. I was supposed to go to bed at 11 o'clock, but I knew all the night
nurses and they knew me, so they let me. It's hard to tell you how upset and
depressed I was, but also how hopeful. Probably the best way for you to get an
idea of what was going on in my head is to read something I wrote at the time.
Some I've already gone over with you, but this is a part of a "self-analysis"
piece that I wrote about the frustrations of becoming a woman.

Self-Analysis

My feminine nature is in some ways like a burning fire, not the consuming
kind, but almost like a miniature sun. It is so much a part of me, it makes up
all of my emotions and some of my intellect. It is in a way all-consuming, yet
it gives so much in return. It is like a newborn child that you want to hold
and nurture, something that gives so much just by existing. This warm and
beautiful thing goes all the way down to the core of my soul. I find it so hard
not to embrace this very essence of myself at this time, but to do so now, as a
man, would prostitute this in my eyes.

God, but it is hard not to bring this part of me out into the open, into the sun
to grow and flourish, be brought into maturity. It is in some ways like giving
birth, and now I suffer labor pains. This is so hard to put into words. Words
cannot tell of the true feelings of this part of me that I have to hide from
everyone else's eyes. This is something that I cannot share with anyone else
as of yet, since as it is not time to be born. It is time to be born, but I am not
yet ready to give birth physically. I have to hold back in such a way that I
suffer extreme mental pain. To bring this into being now would change this
that is inside of me, make it less in some way. I think this is because of my
ethics and my moral nature, but to change that would change the very thing
that I am trying to bring into being. These things are so much interrelated
that in order to change one you automatically change the other. And I want
so much to bring this out into the open and share it with the world. I feel that
now is the time for change, now is the time to bring everything together. I am
so tired of hiding this thing inside of me. I am getting to the point where I am
suffocating in my own emotions and feelings. How I wish I had the money to
do the things that need to be done. To bring this thing into being is the only
thought I have at the point in my short life. This is something that takes up
all of my time, and time is running short. Like everything, to hold something
back in this way will eventually kill it. This I could not take, to lose some-

thing as precious as this would take too much out of me. I have tasted the summer wine that this is made up of, and in some ways I have become an emotional alcoholic. I can't seem to get enough of this out into the open to satisfy my needs. All I get is little tantalizing tastes of what is there. And now all I have is the dream that someday soon I will at last be able to get a fulfillment of my needs. This is all I wish for. To be at long last able to be free, to love, to hold, and to nurture what is inside of me. To love and not be able to give as I wish, to enjoy and not be able to express, and most of all not being able to give to my satisfaction. Is it a wonder that I have remained as sane as I have?

The tasting of the wine and not getting my fill, this is my problem. I can't help but think of the things that I wish to do and be, since this gives me great pleasure and some satisfaction. These things I have found out in therapy, but now how to achieve them. So in conclusion, I have tasted and can taste the wine, but to drink my fill is denied. So some people wonder why I am frustrated and can't stand to think of some things, I just can't stand to only taste.

Who am I that writes in such a way as this? What are my goals, hopes, and dreams? And most important, WHY? In this thing I am not talking of my gender, but the whole person. The why is answered in a way by my background, and the now of me. The more I learn of myself, the more I do not know. I am alive, I exist, I think; therefore, I have the right to be myself to my utmost. But what are my limitations? Not the ones I impose on myself, but the ones imposed by the person that oversees us. What are they? How far can I go?

It was in 1969 that in my talks with Dr. Meed I started spending a lot of time talking about my tatoo. It really started bothering me—it was like my genitals. It stood for me being a man, and I didn't want to be a man. Finally, she did something unheard of, which was to recommend that it be removed for psychological reasons. They did remove it, but not without a hassle. The surgeon who did the operation didn't like transsexuals, and there was quite a bit to do about the whole thing. He knew I was a nut, and they said that I couldn't go onto the surgical ward after the operation, that I had to go back up to the psychiatric floors. Instead of putting an open dressing on it the way they normally do—which is just laying a piece of gauze on it—Vaselined gauze so it doesn't stick so they can keep checking it to see that there are no blood blisters and whether it is healing right so they can repair it, they bound it up tight. It stayed covered for about two weeks. During that whole time I was totally bedridden. So that's why the scar is so ugly. The graft didn't take in a lot of places, and nobody ever checked it.

I had just reached a point in my life when I knew what I was and what I wanted to be, and was starting to implement it. I felt myself changing. I felt the mask that I was wearing slowly breaking down—I was losing the masculine mask. Dr. Meed was helping me by making me feel not so guilty about my feelings and letting me explore them. She didn't push me. Didn't tell me what I should or should not be. I think that if Dr. Meed thought that if she pushed the VA they would have given me the operation she would have, but there was no way they would have. The tatoo was my stigma, much like my genitals. They had reached a point of equal importance. Even though the scar it left is really horrible looking, I am much happier this way than I was with it. I wrote in the "self-analysis" after it was taken off:

> I have just had my tatoo removed. It seems that more than just a piece of skin was removed during the operation, part of my male stigma was removed. This was a self-imposed psychological branding, trying to force myself into a role that I did not want to accept, but society said that I was a male and I had to do something to keep myself in this unwanted role. Now that it is gone, I seem to be more free in my thoughts and actions, at last I have no more self-imposed restrictions on myself. I still have my conscience to restrict me, but not the one I had forced on myself.

I'm a person who loves the water, but right now I won't go swimming. This will be the third summer I haven't gone. I am superself-conscious about my arm, and I'm just paranoid about the scar. It is really ugly, and it bothers me. That's why I won't go swimming, and that's why I wear long-sleeved blouses. I won't wear anything sleeveless. It's OK when it's partly covered up, but when it's fully uncovered you can see that it was a tatoo. I know it was a tatoo, and I think everybody else can see that, too. They didn't get off a little part of the anchor. I'm going to find out if anything can be done to improve it, but I will get another operation before I see about that one. I only have one operation on my mind now.

Dr. Stein really helped me when I was so messed up. What I needed that night on the campus was someone's shoulder to cry on. We became friends after that. I still sat up on my perch overlooking the city and around nine o'clock each night I would wander down by the take-out place. Sometimes he would come by, and we would have coffee together and a hot apple puff. It used to be a regular thing. I like apple puffs. I still can't eat them without remembering those nights. We used to sit there and discuss philosophy and the state of the world and everything else. We never talked about the hospital, or anything concerning it. It was just a friendship kind of thing. A lot of the poetry that I wrote was originally for Dr. Stein. I know how to do script writing, so I got some parchment paper and wrote them on it and bound them into a leather book that I made; down the sides of the poetry I drew vines with flowers on them and then gave it to him. It was really great. I did a beautiful job on it, and I gave it to him for a present.

One time he took me to Leone's (restaurant) for dinner. I normally was given passes to leave the hospital, so there was nothing wrong with it. I just needed to get a late-night pass which means you can stay out till 12. I used to have to be in at 10. Dr. Stein wrote the pass and then walked down stairs to get the car. I hung around the ward looking inconspicuous, and then went up to the nurse and said, "I understand I have a pass." She said, "Yeah, Dr. Stein brought it." I said, "I'm taking it tonight." She signed it, and I went downstairs and got in the car to go to Leone's. He lived in Italy for quite awhile, so we sat around and had cataline pasta, antipasto, and all kinds of things. We had three different wines, and he was ordering them in Italian, which freaked the waitresses out. We had a great time. We went back to the VA, and I went up to bed. I couldn't tell anybody that I had such a great time, because patients and doctors are not supposed to mix. They get upset with patients and nurses or patients and aides mixing.

Our relationship was nice. He treated me like a human being, an intelligent human being, and as a friend. I don't know about him, but I was kind of infatuated with him, which is the reason that I gave him the poetry. I have never said so before, but I liked Dr. Stein romantically. If we didn't change his name in this book, he would probably lose his job. I haven't seen him since I left the VA.

Dr. Stein was a real romantic thing for me. It started out as a friendship; actually, it started out romantic with him holding me. I did have romantic feelings, but mostly it was a friendship, a superwarm friendship-type thing. He never tried to psychoanalyze me or talk about my problems. I told him once, "You know Dr. Stein, I would hate to have you as my doctor. I would lose a good friend." That's the way I felt about it—he wouldn't want me as a patient either. I thought of going out as a date, but that was only in my head and I knew that. I liked him very much and still do. I restrained myself and didn't express it.

The rationale for patients and doctors not mixing is that it is harmful. Christ, it sure wasn't harmful for me. Here I was a stupid illiterate who had only completed the tenth grade, who really felt down, with a doctor with all that education behind him who would rap with me and I with him, accepting me as an equal. It was a fantastic boost. I didn't know anybody at the University before that, and he was the first close friend that had a decent education. None of my family had one. My mother had a decent education, at least she had a high school diploma, but the rest of them didn't have diplomas or anything. I had a lot of ideas, and I couldn't express them because a lot of times my father and my brother, sisters, and mother wouldn't understand. I didn't know anybody that I could talk to on a deep level that could understand me. They didn't understand me.

I really knew that there couldn't be any romantic relationship and that kind of thing. I knew it, so I restrained my feelings; that hurt, but I was willing to put up with the hurt to keep the relationship. I would like him to see me now—what I am turning into. Before I leave for Boston I'll try to get hold of him. It would be really nice seeing him again.

He was very important in my life. He was more of a therapist not being a therapist than anybody I knew. Everybody around the hospital was so interested in treating my problems that they forgot about me as a person. He was a person who didn't give a damn about my problems and was just treating me as a person. That was important to me, it was something I needed. As a matter of fact, I think it was his faith in me that got me out of the hospital as soon as I did.

At this same time I was still in therapy with Dr. Meed. I didn't tell her— that is one of the few times I didn't tell her about something. Dr. Meed knew Dr. Stein very well, so I didn't want him to get in trouble. It would have been hard for her to get a proper perspective on it too, because she would be in a double bind with me being her patient, and she was his friend and he was mine. It would have also been considered unethical by the psychiatrists in the hospital, so she might have felt obliged to tell. I never saw anything that said it was unethical, I just assumed it was, but I didn't want to put her in any bind. It wasn't that important anyhow, and anyway it was my business and not hers.

While I was up on the eighth floor I was having heavy sessions with Dr. Meed about Jimmie, which refreshed some of my feelings toward him, so I decided to take a little vacation and go up and see him to see if my feelings were still there. This was just before I left the hospital and I needed a vacation, so I went to my old hometown for a weekend. I was dressing neuter, and my hair was long. I called Jimmie from the bus station to tell him I was in town. He was working the late shift in the factory. He was married—very typical life he was leading, had a couple of kids. He said, "Come up to where I work." He was there all by himself, so I went up and rang the doorbell. He came out and thought I was Harmony, my sister. It took me about five minutes to convince him that I wasn't her. It was really beautiful. We got to talking about everything under the sun except me. Then I told him that I had something important to tell him. I told him that ever since I was little I wanted to be a girl. He said, "Yup, I know," which blew my mind. I said, "How'd you know?" and he said, "You were just always interested in the wrong things. I kind of expected it. So what's happening?" I said, "Well, I'm trying to get an operation." He said, "That's really great." We had a beautiful time. Jimmie was my childhood sweetheart. I guess I will always love him.

One time I went over to see Dr. Meed one day over a City Psychiatric where she was working. It was one of our regular sessions. I took her some stuff that I had written, some of the things I have included in this book. I wanted her to look at it. I gave it to her, and she put it down and didn't read it. She just sat down and crossed her legs and said, "Do you want to tell me about it?" I said, "Do you want to read it?" She said, "Do you want to tell me about it?" I said, "God damn it, I brought it here, aren't you going to read it?" She said, "Why don't you want to talk to me about it?" I just blew up and walked out. I mean, I had spent a lot of time putting my thoughts on paper and I thought I had done a good job, and she was playing those games. It didn't get through my head at the time that it was important to talk about the things I had written, and you just couldn't expect to write the whole thing out and give it to her, and that was that. After that I gave her other stuff to read, and she would put it to the side and we would talk, and then she would take them home and read them and then give them back the next session. I guess that was more beneficial to me, since I had more time with her and it was more of a one-to-one thing.

One other time I got angry with her, and I said, "You're not my friend." She said, "No, I'm not your friend, I'm your therapist." All of a sudden it hit me right between the eyes what the difference was.

I wanted money and decided that if I was going to be a woman I wasn't going to be able to do it at the VA, so I got a job repairing appliances at Mc-Crory's, which is a department store. My mother had worked there and told me the name of the personnel manager, so I went down there and asked for him. They gave me a job. I slept at the VA and worked during the day down there. I would get up about 6:00 every morning and make my way over to the coffee pot. I had to go down to the store at 8:00 to open up my shop. What I did varied from day to day and depended on what was broken, but most of the time I just messed around. I repaired air conditioners. I was a mechanic in the Navy, so I had a good mechanical background, but I am actually a lousy mechanic. I can tell people what's wrong with something, but I can't handle a wrench. I walked around the store with this big belt of heavy tools on, looking important. I would sit in the office, put my feet on the desk, and take a nap. That was pretty much my day. I worked there for six months. I left just before they were going to fire me. I got bored, and I was just working because of the money. I don't like to do that—I like to be interested in my work. The place got to be a bummer. I was thinking about being a woman and walking around with that belt on—it just didn't fit. I didn't get to know anybody down there either; they minded their business, and I minded mine.

Toward the end of my stay on the eighth floor I enrolled in beauty school. Everybody knows that if you're a beautician and you're male you have got to be "queer." The majority of beauticians are not homosexuals. Because it is a feminine-type occupation a lot of people are very feminine who get involved, but they are not necessarily gay. I kind of made up my own mind that I wanted to start, and then I told them at the VA what I was going to do. They liked the idea, because they thought I would be at home with the other "queers." Actually, they were pushing me to go into vocational training, and I figured it would be better to do that than diesel mechanic school. At least I would get some practical value out of it. I wanted to know how to do my hair, and about makeup and things like that. I already knew something about being a woman, but I didn't really know anything about hair. I also wanted to be around more females.

I had been getting hormone shots for a while before the International Beauty School. As a matter of fact, when I went down for the interview with the director I had my hair at shoulder length in kind of a pageboy fluff. At that point it was difficult to tell at first whether I was a boy or a girl. When I went down he said, "Well, you're going to have to get your hair cut if you want to go to school here. No male should have a pageboy fluff as good looking as that—you'll have everybody wondering, and run into problems." I talked with the director for about two hours at the interview. I told him that I was a patient at the VA, and it didn't bother him one way or the other. He was really cool. I liked him right off the bat, and I figured I might as well be totally honest with somebody at the school. I wanted somebody I could rap with, so I thought it might as well be the director. I told him what the hell the score was—where my head was, what I wanted, and where I was in the process of achieving it. He thought it was great, just as long as it didn't bother my work. He gave me some advice. For one, don't tell any of the students—try to keep things undercover, which I did.

He was very open-minded. That is one thing I found out about people in beauty school; they are like people in show business, very open-minded. He made me get a haircut, which pissed me off, but he was open-minded. You could have been in the hospital or whatever, they don't care, just as long as you can do a good hair style. And I got to be a damn good stylist.

The beauty school worked out for awhile, so I kind of had a job and was feeling good. And I had made up my mind that I was going to leave the VA and go on to be a woman. I just didn't have the schedule. Maybe another quote from my "self-analysis" writing will give you an idea of where I was at:

I have gotten over my guilt. Now, the only thing holding me back is myself, as far as being myself is concerned. Now at long last I can with a free conscience be myself when the opportunity arises. Something alive died in me in these last few days; this was the masculine mask that kept holding me back from any self-expression. I no longer have to fight with myself to do or be the things I want. I have gone out as a girl before, but I do not think that I could do the things I do now without feeling guilty.

The VA wasn't all that bad, I guess. Through people like Dr. Stein, Dr. Meed, and Jane I learned that not all people are bastards, like I thought. I later figured out why I was there for so long, and it kind of bothers me. I was on a male ward and was called Mr. Fry; that's ironic. They used to tell me, "Be yourself," and "Relax," and they kept pumping that into me—"Learn how to express yourself"—and then when I did and when dear old Jane came peeking out from behind her mask, they said, "Dear God, not here." I was constantly uptight because I couldn't be myself. So the reason I was in the VA so long was that the hospital was upsetting me. How about that? I'm not the only one who blames the hospital. After I got out Dr. Nickel and I talked about it, and he came up with the statement: "You got better in spite of this place, not because of it." It was so true.

12

Grand Street

When I knew I was going to leave the VA, I began to think about an apartment. I didn't want to live with my family because I thought I would have too many head hassles, especially if I was going to do what was in the back of my mind—live as a woman. I saw a sign, "Apartment for Rent," over on Alder Avenue which is about three blocks from the hospital. It was kind of crappy, but cheap, and near the beauty school and the hospital. It was also right off Grand Street, where the university freaks hang out. I was kind of glad, getting out of the VA, but I had been on the open ward and going out every day so it really wasn't that big a deal. I lived close to the hospital, so I knew I could go there if I needed help.

I didn't know it when I moved in, but the house had a lot of characters—it was really nice, interesting. Every apartment house has the busybody lady who lives up front, checking on who comes in and out. Ours was Millie, an ex-prostitute and drunk. She was about 70, or maybe even 80. She was receiving social security and fighting with the welfare all the time. Really an interesting person who was fun to have around, except when she knocked on your door at eight o'clock in the morning to have you go down to the store and buy her some beer. The guy who lived across from Millie and on the same floor as me was an exchange student from Thailand. He was as horny as hell. It seems to be the custom in Thailand that when you invite someone over to dinner you have to share everything with them, including yourself, or at least that's what this guy said and how he came across. He was always making passes at the girl who lived next to me, Sono. Sono was one of these people who wants to be footloose and fancy free. She had left her husband and was into Buddhism pretty heavy. She got me into it, too. She and I got along really well; she knew. At this time I had not come out. I was still living as John Fry, but she knew about the whole situation. She was really helpful—it was good to have someone to talk to and someone to be a friend. We both liked to cook but didn't like to clean up. We ate dinner at my place a lot. I had this big, round table that came with the apartment, and we unscrewed the legs and put cinder blocks down to rest the table on. We sat on cushions and ate Japanese style. She was a freak for Japanese food, and I loved to cook it. We were always inviting the rest of the house, too. It got so everybody brought something to eat, and then we would throw it together and cook it.

We didn't get to know the people on the second floor too well; they were freaks who were bums and crashers.The whole house was freaks, but they were street people who panhandled and didn't go to school. There were five guys living on the thrid floor in three small apartments. They were nice—all students. They ate with us some.

I was straight when I moved in, but it didn't take them long to convert me to a freak. I changed my opinions about a lot of things; they changed me, I guess.

It wasn't too long after I moved in that the Thailand guy moved out. I don't think he could handle it. He was pretty straight. It was funny—one night he got smashed, and we kind of cut him off. We invited him over to dinner at Sono's apartment, and he wanted to do some international sharing. He made a pass at her, and when she cut him off he made a pass at me; he thought I was gay. I cut him off too, so he was really frustrated that night.

The way we did it was funny. Sono told him that she was going to teach him some American dances. So she had him up there square dancing. He was really wrecked at the time.

Mr. Engel was our slum landlord. Everybody hated his guts, but I got along with him beautifully. I always get along with people like that, for some reason. I had a combination living room and bedroom, and a kitchen and a bath. I was paying $100 a month. Utilities were provided, and it was furnished. The whole place was panelled, but it was a lousy, amateurish job. I had to put up with a lot of things, like cockroaches, but you learned how to handle those. I had a rollaway bed that I conned Mr. Engel out of. I put that under my bookshelf. I had a big, stuffed easy chair with a hassock, a bureau with a mirror, a coffee table, a couch, and a couple of end tables and lamps.

When I first went there I was going to beauty school and double-dealing. The money for my school came out of the Division of Vocational Rehabilitation because they were very interested in rehabilitating me. I took advantage of their spirit. Because I was in school, I was eligible for the GI bill, so I used to get a check from the government and from the state. Since I was technically married with one child, I got the money someone in that category gets.

I started dressing neuter when I was at the VA, and I continued dressing that way on Alder. My hair was long which was the style. People had to toss a coin whether I was a boy or girl when they saw me, because of the hair, the dress, and that I was babyfaced. I kind of accented my femininity, but I was still John.

The Thai fellow moved out, and then so did Sono. She went back with her husband. Another girl moved into her apartment, Sue McDonald. She was a speed freak doing a lot of speed crystal. She became one of my closest friends. She was a real nice person. I told her my problems about wanting to be a girl, and she told me about her love life and the troubles she was having. She finally moved out too, but sometime while she was there we had this big St. Patrick's Day party.

Patrick O'Leary was one of the local freaks or street people. He never had a place to live—he really did, since he was married and normally lived with his wife—but he was also a wino and went on drinking sprees which lasted a week or two. He did this every two months. He would leave his wife and come to the university section, and then he wouldn't have a place to stay. When he was drunk, he was a hell of a lot of fun. He decided that since it was St. Patrick's Day and his name was Patrick he would throw a party. It was in the apartment on the second floor. He invited all the people on Grand Street. Just went around telling everybody that there was a party at 504 South Alder. All these people showed up with booze and drugs, and the doors to all the other apartments were left open. There was whiskey, beer, grass, acid, wine, and everything going around. I just sat up there and had a good time. Millie came up and got drunk and did a strip—an 80 year-old woman doing a strip to music—right. I finally conked out. Engel was very upset when he found out about the party.

He got pissed one other time. That was because of O'Leary. All these people were very interesting and understanding. They knew what was going on with me, and it didn't blow their minds. They were very accepting people, and that's why I was probably able to come out in the open with them. These were the people who taught me to be open about myself. I met most of them on Grand Street. They were so open that you couldn't help but meet them if you hung around there. People would just come up to you and say, "I'm Patrick O'Leary." Most of the panhandlers on Grand Street knew me; they knew I was good for a touch. I would share what I had—the food in my house, and my money if they were hard up for a bottle of wine. They used to sit on the front steps and get drunk, and I used to sit with them. You also got to know people through knowing other people; it was like a regular chain. I was having a good time, for the first time in my life.

Well, back to Scorpion. Scorpion was really nice—kinda messed up the way everybody else is. He just hung around and crashed at my place a couple of times. The one time I was about to tell you about was in the middle of the winter. O'Leary was on one of his superbenders. He had bought himself a pair of those brand new $30 cowboy boots, and they were too tight. He kept them on for a couple of days and got a blister which got infected. His foot swelled real bad, and Sue took him into her apartment and got a medical student who we knew that lived on the street. He came down and looked at the foot—he was running a fever and everything. He wouldn't go to the hospital, so we told him we were going to cut the boot off. We slit it down one side on the seam, so he could resew it, and took it off. First we got him rip-roaring drunk, because it was hurting him so much. The student cleaned it off and put some gunk on it. They went down to Sam, the friendly pharmacist in the drug store on the corner of Walton and Alder, and got some antibiotics. Sam was really a great guy like that. He gave the antibiotics free. We got O'Leary to soak his foot, and it got somewhat better. He ran around with one boot for awhile.

Engel hated O'Leary's guts because of the party, and Sue was in bad with him, too, so she asked if he and Scorpion could sleep in my place. I said sure and gave him my bed; I slept in the chair that night. I took a shitload of pills that night. I used to take a lot of pills during that time. Sometimes my emotions would get all wrapped up wanting to be a female, and I would get real uptight. If I took the pills, they would put me to sleep and kill the bad feelings. I didn't take them to kill myself, because I knew my tolerance. I took a lot of pills, and O'Leary got shook up. I told him I was going to the Medical Center and popped out the front door, leaving Scorpion and him there alone.

Engel came around that morning. He is the kind of a guy that if nobody answers the door he would unlock the door and walk in. So there was O'Leary, with only one boot, and Engel is knocking on the door. They didn't want him to find them there, so they borrowed my moccasins and beat it out the window into three feet of snow.

Things were pretty good, like I said. I wasn't into drugs or drinking heavily, or anything like that. I was just enjoying myself. Being accepted was good, but there were still things that were going on in my mind that were hard to handle. I would have liked to have sex with some of those people, but I couldn't. I had very warm feelings toward those people. There was no way to express my feeling, and that was kind of bad.

I stayed on Alder for 11 months. After about the second month I started thinking of myself as a freak, too. They integrated me very fast, but I think the raw material was there for them to work on. Their whole approach to life was not having anything blow your mind. If at five o'clock in the morning O'Leary pounded on my door, I would let him in and he would say, "Hi, John. I need a place to sleep. It's cold outside." He would be drunker than a skunk, and I'd say, "Sure, Pat, come on in," and I would throw him some blankets on the floor and give him some space and a pillow and tell him to go to it. Nothing would upset you. If three or four extra people came in for supper, you just threw some more spaghetti in the pot. People just got used to not worrying about the small stuff, and to this day I don't worry about the petty. It was very easy to talk about myself to them in that kind of atmosphere. I mentioned that I was a transsexual, and most people would know already and they might bring it up themselves. I remember once this guy said to me, "John, not to be nosey or anything; it's your own business and you don't bother anybody, but just out of curiosity, are you gay?" I said, "No, I am a transsexual." He said, "Dig it man, that's really great—far out. You know you would make one hell of a broad." That's the way these people approached the whole thing. How could you be inhibited around people like that' You didn't have to explain yourself, just "dig it—far out—and do your thing," and that kind of stuff.

So things were going fairly well for those months, but then everybody started moving out of the house. Sue got thrown out and moved into this dump on University with a whole mess of other freaks. The people on the third floor moved, too. After Sue moved the people who used to come around didn't come anymore. They kind of moved their center to Sue's new place. I didn't get to know the new people that moved in at all. They were students superhung up on getting papers done on time. All the fun people were gone—like, the whole crew of them. I would have moved up there too, but there were no places around. They were too far away for me to keep track of what they were doing. Most of the people who were with Susie were into dope too—not heroin—just speed. Most were speed freaks or winos. Scorpion had been into heroin once or twice, but he kicked it.

Well, anyway, I had gotten to know a lot of people in that short time. You have got to realize that when I left the VA I didn't know anything about freaks. I didn't know one hippy freak. Then I jumped right into it—like, totally got immersed in it. My attitude changed. It was kind of like when I got out of the VA I didn't really have anything. I was like a newborn baby, looking for something new.

I kept going to beauty school after I left the VA, but I found out that the director told his instructors about me and my transsexualism so they could kind of keep an eye out for trouble. One was a female, and I think she told some of the students. She was a very spiteful woman, and I think I made her uptight. The students seemed to be friendly, though.

The way beauty school works, after you have taken a certain number of hours of training, you get to work on patrons who come in. They can get their hair done for a minimal charge. I worked my way up to a first-class hair dresser. The director used to tell me that I was damn good, and everybody else did too. I had my own clients that came in just for me, and I made real good tips. I was also a good "seller," which is important. Most beauty schools don't teach selling your products, but this one did. They encouraged you to sell special setting lotions, and conditioners and other things, and you got a commission. The student who sold the most got a five-dollar prize which I won a few times.

I had about a month to go before I could have taken the exam for my license, but by then I was getting uptight. My seizures were also getting worse. I enjoyed it, but I was under a lot of tension. I was becoming more and more female through the medication, and I was coming outside of myself. My shell was breaking open, like my mask was coming off. It was hard because they saw me as a man, and I couldn't change. One thing that really got to me was they used to call me over the loudspeaker when my patrons came. "*Mr.* Fry, desk please." At the end it used to rile me just to hear "Mr. Fry," because when I left the school at the end of the day I felt like Jane and I was about to become Jane. I was dressing a lot in the apartment. I was right on the border of completely changing over.

After the freaks moved out I began getting very, very, very depressed. I just couldn't handle it alone. I hadn't made the change over to living as a female, but I was hanging on the borderline—so close. There was nobody to support me for changing over. I was really uptight. I had quit beauty school and had nothing to do. I used to spend my days sitting alone in my apartment, day after day. I was still pretending to be a male, but people were recognizing me as a female or mistaking me as a female since I did look so feminine. That made me feel good, but I didn't want to be mistaken for a female, I wanted to be one. They were just really uptight. It was making me uptight. They would call me "Miss" and then correct themselves. That would upset me. I knew I couldn't be a man any longer, but I couldn't move forward. Sue was about the only friend I had.

This one day I went up to the hospital to pick up my new set of pills, my Mysoline and Valium, and then went up to see Sue on University Avenue where she was living. I was really dragging, and she knew it. She tried to boost me by saying, "Well, why don't you get your ears pierced." She was more or less trying to help me. So I went out and bought a pair of pierced earrings, and I lost them. I was going to get them pierced. That even bummed me out even worse.

Sue was real nice. She was just a street person—a speed freak. As a matter of fact she is in the county penitentiary right now, for speed. So I was at her apartment and just sitting around and all of a sudden I said, "The hell with it.

Let's do it up right." I wanted to end it all. I figured I'd take the pills at her apartment and then start home. If I couldn't make it home, there were a couple of places to stop along the way where nobody could find me but if I made it home, I was going to lock the door and lie down. For some reason it hit me that I should take the pills right there. I did. I took all of the medication which was a month's supply of Valium and a month's supply of Mysoline. I went into the bathroom and took them and walked out, my knees just gave out. They hit me so hard—I didn't realize it would hit so fast. She said, "What's wrong?" I said, "Nothing, I'm just a little weak." She said, "What's wrong?" I said, "Nothing," again and started toward the door, but she wouldn't let me out 'til I told her. I wouldn't tell her. She fought to get into my pockets and found the two empty bottles and freaked. I lost consciousness and don't remember the rest of it, only in pieces and what she told me later. She got me outside and flagged a cab and drove to the Medical Center emergency. She said that I was saying in the cab, "You don't think I'm a slut do you?" For some reason that's all I was saying to her all the way down in the cab. That freaked the cab driver out completely. When we got to the Center, I had to make sure that I paid the cab driver and tipped him. She was trying to get me into the emergency room and said, "To hell with the cab driver." I got in and I'm still standing, and they say, "What is your name and address?" Sue yelled, "Don't fuck around, will you. She just took a whole lot of pills." (She said "he.") Would you help him out?" You know how the emergency rooms are—they have to take the name and Blue Cross and Blue Shield and everything like that. At that point I collapsed on the floor, and a doctor coming down the hall saw me and grabbed me. He took me inside and pumped my stomach and shipped me to the VA. There I was in intensive care, and then back up to psychiatric. I was there for three days, and then they released me. By that time the doctors had decided that the hospital had done me more harm than good.

After I got out I went over to see Sue to apologize and find out what the hell happened. When I saw her, she was glad to see me. She hadn't been able to see me at the Medical Center, and they didn't tell her that I was transferred. They didn't tell anybody anything. So I saw her, and we began rapping. She said, "What you need is to meet people—people that would understand you. The Gay Liberation League is starting up here in Central City. I know you're not gay, but perhaps these people would understand you a little bit better than straights would." So I said "OK."

13

A New Life

The Gay Liberation League was having a meeting the next night up at the University. I went. I didn't tell anybody right off what I was about, and they took me not as a guy but as a gay female. It blew my mind totally to be accepted by them like that. After they found out they totally accepted me too; that helped me in a lot of respects. That night I decided that I would do it—I would live as a female. I decided that right there and then. It was the first time people actually recognized me and treated me as I was.

They came up to me first off and said, "Hi, are you a new member?" I kind of nodded my head. Then they said "The women's section is meeting over there—why don't you go over." I went over and sat through the whole meeting. Then someone came up to me and asked me my name. I said "Jane." It was like a click—it was like a switch. That settled it in my head. I went back and told Sue, and she said "Great, Jane." And she called me Jane after this. I have been Jane ever since. That was the most important moment of my life.

Changing from a male to a female is not easy. It's like changing your whole life at once, and you have to do it all at once. You have to break all your ties—like you pick up a totally new life. You have to build yourself up for it. You think about what you're giving up. Are you willing to give you everything that you have ever known? Your family? Your friends? Just prior to the change I walked in a halfway world—kind of like you still have got one foot in society but once you cross that line you can't go back. That's when you have to make a choice—a big choice.

I had some women's clothes from the VA that I had there. I went downtown and picked up some other things. The first time I ever went out in public dressed as a woman in front of a group of people was a speaking engagement at Wescott Hall at the University. The meeting of the Gay Liberation League that I went to was only their second, and they had been asked to speak to this group of students. They asked me to come along. I was so paranoid it was unbelievable. I walked up the street thinking that I might get arrested for impersonation. I was very, very nervous, but I did a good speaking engagement. It seems that I have a natural thing for rapping, and the people we talked to were real open. I was so relieved when it was over, but more important was that I was so relived that my hiding myself was over. I felt like a new person.

I dressed twice more after that, going out in public with my friends. I still felt very self-conscious doing it. I didn't feel like going downtown, either. I knew that if I went dressed it would be so much easier to buy clothes, so I said to hell with it and had the final purge. This time, instead of ripping up all my female clothes, I ripped up all my male clothes and threw them away. I just took them out and started ripping shirts, pants, underwear—everything I could get my hands on. That finished it—the change had been made.

One thing that was tough was living in the same place I had after the change. The people there knew me as a male or as neuter, so when I started wearing skirts and blouses they began to wonder. I remember one time two gay guys from the Gay Lib came over to pick me up. I put on a skirt and a blouse. I was walking out of my apartment, and there was Millie sitting in the window where she always sat. I was walking out, and she had the door open. We started walking out, and she said, "John, you've got a skirt on." I said, "So what, what the hell's the difference," and kept right on walking. I was red from the top of my head to the tips of my toes. She always knew me as John. She would be very embarrassed now if I told that story to her, because she does accept me.

I decided that I had to move out, because my head just couldn't handle it. I just kept saying to myself, "Use your common sense—you can't live in the same place that you did as John and expect the people to accept you. They just won't do it. It's against human nature." I eventually did move out, but that wasn't until after I got involved with Crisis.

Every time I think of the Gay Liberation League I have to laugh. It brings back funny memories, both good and bad. I really enjoyed the people there and got over some of my prejudices against gay people, but I felt like a den mother. As a matter of fact, they used to say that I was the only straight member in their organization. They opened up a coffee house, and I was put in charge. The idea of the coffee house was to provide a place where the gay community could get together and not have it as a pick-up place. There wasn't any cruising down there or anything, but I still felt like the matchmaker, since I wasn't eligible for any romances. There was nothing going like what goes on in a gay bar—"meat racks" as they call them, with people leaning against the bar waiting to get picked up. There wasn't that much matchmaking going on, but there were always sexual undertones. I don't think you can get that out of any gay group. Gay society has been oppressed for so goddamn long that the only thing they actually have in common is the sexuality and being oppressed. So when homosexuals are together, sexuality does enter in. It can't be helped.

While in the Gay Liberation League I didn't get involved in any sexual activity, except this one time which wasn't really sexual. There was this one person named Bret. I was in charge of the coffee house for about four months. I was open late one night—we stayed open until 12—and this guy came in and we got to really heavy rapping. Didn't close the place until 3. He and I were the only people there. I suggested that he come home with me to finish our rap. After we got there I thought, "What the hell is he going to think—that I'm gay? If he comes in, he is going to think automatically of sex." So I turned around and said, "Look, I hope you know I don't want sex. I can't have sex." He looked very relieved, and said that that was really great. This guy was psychologically impotent and had been playing the role of being able to do something. He was really relieved not having to play silly games. So we just sat on the couch and just rapped. I got feeling cuddly, which I do every so often, and we just sat there—my head in his lap—talking and very lightly kissing. We talked all night long until nine in the morning, when he had to go to classes. It only happened once, but it was beautiful. Something that couldn't have happened if he wasn't hung up. It was the type of thing that normally happens in story books. It was very beautiful.

I liked him a lot, but he left the area. He wrote me, but I didn't write him back. I saw him recently, and I was really glad to see him back. I don't want to start up anything, because I knew he would just be going back and I don't want to get hurt. That's why I didn't write him. I couldn't get more involved than I was.

I enjoyed my job at the coffee house, but somehow I didn't feel completely like I belonged, and they felt that way too, I think. I did some speaking engagements around the University, and when we went out quite a few people would concentrate on talking to me instead of the gay people—they always introduced me as the only straight person in the whole group. That's actually the way they saw it, and the way I saw it, too. Most gay guys don't have trouble understanding about the difference between homosexuals and transsexuals, but it's very hard for the straight society to see it. There aren't many transsexuals in homosexual liberation groups—they concentrate on liberating themselves first. At the speaking engagement I would get a lot of attention, and the gay guys kind of put you off, and then society puts you off. So you kind of get it from all ends. You don't have any alternatives except to go your own way the best you can.

About three months after I got into Gay Lib, which by the way was the most important single event in my life, I was sitting around the coffee house that I helped start and somebody brought down a bouquet of flowers. I don't know exactly what kind they were, but in the night shade family—night shade is poisonous. I was shitting around, putting the flowers in my mouth and dancing like a Spanish gypsy. I was crunching on the stem. It was really bitter, but I didn't think anything of it. All of a sudden I started feeling sick. I passed out and then woke up, and then passed out. I couldn't focus, and the world was bulging in and out on me—I was tripping. There was belladonna in those flowers. Of course I didn't realize this, so they took me over to the Crisis Center; but I told them that I didn't want to see anybody except this medical student that was really a great person and who knew about me. She worked there, but she was home. So I had them take me to my house—they practically carried me. The guy put me down and told me to wait there while he went back to Crisis and told them where I lived, and everything else. They located the medical student, and she came down and took my pulse and respiration and asked me what happened. I told her, and she took me up to her house to sleep the night. The next day I dropped down to Crisis with her and started rapping with the people. We talked about what had happened, and things like that. It got so I started to know them, and I kept dropping in. They got to know me and where my head was at. After a while I got to know what was going on there. They did various crisis counseling—overdoses, bad trips, suicide, and that kind of thing. I asked them whether I could so some volunteer work and they said, "Yeah—glad to have you." So I became one of their volunteers. "Ace Volunteer"—that was my tradename. I was reliable and practically there 24 hours a day. I used to go home just to sleep. I spent all my time there.

The people there were really terrific, much like those around Alder, only less strung out. As I spent more time at Crisis, I spent less and less time with the Gay Liberation League. I was really busy for the first time since the VA, and it was good.

I did drugs during this period, but I was a supermoderate dabbler. I have done grass, which everybody has nowadays, and acid. Actually, I only took acid three times in my life. The first time was about three months after I did the major suicide thing. My head was pretty clear, then. It was after Gay

Liberation and I was working as a female at Crisis. The first two were very, very nice, but the last time I got too happy for me to handle. After that I decided I wouldn't trip for awhile. That was just before I went to Medical Center psychiatric. The thing that makes acid important is the reason I tripped. When you trip, you can't lie to yourself. I wanted to really find out what was actually going on inside my head about my feelings about masculinity and femininity. I wanted to find out exactly what I was.

I used to do it with friends at their place. I just liked to sit there and rap. I got acid from friends, because that was the only way I could buy them. You cut drugs with other items, some of which are good, others bad. Since I have these seizures, I have got to watch what I take. Sometimes acid is cut with speed, and it's extremely dangerous for me to take speed. I bought it from friends because I wanted someone I could trust. I probably won't trip anymore, but it depends on what this summer brings.

Like I said, I used it as a test—not really to find anything out new about myself. You can't find out anything new about yourself or the world from drugs, but it can bring out a lot of things inside you that you don't know are there. The first two trips were light, and I stayed in touch with reality. This one time I tripped with a bunch of friends, and afterwards one of them told me, "You know, I've always accepted you as a female but always really basically as a male. On acid I got superfeminine vibes from you. You had feminine charisma, for some reason." Any time you trip you have a sexual part of it. My sexual part is very feminine.

The last time I did drugs it got so heavy I couldn't handle it. I started going through white-out. I sat in a chair and got these bad vibes. I kept saying "Who am I, what am I." I don't remember it exactly, but it was a bad scene. I was just a head without a body, floating around toward somewhere that I didn't know where. It was just too heavy for me to handle.

Drugs are funny things. Just because doctors give them to you doesn't make any difference. They prescribe drugs and they call it medicine, but it's the same. I've seen many weird reactions from tranquilizers—ups and downs. I have seen worse freak-outs in hospitals due to prescribed drugs than I have seen from LSD. They lock you up for taking drugs, and then they force you to take them after they've got you.

As a volunteer I counseled people—just talked with them. I was particularly good with suicide attempts. When you talk to people straight, and they know where you are and where you have been, it helps them. I never spoke to them from a textbook. I spoke from experience. It was more like the role of a friend, instead of a counselor. It was immediate crisis counseling. I would try to put myself right over as a friend. No lines between me and them—no professional-patient line—I don't draw lines. It's the worst thing to do. A person would come in, and you would see them once or twice. They would be like people that were trying to get into a hospital—then you might see them for a week. You try to act like a crutch until they can get someplace else or get it together.

The only other transsexuals I had met up to this point were those in New York, and probably some of those were transvestites. While I was working at Crisis I counseled two. One I didn't quite counsel, I just helped him a little bit. He had seen Dr. Moore and was mixed up. Someone sent him to me, and I gave him the name of some doctors where he might get help. The other person was totally mixed up—I don't know what he is. We had a code name for that person—Mr. Judy. This person came walking in one day, sent by a regular customer. This person was hard to figure out, no less try to help. She was blowing everybody's mind, and I walked in in the middle of it. They immediately said to me that they needed my help because, "If anybody can figure this person out, it's you."

So I got stuck with Mr. Judy. Mr. Judy was the most interesting person I ever met. In some ways totally beautiful, but in others totally fucked up. The opening statement was that she was a hermaphrodite. She had all the identification of a normal female she said, but she was a hermaphrodite who needed sperm to live and she was trying to find donors. I never heard a line like that in my life. I worked with her for about two weeks.

His mother lived out in Seleta, and was very fucked up. He lived in his own apartment and traveled all around the United States seeing doctors. He was on VA disability and was functioning as a male most of the time, but thought he wanted to be a female. When he came in, he was dressed as a female, with a five o'clock shadow and a wig that kept sliding forward and about three tons of makeup. Just looking at that just kind of made me freak. I finally had to drop the whole case. There was nothing to be done on the short term. I was kind of glad. He'd got an apartment down city. He met some friends and he got away from his mother. We got him a shrink who will see him.

One reason I was glad that I stopped seeing Mr. Judy was I started identifying with him. He was freaking my head, because here I am a biological male in the process of becoming a female trying to counsel a person who is so fucked up over being a man or a woman. I said to myself, "Oh my God, am I like that?"

Some time along in here I went to a meeting of Sisterhood which is kind of a radical women's liberation group. I like women's liberation, but there were certain things about this group that I just couldn't go along with. For one thing, I wore a skirt and blouse and someone made a remark about it—everybody had on pants or dungarees. I said, "I feel that if you're liberated it doesn't make any difference what the hell you wear—the whole idea of liberation is wearing what you feel like wearing and being what you feel like

being without society or anyone else putting stops on you. Here you're supposed to be liberating yourself, and you turn around and criticize me." The
way I feel is that if a guy whistles at me I am not going to haul off and belt
him, because sometimes I think that it's a compliment. I walked out of the
meeting.

A friend of mine talked me into going. She would say that there are no differences between men and women psychologically that they are born with, and
I think that that is a lot of horseshit. I think there are a lot of differences. I
don't think that males are superior to females, or vice versa, but I think they
have different positive characteristics. I feel that women are different emotionally. They are like different colors. Men are more like red—more angry.
Women are more like pastels. Their moods are more subtle. I went back to
one meeting after the one I walked out of. I thought maybe the one I went to
wasn't representative, but it was.

Somewhere around this time Dr. Meed left town. I still was seeing her
during this time on a regular basis. Even after I left the VA and was living as
a female, she would call me Jim. I never went to therapy dressed in a skirt and
blouse. I always wore slacks and a pullover or some kind of a top. I don't
know what it was. I just couldn't do it. When I found out she was leaving, at
my last meeting with her I wore a skirt and blouse for the first time. She just
came out like she always did and came to the waiting room and nodded to me
to come in, and I walked on in and sat down and we talked. She said, "How
come you're all dressed up today." I said, "Celebrate your leaving, and all
that." We talked quite a bit about her leaving, and mostly what I was going to
do. As I was leaving, I was going by the secretary's desk and I turned, and she
said, "Goodbye, Jane." It was real beautiful. The first time she called me
Jane. That really meant a lot to me. I was always trying to get her to say that
the decisions I was making were right, and she wouldn't do that. So this
saying, "Goodbye, Jane," was like saying, "Everything is going to be alright."

CHAPTER

14

Trials and
Tribulations

While I was living on Adler I continued to do some writing—poetry and "self-analysis," mainly. My spelling was still terrible, but besides that I liked to write. I wrote this after I had changed over and was settling in. It was at a time when I was starting to take a turn for the worse.

I am now living as a woman, but the psychological hell I went through to achieve this is something that I will never forget. Why did it take so long? If I had done this 10 years ago, my life would have been much easier in all respects. When you fight with yourself, you learn a lot about your-self. I think that if I had known before that I could be a whole person I would have done this before, but the combination of being in the hospital and finding the people (doctors) to go to while in there didn't give me much chance to be myself.

The change came about because of not being able to accept myself as a male and not wanting to hide anymore. It is something that you have to find out for yourself—there is no magic solution to this. My mind told me that it was bad to dress as myself, but this conditioning was some-thing that I had to rid myself of in order to be happy. When you try to kill yourself because of what society says about your behavior and your needs, something has to give. I am glad that I was stronger than society, and this is what you need more than anything else—the strength of your convictions. To become in some ways your own master and guide in what is right and wrong.

Some people can just go out and do their thing, but I couldn't. I was paranoid about what people thought of me and what I thought about myself. I went out of my way to try to explain my situation to everyone, but the only one I was trying to give excuses to was myself. I used to spend too much time trying to make "converts" that I forgot about me, and in reality the only convert I was trying to make was me. Like a small child with a new insight I was looking for acceptance and approval, and yet I couldn't even give it to myself.

Now that I have made the "change" and I am *living* for a change instead of hiding, new problems are cropping up all the time. I had to put away my mask, but that was my security—my hiding place. Now I have to face the world alone. I felt psychologically naked, stripped of all pretenses. When I made the gender shift, I did not have any new masks or defenses—I had stripped myself of everything. But I had forgotten to leave myself a new identity. One day I was in the hospital recovering from attempted suicide as John, and the very next day I was Jane. No stopping to think. I do not think that anyone knows how lonely a person is in this position—not even having yourself to relate to. You are left with nothing. No point of reference. All you have is a hope—a dream of yourself. The thing that you need most is someone—someone to orient yourself to relate to. But in most ways I could not have anyone—my morals are still in the way. I cannot reconcile myself to the fact that I might be able to have a man. Someone to hold me and console me with the problems I have. Someone to relate to and be able to understand what I am going through. This is something that I want very much, but I don't seem able to to let myself go into—have an emotional relationship with another person, man or woman.

I have heard people talk about loneliness, but few have experienced what true loneliness is. Take a person and put them in a body they can't accept fully or relate to, and strip them of their past and then place them in a room where they can look out and hear but no one can see them—that is somewhat what I go through each day. My days were spent trying to reach out to anyone, but I can't quite make it. I have no common ground to meet people on. My hopes and frustrations are held inside me, because others have no experience to base what I say on. It's like talking a different language to a person—the things that mean the most to me mean the least to them. I spend my time making small talk, but at the same time trying to weed out the things that would give me away—watching my voice and how I walk, my gestures, and everything. It did not bother me for a while about these things, but my friends keep reminding me to watch them, and I have become much more nervous—there is so much to watch. Why can't people just accept me. I knew about these problems but was taking care of them one at a time. Them constantly reminding me is making me so self-conscious that I can't function as I should.

I started working at Crisis around August of 1971. I had taken that large overdose in April or May, and then I continued to live on Adler until September. I already told you what a drag it got to be living in the same apartment with not many people around and people not used to seeing me as Jane. So I moved out, and in with three girls who weren't freaks. What I mean by freaks is free people—people not confined to the morals and ethics of the society. Two were lesbians, but they were uptight about most other things. These girls were much more conventional in their living patterns. The way I got set up with them was I put a notice on the bulletin board at Crisis: "Unusual unwanted female wants roommates to want her—Looking for a place to stay," and I signed it, "Love and peace, Jane." Everybody knew who Jane was, so the note was kind of a joke. Dee and Lois used to drop in at Crisis, so they came down to my place and said, "We found a beautiful house. Would you like to move in with us? We're looking for other roommates." I said, "Sure," and went over and took a look at the place. It had three bedrooms, a living room and a dining room, a view that overlooked the city, a garbage disposal, a brand new kitchen, redecorated floors, and everything. It was a really beautiful place. It was $200 a month with heat and utilities. So it was 50 bucks apiece with the four of us. I moved in. Lois worked for the country as a social worker from the same division that I was getting my welfare from, and Miriam was the other girl and she worked in the children's division. Lois filled Miriam in on me.

It was interesting. Lois pulled my records down at welfare to read them and told me about them. She told me that she couldn't even unravel the double talk and wouldn't have understood it if I hadn't explained.

At first it seemed like a good idea moving there, but it worked out lousy. At first I stayed home a lot. I used to do a lot of cleaning, and they took it for granted. Dee used to yell at me for not cleaning. They didn't clean, but no one said anything. They also used to go out drinking and places and not invite me. I was like ready to climb the walls after a while. Actually, I ODed (overdosed) on purpose while I was there. I wrote in a "self-analysis" piece:

> . . . I am still under its effects (groggy). Why did I do this when there are so many other outs? To get attention? No. Think that I did this to try to cope with the hurt that is in me—the hurt that comes from not being anything. All I have to do is to hold on to the fact that someday I will have something. I constantly go around and try to prove myself to the other girls in the house when I sense that the only one I am trying to prove my femininity to is myself. But they treat me like I have no experience in things that count, like

shopping and planning dinner. I get vibes like "You have a lot to learn before you are a woman." I think that telling them the whole story would make it easier, but it hasn't. I called Dr. Nickel, and he is going to give me the name of a good shrink to go to. The problem is one of not being able to relate.

I don't think that ODing was fair to the other girls in the house, even though I really didn't try to kill myself. The mental anguish I put them through was too much to bear. I must apologize to them.

The girls would do things like have snacks at night and leave the dishes around. "Jane will clean up." I should have spoken up for my rights. Also, they would get mad at me because my tastes in music and things were different. I found out that they were not really freaks, but superstraight and conservative in many ways. They are kind of like the princesses at the University who spend a lot of money buying imitation hippy clothes but are basically uptight.

Miriam was a farmgirl, actually. Dee had a boa constrictor that she kept that was about four feet long. I had a lot of fights and arguments, especially with Dee. We finally sat down and had a talk, and I told them I would have to leave. No malice—they were unhappy with me, too. Actually, it was just Dee and I that didn't get along, and Lois and Miriam tried to mediate. The real hassle for me besides Dee was that Lois and Dee were gay and they had this thing going between them—they were all lovey-dovey—and Miriam had this boyfriend Ray who came over constantly. So they all had someone, and I was left with no one. They were affectionate with each other, and the whole bit. I just couldn't handle that on top of everything else. I began going back to Crisis, but it was so far away from the apartment that it was tough with transportation. So after a few months I called it quits.

The night that I was leaving Miriam asked me if I wanted to go out for a drink with her, which led to an interesting thing. She had never gone out drinking with me before this—I guess it was for old times, good-bye sake, or something. We went up to the Bridge Inn which was pretty packed, as it usually is. We were up there drinking our beer, and two guys came over. Miriam knew one of them, so we got to talking. One of them started talking to me. I figured, "Great, this is as far as it is going." I don't like drinking, because it's hard to get out of being picked up. Miriam wanted to go out for coffee afterwards with this guy, so I didn't want to be left alone with the other guy so I went with them. So after coffee they drove back to Bridge Street to drop us off at Miriam's car. This was 4:30 in the morning. All of a sudden the guy I was with (I was a little drunk at the time) said to his friend, "I'll take Jane home and I'll pick you up at your place in about an hour." I wasn't swift enough to pick it up fast, and before you knew it I was driving off with this guy—right? He pulled into Bridge Park and parked on the side. He said, "Did you ever see an elephant tree?" I said, "Nope, and I really don't want to. Let's go home." He says, "No, I've got to show it to you." So we argued for about 10 minutes as to whether I wanted to see the elephant tree, and by that time we were at the elephant tree. So, one thing led to another, and before I knew it we were making out. I was trying to keep an octopus off me, and finally he just grabbed something he shouldn't grab and he freaked. All this time I'm trying to fight him." "Look, I didn't want to make out. Get away! Look—no making out! I want to go home." He just kissed me once more and then sat back and said, "Do you take hormones?" I said, "Yes." I wasn't going to tell him anything. I wasn't sure whether he had really found out anything or not. I was half waiting to get belted. I'm gritting my teeth. He said, "You've heard of Christine Jorgensen, haven't you?" I said, "Yes." He said, "Are you in the same boat?" I said, "Uh huh." He said, "My luck." I never came so close to getting beaten up, but I was the one who was lucky. This guy was really cool. I mean, I could have been with somebody who could have kicked the shit out of me. You hear about that happening. I found out something about him later. He had done a lot of bumming around the street— pimping—and was out with an "emerald," that's what they call a male prostitute. Like, he had seen everything, so it was a lot easier for him to deal with me. An average person would have hung me from the elephant tree. That's why I don't drink and don't get picked up and don't date. I don't hitch-hike or anything like that. If just try to avoid anyplace where I might get into a situation like that one.

Because the people around the University, and especially the freaks, Gay Liberation people, and the people at Crisis, are so open, I was pretty much accepted. But that doesn't mean I didn't have my problems. This one time last summer I had an appendicitis attack. I was at Crisis, and nobody was sure what it was, so they took me down to the emergency room at the Medical Center. At first I refused to go, because I had been to the Center before and I knew they would give me a hard time. They would always recognize me as John Fry, no matter how I dressed or who I told them I was. They admitted me with a possible case of acute appendicitis. They fussed around a lot. I gave my name as Jane Fry, and when they asked for my ID—my Medicaid Card— it said John Fry. They put in parentheses John on the top and wrote my number down. They pulled out John Fry's record with the suicide attempts on it and called me Johnny. There was no way to get around it.

They just totally pissed me off. The doctors treated me like some kind of a freak and not the good kind. The nurses, the aides, the attendants, the cleaning staff, the people that served the trays—they all giggled and laughed.

The doctors didn't laugh—they were too professional for that, but everytime I got examined it was by a different student, and they never seemed to be examining me for appendix problems either. They kept me in there for a week without doing anything except giving me a barium enema, which is something you should never do with a person with possible appendicitis. An intern who works there that I know told me that I was the worse-treated patient he has ever seen there. They thought the appendicitis attack was mainly psychological. Can you imagine that? A psychological appendicitis attack? I got out of the hospital and went home. About a week later I had another attack, only this time worse. I went back in, and they yanked it right out.

I had a semiprivate room the second time. For awhile I shared it with a little old man about 95, who was too far gone to care about who I was or what I looked like. Then they put me in with a 22-year-old guy who just had had heart surgery. He started pacing the corridors when I moved in. I made him nervous. It really wasn't fair to the other patients to have me in with them. It's not fair to whoever I'm with, or to myself. The first time I was in they put me in a ward for awhile with eight beds, which was kind of ridiculous. It was a men's ward, of course. The woman doctor who admitted me was very sympathetic and tried to get me in a private room. I find women much more understanding about this than men. Men doctors take the attitude, "I'll show him,"—spare the rod and spoil the child kind of approach, which is totally ridiculous. She did get me into a semiprivate, but even at that it wasn't good. My room overlooked a blank wall, but people kept walking in, pretending to be looking for things out the window. The cleaning ladies keep coming in, too—I had the cleanest floor in the place. They were just coming to get a look at the freak.

I was like a side show at the place. I was going to write the hospital director, but I never got around to it. Transsexuals are in a very funny position, because they don't want to have themselves at the center of attention by disrupting the flow of things or complaining. So they don't confront people and complain—they hold back their anger when people treat them like dirt. I found out that that was a bad approach to life, but you don't know how to handle it.

I'm angry with people who treat me like a freak. I was angry at the staff, but I am also very sympathetic to the patients that have to be with me. Since they are there with their own problems, it would be better if I was in my own room. It kind of blows people's minds to see a feminine person on a male ward, whose friends call her Jane. It makes me uptight to be called Mr. Fry, too.

During this time I used to go back to the VA to get medicine and stuff, but that was bad. I was having my seizures and they were increasing, so I set up an appointment to see one of the head doctors. The doctor said to me, "You're going to have to cut out these female hormones. They are going to give you a thrombosis.'' I didn't go up to see him about that, but that's what he told me. I got scared because I knew what a thrombosis was—it's like a blood clot. He told me that what I was taking would cause things like blood clots that would float and wind up in my lungs, heart, and brain, and kill me. You know, lodge some place and wipe you out instantly, or make you a vegetable for the rest of your life. It was the head of the department that told me this. They were very uptight over me down there. They didn't like *Miss* Fry at all. They would have rather had me as a number, or at least as John. I don't know if they were purposely trying to scare me, but they succeeded.

After that I stopped going to the VA for medicine. I was on Medicaid, so I went to my private doctor. I went down to see this new neurologist that I found and wanted a prescription for Mysoline for my seizures, and we got to talking. He knew a little about transsexuals, and it didn't blow his mind. He called down to New York City to find out exactly what the hormone did to me, and about the operation and things. Then he called the VA to find out about the seizures. I didn't mention this, but finally after years of telling me that the seizures were psychosomatic they finally said that they were phototropic. So he found out all this information, and I told him what the doctor had told me about thrombosis. He checked the whole thing out. He told me, "Look, thrombosis was around before Jesus Christ and they didn't blame that on hormones." He told me that he didn't think the hormones would have any ill effect on me. He also told me that he thought that Wexler, the doctor who told me that, had a castration complex and to ignore him. He is on the faculty of the Medical Center, and they don't like me. It was great to have someone on your side. This was the first doctor who took the trouble to really look into my condition, instead of giving me a lot of bullshit.

He was interested in my bust development, and said that I had quite a bit. I told him that I would like more, and he said, "You transsexuals are all alike. You are like religious converts—you want to be perfect. You want to be the best, and second best won't do." He kept telling me that. I think to some extent it is true, just like it is for everybody. I don't really want to be the perfect woman, but before you're something you always have an ideal you are heading for, and you try to attain that ideal. You normally don't make it, but you strive for it anyway. Well, anyway, I think that Wexler is a damn good neurologist, but because he thinks of me as nuts, he sees it as psychosomatic and that he is going to play little games with me that he sees as white lies. He doesn't understand what those hormones mean to me. He is just terribly threatened.

I remember around this time with Wexler I went up to Thomas Mall Clothing to buy a pair of jeans. I used to buy there when I was John. I was wearing a skirt and blouse. It really pissed me off. I went in, and the clerk said, "Can I help you, sir." I hadn't said a word, and I was wearing a skirt and blouse. Sometimes when I open my mouth people think I'm a man because of my voice. I said, "Miss—it's Miss. I'd like a pair of jeans." I gave him the size and the type I wanted. He went over to the counter, and he didn't even look up and said, "Men's jeans will fit you better, sir," and handed me a pair. I threw them on the floor and walked out. That was a very bad experience. I won't go to that place again, or any place that I feel doesn't accept me. Everytime I walk by that place I feel like ripping the clothes they have hanging outside on the sign. The guy is an asshole. I don't know what he is trying to prove.

At this point I was still taking hormones, but wasn't making any progress on getting an operation. Dr. Meed was gone, and I didn't have a psychiatrist. Someone had told me about the Richardson Foundation that helped people with problems such as mine. I wrote them, and they sent me a list of doctors in my area that I could see. One was Dr. Roper in Lake City. It was at the Children's Hospital, the Psycho-Endocrinology Clinic. She is very famous, and I went up to see her a couple of times. She gave me a whole lot of tests and what have you. They were pretty good about the hormones, but not about the operation. They gave me my own syringe and a prescription. I carry a letter around with me, so that I can give myself shots and not get into trouble if they pick me up. She told me that in order to be eligible for the operation I would have to work and live as a female for at least two years. She said that I couldn't even start thinking about the operation until I got the money that was needed, which was over $3,000. They told me that paying for the operation is part of treatment. I asked Dr. Roper about the operation, and she said, "We shouldn't discuss it until you have the money." I was working up at Crisis for over a year when I first went to Lake City, and I told her that I was working at Crisis and that even though I wasn't getting paid for it I was working. At first she said that she wouldn't accept my working there as part of my requirement for the two years as a woman. I had one of the professional staff who worked at Crisis write her a letter. I found out just before I went into the Medical Center psychiatric ward that she definitely wouldn't accept it. What I was doing wasn't considered honest work, because I am not getting paid for it. I'm not living up to the image of a female, even though I can relate to people who are bumming out and who are supersensitive. This working as a woman for two years is pretty much standard among all the places that do the operation. I think Johns Hopkins set it up, and many of the doctors who do the operation were trained there.

I guess the way they figure is that I have to prove that I am going to be an asset to society by showing them I can make money. I think each doctor has a lot of discretion. I have to provide I'm an asset to society the way she sees so-

ciety. My doctor is judging what she feels society is—she is not judging the society which I am in. In order for me to fulfill what she wants I have to become
a totally different person—very unfreaky, very straight. Get a nice, respectable
apartment and a car, and work really hard as a secretary or some idiotic thing
like that and get my mind totally blown. They say you have to prove you can
function in society. "Functioning" to them is making a minimum of $6000 per
year and living up to their standards. Why should I live up to their standards?
Their standards are what makes my life so damn miserable. Why should I join
them? I just won't do it. I can't compromise that much. The freaks, the people
that accept me—who made me feel like a person—they are asking me to reject.
The people who have accepted me know everything about me. The
professionals have never bothered to find that out. They just want to know
how big my bankroll is. They never bothered to find out what I'm like and
what and how I think. Just as long as I have the money, everything is hunky-
dory.

I'm not very moralistic concerning other people's sex. If it turns you on, do
it—as long as it doesn't hurt anybody. Life among the freaks and the people at
Crisis was a beautiful thing. It is really a nice thing they had going, and it was
only through my own choice that I was left out. It was because of the situation
I was in. For one thing, I just couldn't participate in sex. I couldn't go to bed
with a female because I am not a homosexual, and I couldn't go to bed with a
male because he would treat me as if I was a male. There is no way I could
function as a female in bed, so I wouldn't be satisfied. So therefore I just steer
clear of all sex.

Not being able to even hope of romance, I felt left out. People who were
volunteering there as long as I was were accepted as members of the family—
which is what it was like. But I couldn't. I started getting very paranoid about
it—about my transsexualism. I was having emotional difficulties. I was unable
to express myself in all ways, not just sexually. I had so many feelings inside
me that I couldn't get rid of. I didn't know how to handle it. I couldn't get
angry. I would hold my anger in. If I would feel love and joy, I would hold it
in. Having hassles in the community and what happened about the operation
in Lake City added to it, but I think not being one of the group is what pushed
me. I was starting to psychologically freak out.

I just got to the point where I knew that I wasn't in any shape to help anybody else, especially in a crisis situation where you have to be quick, so I
submitted my resignation to Crisis around the middle of January. I told them
that I was not volunteering for a while because I wanted to get my own head
back together.

I go back there, but the vibes aren't the same. The people there think that
they were responsible for the breakdown. They did help this last breakdown,

more or less. I used to go there 30 to 40 hours a week, which was more than any volunteer. That's why they called me the Ace Volunteer. I was super-dependable.

When you work there as much as I did, you can't help but get wrapped up in it. For a person that couldn't get involved in it, it starts bugging you—it starts tearing you apart. Basically, it was not their fault. It is just the way the operate—they are a superclose group. I was a semimember of a very close group. They helped me into the breakdown. They kind of pushed it along, but that might not have been the only cause, since usually with a breakdown there isn't any specific cause. They don't feel guilty so much as feel that I should have backed off sooner. I'm kind of stubborn, and I didn't. Most of my friends are still there, and I go and drink coffee and help out. They got me listed in their files as a community help person—not a volunteer, but it's about the same thing. I would like to counsel again, but they won't let me do it and there is no group in town like that. All other places you have to have letters after your name. I am damn good at counseling, especially suicide and depression counseling.

So in December I moved out of the apartment that I was sharing with the three girls to one on Frost Street, right next to Crisis. Some friends had told me about it. I also dropped out of Gay Liberation. I couldn't play cupid and mother to 28 guys all at once. It was a kind of 150-year-old haunted house with lots of room. We redecorated practically the whole thing with bits and pieces from various places. Sandy was an egotistical bitch, who was a good singer and an artist and made money doing that. Mary was a real nice girl, a student, and was getting support from her parents. Carol was an unwed mother and on welfare and was a bitch to live with, too. I lived there from early December until I went to the Medical Center.

I was mixed up emotionally. It was hard for me to relate to people. Sandy made life no easier for me. She didn't like the painting and poetry I was doing, so was always putting me down. I was friends with Carol and Mary. Carol disliked Sandy, too, and so did Mary. Mary finally left. I wound up babysitting for Carol's daughter, Kate, a lot. She was over a year old. She kind of tied me down, so I couldn't go anywhere. They all knew a lot of people, so there were parties all the time until four and five in the morning. They would keep me up, and I felt out of place at them—I was starting to feel very insecure around people. I was feeling very paranoid. It was just a bad scene. I thought it was only me at first—that I was imagining all this stuff—but I talked to people since and they told me I wasn't and they don't know how I stood it. They were all into drugs. One night Miriam came over, and there was an argument and it just got to be too much. Everybody's tempers were short. I was all uptight and I was taking care of Kate all the time and Crisis was such a strain, and Roper, and everything. So this one night I don't know what got into me but I went crashing through the French doors on the second floor onto the balcony and then flipped right off the edge of the balcony. I landed on my back. I could have killed myself but I wasn't trying to. Just acting out. And that was the beginning of the trip to Central State Mental Hospital.

It was the start of a move down, but I had been up. I had met new people and was accepted. I had made the choice of being a woman, and I did it.

When I cracked up it was the beginning of January. They took me over to Crisis, but nobody knew where to take me from there so they took me to City Psychiatric. Actually, I went to City three times. The first time was with Mike Erickson, who is a close friend of mine. They wouldn't admit me, because I was outside their catchment area. I went back to Crisis and was freaking out more and more. They took me back, and they told them that they would only admit me if I was psychotic. Jill Popoff, who was doing some work at Crisis, called them up on the phone—she is a trained social worker—and told them that I was getting pschotic, and I was, kind of. They overemphasized what I was doing. That's the only way I could get in. I don't remember this whole episode too well, but I do remember being at City. From what they told me afterwards I was having these dreams that I was talking about jumping off the top of Barkley Hall into the toilet bowl. I was talking to people that weren't there, and a few other things. So I was finally admitted. I was only going to go in for over the weekend from Friday night to Monday morning.

When I arrived they admitted me under Jane Fry, then on Saturday morning a friend of mine who works there, Doug, who also works at Crisis, came up to me and said, "I picked myself to be the teller of bad news. I'm at least your friend. The staff had a conference, and they decided you had to be a male while you were here. You can dress however you please, but you have to be known as Mr. Fry and use the men's room." I found out later that some of the other patients were upset about me using the girls' bathroom. I never told anybody that I was a transsexual, so I know that the staff must have told the patients, which I thought was totally medically unethical.

I didn't get too much of a chance to get to know the people at City, the staff or the patients. You have to convince people about what you are. They just thought that I was some kind of "queer," or I didn't know what I was—a drag queen of some sort, or something like that. I get that quite frequently. It really pisses me off, especially from professional people who are supposed to know better. Professional people are very quick to make judgments like that. They can rationalize what they are doing to you a lot easier that way.

So the staff had a conference about me on Saturday morning. At least I thought they could have invited me and asked me what I felt, so they could tell me how they felt. So I went up to one of the nurses and said, "How do you get out of here?" She gave me a form to fill out, one of those that they have to act on within 72 hours. I wrote a letter stating that I wanted to get out. They were very good over at City about letting you out, but not very good about helping you. If they didn't want to help me as Miss Fry, why add insult to injury. I went because I was having problems. Not really transsexual problems, although that was part of it. Transsexualism wasn't why I sought admission. So I wrote the letter and mentioned the bathroom. Actually, I didn't have to use the men's room all the time. One aide took a liking to me. City had two floors, so when I got up in the morning to have breakfast he let me go down to the second floor where nobody wanted to use it. It doesn't really matter to me which toilet I use, just as long as I have privacy. I don't like walking in front of a lot of guys.

On Monday morning my doctor came, and I was sitting upstairs waiting for an answer to my letter when this man came up to me and said, "Are you Mr. Fry?" I said "Yeah." He said, "You don't mind if this interview is with a one-way mirror?" I said, "No," but I was pretty pissed because you feel kind of weird. Here it is the first time I have ever spoken to this doctor, and it's with a bunch of students watching on the other side of a one-way mirror— right. It's a beautiful way to build confidence in each other. I didn't want to say, "No, you can't have me watched," because they might think I was a trouble maker. So I spoke to him and talked about my problems, and he looked at the letter and said something intelligent like, "Did you send this letter?" I said, "Yes," and he said, "Do you want to leave?" I said, "Yes." He said I could go. I was like tied up in knots inside—terribly impulsive. I had been through this before, so I knew the danger signs. I went back up to Crisis, but I was still freaking out. While I was at the hospital I was getting medication to calm me down, and the minute I was off I started getting worse again. I stayed at Crisis about three weeks, totally flipping out, while people were trying to get me into hospitals as *Jane* Fry. Places wouldn't take me unless I cut my hair and went as Mr. Their treatment would only fuck me up more. Help is sometimes worse than the sickness. You need help, and the treatment makes you worse. I didn't go back to my place next to Crisis, because at that time I was doing impulsive things like trying to take too many pills and jumping out the window. I was doing what they call hallucinating. I had somebody talking to me, but I really knew it was only inside my head. I knew it was a hallucination, so it wasn't a hallucination. I wasn't quite right, to put it bluntly. It was like getting supernervous and then kind of breaking with reality. I started to break with reality, but I knew it. What I had was what they would probably call a psychotic break.

One thing I forgot to tell you that happened at City that scared the shit out of me. Sunday morning I got up and went downstairs to the day room, and there was this big colored woman there sitting on a chair rocking, and she looked awfully dazed. She was a patient. A couple of girls were still there talking to her, and somebody said, "Your hair is still wet." I said, "Did you take a shower?" She said, "No—it just got wet from the shock treatment." Like, you know, it's like you get your morning dose of pills, only they're giving shock treatments. It just freaked my head. You hear all kinds of bad things about shock, and nothing about it doing anything for you. You really wonder—I was just glad to get out of there.

After I stayed for three weeks at Crisis I was still in bad shape—but I was finally admitted to the Medical Center. It was very hard to get me in, but finally Jill Popoff, who was watching after me, called Dr. Roper in Lake City who knew where my head was at and knows that I am in pretty good shape gender-identitywise. She had no idea what was going on. Jill talked to her, and she called down to the Medical Center and talked to the head of the ward, and that's how I got in.

Compared to the places I had been in, the Medical Center was really good. There was no hassle over being Jane. The only problem was one psychiatrisit, Dr. Regan.

Dr. Regan was something else. He was out in left field. He had only seen me three times and insisted that the problems of transsexuals were related to repressed anger, and that my father was a very angry man—a very violent man—and that in trying not to be like him I was supressing my masculinity and anger. That was his pet theory. I thought he was full of shit. When I got angry at somebody, that was a sure sign he was curing me according to him, until this one time that I will tell you about later. He never even called Dr. Meed, my therapist. I had been with her for almost three years, but he didn't try to find out what she thought. I used to think a lot of therapists. I used to hold them up on a pedestal. Now I know they are just a bunch of educated jerks like everybody else—just trying to make a living. I thought Regan was a real egotistical bastard too. I had had so many diagnoses by then, and most of them by male doctors, that I was just fed up with it. None of the doctors could separate my emotional problems from my transsexual problems. My emotional problems were always seen as being part of the transsexual "sickness."

Even though I have some feelings against certain people at the Medical Center, I think that the place is basically good. Their philosophy is get people out as soon as they can, and it serves as a temporary escape or resting place for people who need it. The other psychiatric hospitals are supposed to be resting places, too, but this is the only one where it wasn't so bad that it gives you more problems than you went in with. I liked the way people were given individual attention. It was a small ward with about 16 people on it, and part of a regular hospital. It is very nice physically, and there is a lot of staff. If you want to sit down to talk with someone, you can; as a matter of fact, they are just standing there waiting for you to talk. You have private rooms, and you can come and go as you want.

I was beginning to get my head together there. They gave me support. One day when I was in the hospital, I called my caseworker from the welfare and said, "Look, my checks keep coming in to me as John Fry, and I've been living as Jane for almost two years now." I was having trouble getting my checks cashed, because nobody would believe that I was John, and nobody will take a two-party welfare check. I couldn't get food stamps, either. I called her up, and told her. She didn't know about the transsexual thing up to this point. I guess I didn't freak her out too much, because she told me that she would change the names on the check and on the Medicaid card and on all the other stuff she could. (I just got an ID card today with my picture on it from the Central County Social Services, matter of fact. It's beautiful.) So I got the letter in the mail that I could go down to get a temporary ID at the Social Services. I got there and told the clerk that my name was Jane Fry. She went through her files and said, "There is no Jane Fry listed here." I said, "Keep looking, I'm there." She looked again and said that there was a John Fry and said that the numbers matched. "Is that you?" I said, "Yes, a lot of things have changed since the last time I was here." Here I am in the middle of the County Building and she said, "Well, are you a female?" All these people were around and she said that kind of boisterously. I said, "What do you want me to do? Strip and prove it?" Of course she got flustered. She wasn't going to have me strip, and I wasn't going to. So she gave me the ID card. That is what you call getting some gall for a change. That was beautiful. I never stood up to people like that before. I am getting more and more that way. You can tread on people's toes, especially in matters of sex, because they don't know how to handle it. If you want, you can blow people's minds and get anything you want. Everybody is so frightened when you confront them with sex that they don't even talk to you. They just try to get rid of you as quickly as they can. I don't usually resort to doing things like that only when it's really necessary.

CHAPTER

15

The State Hospital

I was on the ward for about two months at the Medical Center when I got into a group therapy session that was very heavy—very hard for me to take. It was about suicide, which I had tried a few times. The other patients who were talking were very down on all types of suicides. There was one guy who had a totally negative attitude and wouldn't let himself understand what the whole idea I was trying to get across was. It just so happened that this patient looked just like my father. Just a couple of months prior to my going to the Medical Center my brother had tried to commit suicide and messed it up. He tried very hard; it was an honest attempt. It was an accident that my brother was found. My father's comment to me about it was, "Your brother did a better job on it than you ever did." This person who was talking in this group was physically like my father, and the same thing was coming out of him. When I got up to leave I walked out the door right next to him. I didn't plan to do that. Well, anyway, I hauled off and belted him. Doing something like that is totally unlike me; I had never done anything like that before. I didn't hurt the person, just scared him.

Dr. Regan, who was in charge, grabbed me by the shoulders and threw me out into the corridor and shoved me against the wall. He said, "I'll make a human being out of you, one way or the other." Those were his exact words. He wasn't worried about me being violent. I mean, I didn't swing at anybody else. He is a psychiatrist, a senior psychiatrist, at the Medical Center, which is supposed to be one of the best psychiatric institutions on the East coast. He was angry. I have never seen a man so angry. His face was red, and his veins were showing.

He told me to go to my room. This was at 5. I went to my room, and at about six Dr. Regan came and said, "I called for Dr. Long. We can't handle you. We are going to send you to Central." I had never met Dr. Long, but I knew from hearing about him at Crisis that he was the county examining doctor who did the psychiatric exams for involuntary commitments. He was supposed to be a real bastard. He isn't even a psychiatrist. He gets a fixed rate for everyone he examines. I also heard quite a few stories about Central, which is the state hospital about 40 miles from Central City. It was generally known as a hole.

I was very frightened, and I was crying the whole time. I asked Regan, "Don't you want to know why I hit the person?" He said, "No," and walked out. At 6:30 Long came in. He just said "I'm Dr. Long; I am here to examine you." He asked me my name, address, and sex. He had it all written down when he came in, but he was just testing me, I guess. When they do that, it really annoys me. He asked me to count backward from 10 to 1, which I did. He also asked me if I wanted to be referred to as John or Jane. I said, "Jane." So he called me Johnnie. He kind of slurred it. He couldn't bring himself to call me Jane. Since I am a transsexual, I am automatically sick and in need of help—especially to a guy like Long. He left. Regan came back later, and I told him why I hit him—I got that in. He told me that I was going to Central anyway—tomorrow.

The only time I stopped crying during the whole time was when Long was in the room. I started crying again after Regan left and cried for most of the evening. I cried myself to sleep. In the morning some friends came from Crisis and sat with me, till about two in the afternoon when the sheriffs came. My friends were shook up because they couldn't see why the people at the Medical Center couldn't handle me, even if I was psychotic. They take psychotic patients there, too. They couldn't see any reason for sending me to Central. Everything was all piled up against me, and then the sheriffs came. They were going to put these handcuffs on me that were attached to one of their belts and take me down the elevator. The head nurse was very angry at this whole thing and blew up. He said, "You aren't going to put cuffs on that person—that person is not violent and you don't even have to guard her." I caused a feud among the staff, because a lot of them were on my side and thought that Regan shouldn't have done what he did.

The sheriffs were very nice—very sympathetic. They wanted to stop for coffee but thought that that would be too much. When I got there, I found out that I was the only person who ever came from Central County up there without cuffs on. It's an automatic thing—once you get a health officer commitment the cuffs go on you. If you're not in a hospital already, they don't take you to one. They take you to the Public Safety Building. You stay overnight, and then they transport you up there in the morning. You're not booked at the Public Safety Building. That is the only difference in going to Central and going to jail, but once you get to Central you are mugged, fingerprinted, and photographed. My fingerprints are on permanent records with the FBI that I was a mental patient.

I felt very confused, frightened, and angry. I also felt very conspicuous. I knew I wasn't nuts and said to myself, "What the hell did I do to deserve this?" I mean, you feel ridiculous in the back of this big station wagon with bars all around the windows and bars separating you from the front. It was very conspicuous going there. The main building is six stories high and made of red brick. It stands on the top of a hill in the middle of a cow field. There is no other building over two stories within about three miles. It's a huge tract of land in this rural area. There are other two-story brick buildings all around, and over 3000 patients there. The whole thing is just the State Hospital for the Mentally Ill, that's all that's there. I couldn't see any sense of building the building that high—it's made to stick out so. The place is the most perverting place you would ever want to see. There were no bars on the windows, but the windows are made out of the glass with wire mesh inside and the panes are about four by six inches square, so if you did break them you couldn't get out anyway.

I was petrified. I was too afraid to do anything. When I walked inside, it was somewhat like a hospital. There were people walking around in state clothes which are supposed to look like regular civilian clothing, but they are mass produced so they don't fit. People walking around with pants that didn't fit, dresses that didn't fit, and everybody looked superdrugged up. You know that you are going into something that is really overpowering.

I was admitted in a bare office. The doctor came down who was going to be my physician. He wanted to put me in a female ward. There are two admitting wards; 25 is a female ward and 22 is the male ward. The female ward was under the head of one doctor, Dr. Faro, and he didn't want me in there. They made me strip and tried to figure out where to put me. Finally, they had some state clothes sent down. When I went, I wore a regular skirt and blouse, what I normally wear, but they couldn't have that. My own clothes were with me, the ones I had at the Medical Center. They kept my clothes and made me wear state clothes and sent me upstairs. The state clothes I wore were green work pants and some kind of a work shirt—no belt or shoes. I requested female clothes. Dr. Faro and my doctor discussed the whole thing in front of me, only I wasn't part of the conversation. Both of them had foreign accents. What they did to my clothes really pissed me off. I didn't have that much money, so the clothes that I did have were important. They either stenciled my name on it, or put marking tags with my name in them. Some of the things they just ruined, one nightgown in particular. I can't get any of the marking off now. I call them my Central clothes.

Dr. Faro called me "him," but Dr. Lee called me "her." There was always a controversy about that. Dr. Lee called me Jane, and Dr. Faro always called me Mr. Fry. When I got up on the ward, the first thing they made me do was strip again and take a shower in front of some of the staff. They had three aides in the shower in case I got violent, supposedly. I was a little overly developed for a male, so that was one thing in my favor because after that they made me take showers by myself. Everyone else had to take showers in a group where everyone could see everyone else. Whatever you did in the ward, you did as a group. You got up together, you took showers together, you ate together, and you slept together.

When I first got there, they showed me into the day room. I sat there for about an hour, and no one said anything to me. I was too scared to talk to anyone else. Then they came and told me to come and take some medication. They doped me up pretty heavily. I think it was 250 milograms of Thorazine and some Seconal, which is quite a heavy dose of medication. Everyone was overdrugged. They didn't even bother to ask me if I was allergic to anything. The only thing they asked me was if I was into drugs. I said, "No," for a very specific purpose. If you mention at any time at any state hospital that you have taken anything, including smoking grass, all your problems would be connected to that. That's what caused it. That's an easy out with doctors.

I never found out what my diagnosis was there. I didn't have any idea what was happening, because they never even talked to me—the doctors or their aides. I saw a doctor three times in 15 days and talked to one aide for three minutes. The first time with the doctor was about one-half an hour, the other times were 15 minutes. You just sit around and play cards.

Some of the staff were good. Some of them really tried to help; like, they tried to get the patients interested in things. There were a couple like that. Like, they made popcorn on the ward one night. Others just tried to ignore the patients by sitting in the staff lounge for their whole shift. You don't see them, except during meal times and during medication.

They wake you up at six in the morning—this is the routine I went through every day. The dorm doors are opened at 8:30 at night. You can't go in there from the morning until 8:30. You have to go to bed between 8:30 and 10—10 is the latest you can stay up. You have to be up by 6:00—you make your bed and you walk down to the clothing room where you strip together and change into clothes which are hanging in the clothing room. Nothing is kept in dorms.

Then you file out of there into the day room. Once you're in the day room you hang around there, till 7:30, when it is time for breakfast. Right after breakfast, which is about ten to 8:00, you go back to the day room and start cleaning. You have to sweep, mop, and buff all the rooms, the hallways, and the doctors' offices. After that you are done working for the day.

The ward is locked, so the only thing you have to do is play cards or watch TV—the reception was terrible, only one channel that you could actually see anything, but they left the thing on all day, anyway.

There wasn't anything to do, really. I went to what they call occupational therapy two or three times. It's a room about 9 by 12, and they take four patients down at a time. They try to give you something like crafts to do, but the state doesn't give them any money to do anything. In some hospitals they have good ones, but in this one they didn't have anything to do. The first time I went down there it was real funny. There was this girl working there who by looking at her you automatically knew that she never went to college so she wasn't a certified OT instructor. She gave me this piece of paper and said to fold it in half for her and draw certain pictures on it. First I was supposed to do it in pencil, and then do another on it just like it in crayon. Then I was supposed to tell her what the pictures were about. After I drew the pictures I just refused to tell her. I asked her if she had a bachelor's degree in psychology. She said, "No." I asked her how she could go around giving any TAT tests if she didn't have any training. I told her that I was going to sit there and draw, and I didn't want her picking my soul. She was very angry at me and told me I was irresponsible—resisting therapy. I only went down there about three times—the first time a half an hour, and the other times about 15 minutes. She could have gotten me in trouble, but she was probably scared. I knew my rights.

In the dormitory where I slept there were 25 beds, with approximately two feet separating each bed. There were no night stands or anything—just room enough to walk sideways between the beds. The day room was a great big room with chairs around the sides, a TV up in the front, and a group of chairs grouped in front—about 10 chairs. There were tables around for people who played chess or cards, and a ping pong table. There were some books. They had a library, but nobody was enthusiastic about it because there weren't any books worth reading in it. There were approximately 50 westerns and 28 children's stories—that was it. There were some *Reader's Digests*, which were interesting, and some magazines.

There weren't any seats on the johns. You sat on the bare porcelain. Sometimes there was toilet paper, and sometimes not. If there wasn't any toilet paper, you tried to talk an attendant into letting you go to the place where they kept it. If he didn't feel like doing it, he didn't. It was totally up to him.

The whole thing was so humiliating. But the thing that used to get me the most was the eating. Grant you, the specific ward I was on had food that wasn't that bad, but the way they slopped it on your plate was terrible. They had a plastic tray that you picked up, which was divided into six segments or recesses. One had a place to put a cup, the other silverware, and the rest for food. They just yelled "chow" down the hall. You walked down to the end and waited to go into the room where that ward ate. If someone didn't want to eat, you had to go down anyway and just sit. If someone was sitting depressed, they didn't ask them what was the trouble, they just forced them to go. You filed in past a counter window, and the food was slopped on. There was no choice. If you said, "I don't want potatoes," they gave them to you anyway. They don't ask you how much you want, or anything. You walk over to the table and sit down. There were certain tables reserved for staff to sit and watch you. There were artificial flowers on the table and curtains in the place, but they were the minimum and even at that were out of place. There wasn't any pepper on the table because, I was told, one patient had blown it at an attendant's eyes way back when.

One patient had his wife smuggle in a can of pepper that he kept in his pocket. There were a number of such contraband items smuggled in, such as matches—so when there wasn't an attendant around we could light up—since we weren't allowed matches. If you wanted a light, you had to ask the attendants, or usually you got a light off somebody else's cigarette. There were a lot of patients smoking, since that's all you had to do, so there was a constant lit cigarette someplace. But it was a bummer if you wanted to be by yourself. I couldn't sit by myself and read. It was better anyway, because when I went to get a light they thought I was being more social—participating—so they thought I was improving.

The rationale for not having matches was that you could set a fire, but you can set a fire with a cigarette if you try hard enough. You can take a page from a book and light it up. There were a lot of inconsistencies in the rules.

Well, back to eating. On this ward we did get knives, but they counted them. At the end of each meal you have to remain seated until all the knives and forks and spoons are counted. These people are worried about mental patients committing suicide, but if you want to commit suicide there are many ways to do it in a place like that. Light bulbs were readily accessible to cut your wrists with—all you had to do was unscrew them—but they counted the knives.

You couldn't smoke in the dining room. Usually, after a meal is when you want a cigarette to relax with your coffee. You had to wait until everyone was through, and then you walked over to where another window was and you scraped your tray off and stacked it up. After that they handed out rags and you wiped off the tables, and then you were released. They would say, "You can go now." If there were geriatric patients on the ward, who were extremely slow, we would be dismissed before they were finished. The staff didn't eat there—they sat by themselves.

There was no way to get snacks or anything there, unless a staff member went down to the canteen for you. When I was first there they used to send somebody down for coffee for the patients in the morning. A patient would come around and take the orders. After you finished it, you would save your cup and hide it, usually in back of the books, and then at night you would take it with you when you went for supper. At the end of the meal you could pour your cup of coffee into the cup, cover it, and put it on the floor, and then go get another one. Then you had a cup to take back with you to enjoy with a cigarette later. The way you kept it warm was by putting it on top of the radiator in the day room. Someone would lie on his back on the floor and reach up and unhook the radiator cover and put the coffee there and then shut it. You could get it out later. It was hotter than when it was first served.

Since Central is in the country, most of the attendants have been raised in the boonies and are not as educated as they should be. Some of them are fearful, so I let them know right off the bat that my head was alright and they had nothing to fear. I used to volunteer for things, so they would get to know me and do me favors. They would come in and say, "We got to clean up the doctor's office tonight." I would walk right out there and get a bucket and pail and whistle like nothing was bothering me. It pays off.

While I was at Central, I sent a letter to Dr. Regan. It was a very nice letter. I thanked him for helping me, and it was just all sweetness. I told him that now I knew that I was having emotional difficulties and thought that Central could help me through my difficulties. The people at Central knew that Regan had put me in the hospital, and they were thinking that I should be violently angry with him if I was nuts. If I was seeing the light, so to speak, I would be "reasonable." So I just went to the nurses' station and asked for an envelope and gave it to them. You are allowed one letter a week that they will send free of charge. Every letter that is sent is read by the head nurse and OK'd, so I knew they would see it. You can use it the way I did, but because they read the letters you can't write anything personal or anything negative about the hospital because they will know your business or think you're a trouble-maker. If a letter really says bad things about the hospital, they don't send it. They don't always tell you if they sent your letter out or not. You can always get a letter out by giving it to a visitor, but you have to be careful they don't turn them over to the nurse.

One of the big crimes about Central is the way the director lives compared to the patients. The guy who is there now has been there for 20 years, and he has this huge house with a swimming pool and a chauffeur-driven car. They have the patients taking care of his house, and the garden, and everything else. It's part of the vocational training program, supposedly, which is a joke. Central also had this huge golf course that the patients kept in beautiful condition. It's part of the recreation program, only it's staff recreation. Patients aren't allowed to use it. When I went to Central, I thought that patients got paid for working around the grounds, but it's not true. The way it works is that they give you special privileges, like passes, if you cooperate.

Medication times are 6:30 in the morning, about noon, and around 5:30 at night. Then they give you medication right before bed hour. Some of those people were on fantastic amounts of medication. I know my medication, since I have been on so much of it for so long, so I know what I am saying. I took all mine until the third night, and then I put it underneath my tongue so it looked like I took it. I walked out and spat it out and then went to the doctor's office and asked him what they were giving me. They were giving me something different that night. He said Mellaril. I told him that if I was totally freaking out that he should give me something, but if I don't need anything don't give me anything. I told him not to fool around with me by giving me 10 milligrams of this and 5 of that—it's asinine. They don't know what they are doing. They can't keep track of the effects when they give you all these different things. Central has a philosophy—if they aren't giving you medication, they aren't helping you. If they can write in their records you're getting medication, they can say they are doing chemotherapy. It looks good in the state books. They'd just as soon give you medication as not.

At medication time they call "medicine" and you line up. An aide would come with his cart and proceed to hand out the pills. You go up and tell them your name, and he gives you what you are supposed to get. If you ask what it is for, they say, "Go ask your doctor." Most of the people know what they are getting anyway. If you have been in a psychiatric hospital, you know your antidepressants and your tranquilizers. This one guy there used to save up his Thorazine. He would stick it under his tongue, and then he would sell it. Other patients who would want to get really wrecked watching TV or something would buy it. You can get a really good jag on Thorazine if you want to. He sold them for cigarettes, because nobody ever brought him any money. The state does supply you with cigarettes—not actually cigarettes—they supply you with state-grown tobacco and rolling papers the same way they do in prison. You are entitled to a bag of tobacco and a thing of papers everyday. If you can't afford cigarettes, you have to fall back on that. So he would sell them for real cigarettes. Now you have to understand that what I am talking about is the admissions ward. So you can imagine what it is like on the back wards.

This one guy really didn't need the medication, but everybody thought the medication was doing such wonders for him—even though he wasn't taking it. The aides didn't even know. When he left, he dumped his supply down the toilet, because he didn't want anybody to get their hands on them. He was careful who he gave them to, by the way; he had more sense than some of the aides.

As soon as you get to the hospital—the first day—they dope you up. I don't understand how they can ever observe your behavior; you're so out of it all the time. The medication fucks you up as much as anything. They start you with a very high dose and then work you down, or at least that's what they are supposed to do. On my ward you were supposed to be there for observation, so they gave you a high dose and kept you on it. I saw a guy come in, and they gave him so much medication that it made him so sick they had to keep him in a side room.

It was a depressing place. I think they could easily force a person to commit suicide in a place like that. The only thing that held me together was the thought that they never could take away from me what I was or what I had become. I saw one guy who committed suicide. The funny thing about institutions is that you become so self-centered—the only thing you think about is you. To survive, that is the thing that goes through your head. I have to survive this; that is what I was thinking. You don't bother to think about anybody else, you are the only thing that is important.

At Central most of the patients were just thinking about ways to get out. It seemed like even the people that came in voluntarily were just lost, with no hope of anything happening. There is no need to be on a ward like that. Being confined in a ward like that for 15 days for observation is totally asinine. They could have had all their tests done and all that stuff done in three days if they put their minds to it. By the time people left that ward, they were close to broken—some had just lost hope in everything. The state system is crazy. The system is so filled with red tape, it breaks everyone, patients and staff. It tries to take a mental patient and boil him down to a number and fit him within a system. You can't do that. Most of them are in the hospital because they can't fit into the system. The hospital dopes them up so that they can fit. By the time they come around to fit into the hospital system, they are totally dependent on it and they probably will never get out. It's just a vicious cycle. I know someone—a close friend of mine—who went through 26 sessions of electric shock by the state. Supposedly, it was to have her forget something in her childhood. The only thing she forgot was the one thing that gave her joy, and that was playing the piano. Everything else became clearer. The one thing in life she enjoyed, playing the piano, she doesn't even have that anymore. Most people don't realize it, but there are a heck of a lot of things going on in the state hospitals with people not knowing what the hell they are doing. They are still doing this psychosurgery—lobotomies and all these other damn things. There are plenty of people advocating it.

There are things that go on in mental hospitals that are hidden even from the psychiatric staff. A lot of the psychiatrists don't know what is going on.

They think the hospital is well run, when it actually isn't. They don't know the way attendants act around patients, the way they treat them. The psychiatrists never get out of their offices. My doctor at Central had his office through the second door after you got to the locked ward. He never actually went down on the main ward; very few of them ever did. Once in awhile you would see a student wander down looking for someone, but they were never there in the evening or at night. The doctors set policy on the ward, but there was no way of enforcing it. Anytime a patient complained, it was automatically taken as part of his illness and not taken seriously. When you go into visit an institution, you just don't see what's going on.

If you haven't seen the film "Titticut Follies" you ought to. It was taken on the wards of a state mental hospital for the criminally insane. When I first saw it, my reactions were of shock. I had been in hospitals, but "nice" hospitals like the VA, and general hospitals where they don't go to extremes. This time I saw the film after I had been to Central State, and this time my reaction was different. I had to laugh, because if I didn't I was going to cry. The people portrayed in there were similar to the people I was in with—so doped up they didn't know what was going on. Drugged up to the point of not wanting to get out. I have been in three different types of hospitals—good, medium and bad. The VA was the medium, the Medical Center was the good, and Central was the bad. I feel that in some cases people need a resting place to get away from society, but the resting place should not be so bad that it causes more problems. Watching "Titticut Follies" was like having a drug experience with flashbacks—Central kept flashing back. In many ways it is an accurate portrayal of large state institutions, even though it was a place for the criminally insane. There are isolation cells at Central, but there are more subtle kinds of confinement. Like, in the geriatrics units there is a big day room, and all these old men are let out in the morning and placed in these chairs—kind of like high chairs with a tray on them. The tray is locked in, so they can't slide out. But the person can't get out of his chair. They are left there until it's time to go to bed.

They are trying to clean up back wards in state hospitals, because there has been so much stink about them. They are the most blatant horror, the most obvious thing to clean up. But it's hard to get people to see beyond the back wards and look at the hospital as a whole. The old men are not on the back ward, and I wasn't either, but what went on there was the same even if it wasn't as obvious—the way you're treated, and the way the attendants call to you or don't talk at all. If you are depressed, they put you in those extremely depressing surroundings. And what does it do for you? It just totally blows your mind, and then you're supposed to be thankful for treatment. There is no treatment. Your sense of dignity is robbed with those plastic trays and the food slopped on the trays. It's robbed by taking your matches and your clothes away from you. Every human right that you think you have and some you can't even think of are taken away from you when you go through those doors.

While I was there, I felt less than human, but you could never say that. The one thing that you don't do there is to tell people the way you feel. If you complain about something, you're through. The say you're fighting the system. They tell you you're not cooperative. The worst thing you can be in uncooperative. That means doing anything they don't want. It goes on your record. Can you imagine the big book in the office—it's like God sitting up there scoring you. That is exactly the way a patient feels in the hospital. Everything that you do gets put on that chart. They watch every move that you make. You try to make your record look good. Forget about being human—you can't.

Some people are going to read this and not take it seriously. They are going to say I am just bitter. I feel that I have a right to be bitter, and I'm not the only one who is bitter. Almost every patient comes out at least a little bitter. A lot of institutions aren't as bad as Central, but they are bad in subtle ways. The people who graduate from these institutions don't dare open their mouths—for one thing they don't want anybody to know that they are nuts. If you're a nut, they don't listen to you anyway. You say things like I'm saying, and you're told you are paranoid. The truth automatically comes back on you as a diagnosis.

After the receiving wards you are changed to a ward that is for your county. The wards are set up according to your county, except the violent wards. People actually dread leaving ward 22, because they are going to something worse. My social worker told me that, if I didn't get out while I was in B building, forget it. You can get out easily within the 15 days from B, but once they put you in one of the other buildings, in order to get out they have to do a complete reevaluation. It's a long and tedious process, and by that time you're so fucked over from having been in there that it's almost useless.

At the end of 15 days your case is supposed to be reviewed, and if they are going to keep you involuntarily longer you can see a judge if you request it. The patients aren't told this, but I happened to know from the work I was doing at Crisis. I told them that, if they tried to keep me longer on a "two-physician" hold, I would take them to court on a sanity hearing where they would have to prove me insane and incompetent and dangerous. Since I didn't act that weird, they didn't push the issue. That's how I got out basically—by pushing the issue. Central was tough for me, but I was stronger than I ever was before. It was hard on me, but I think it made me strong. I stood up to that shit and faced it. I was sure of who I was. It bothered me more when I got out than when I was in, but I knew I had hit the bottom and I was on my way up and not even Central could hold me down long.

CHAPTER

16

The Present

When I was about to be shipped off to Central, one of the people who came up to see me was Jill Popoff. I know her through Crisis. Actually she babysat me totally from the time I started to try to get into City until I got into the Medical Center. She is finishing up a master's degree in social work with an emphasis on counselling—and is really good at it too. She makes herself available to people 24 hours a day and lets people open up to her, and she opens up to them. She treats people like people, which some people consider unprofessional. It worked with me.

There was a social worker up at Central that she knew, so they got in touch, and when I got out Jill picked me up and helped me get on my feet. I took a room down on McGeorge Street, but I only stayed there a night or two and then moved in with her. I just couldn't hack it down there with all the strangers, and it was in a pretty tough section. I've been living with Jill near the University for the two months I have been out, except for the week I spent in Boston.

She has been really good for me. She is totally against moralizing. Jill totally involves herself in her work—she immerses herself in the other person's problem. In a sense you share things that are bothering you. Like this one time I was very silent and I started freaking out. She sat down and talked to me and told me things that she had been through, and I knew that she had been there before. It's a lot easier to relate to a person like that than to a psychiatrist who refuses to tell you anything about himself or herself.

I mainly eat at Sloppy Joe's nowadays. This is mainly because we don't have anything to cook with, and I usually don't feel like making sandwiches. I'm around the university area a lot, too, so I just stop in. Sometimes I alternate between Sloppy Joe's and the Pizza Shop, and once in awhile the Last Stop. I only eat once a day, which I know is bad for me. I drink a lot of coffee, though. Sometimes I have something in the morning, like toast.

I get up at different times, depending on what time I go to bed. My life is very haphazard, but normally I have a routine that I stick to. Jill is trying to finish a lot of work to complete her degree, so I help her and live by her schedule. She is working nights over at the Community Projects Office. It is very hard to do anything at the house, because of the music and other noise. So she goes over there until all hours of the morning, and I stay over there with her.

The place that I live in has a lot of people and is very disorganized. It's an old building that the landlord made over into a mess of apartments. I don't know how many there are in there now. We have an apartment with five bedrooms and a living room and a dining room and kitchen. There were six people living there, but two of them have left because of the end of the semester. I moved into one of the bedrooms, but before I was sleeping on the floor in Jill's room. I wasn't getting too much sleep, but I wasn't paying anything except the work I was helping her with. The Urban Renewal took it over, and they will be knocking it out soon, which means that we will have to move. I should be back in Boston before that happens, though.

I am an organized person, and when I get disorganized I get uptight. I'm kind of sloppy-neat, that is, I know which pile what's in. Living by myself I know where everything is, but now I'm living with somebody else and it's blowing my mind. I don't mind living with another person, but I like to have a place to keep myself so I know where things are when I want them. I don't like living out of a suitcase. I'm one of these people that is constantly writing down things to do. I find it a lot easier to keep track of things that have to get done. It's a habit I got into since I changed roles. I changed somewhat my personality, too. I was much more disorganized before. I have more to do now, so that might be a reason for it.

I still have one bad habit which I've gotten a little better with but not much, that is, that I trust everybody. I'm always looking at other people's side of the story and think of them before me. I almost have to get belted in the face before I know I'm being taken. Dr. Meed used to say that if she didn't know me better she would swear that I was a masochist. It's just that I'm too stupid to realize when someone's doing me no good.

I pray in my own egotistical way. I'm even into meditation—yoga. But every time I ask God for something I usually don't get it, so I have stopped asking. I've even tried a little reverse psychology in praying—ask for something, knowing that I might get the opposite.

Most of the people I would call my friends are at Crisis, or do things for Crisis. I just go up there and drink coffee. When I feel least forced into a mask is when I'm there with people I have known for some time. When people first know you're a transsexual, it's hard for them to get it off their minds, but after awhile they just take it for granted and that's when I feel like a human being—it's when the mask comes down. Also, when I'm alone I feel like myself. People tell me it's bad, psychologically, for me to spend a lot of time alone, but I like to be alone and think and read. It's not so much that I dislike people now as it's I just like it better.

I'm not a volunteer at Crisis any more. They transferred my card from the volunteer's box to the community people's box. Community people are people they know in the community, who are friends of Crisis and who are willing to do things for them—like help in special crises.

I very rarely go out on a date. The few that I have gone out on were very conventional. I will go out on a date as long as there are people who go along that know me. I have kind of gone out with guys that are basically gay but are not looking at me sexually or anything. It's like they have to go some place where it is socially mandatory to have a female date. Like, it would be ridiculous if two guys went. I do them a favor, and I like it. Those kinds of things are like junior high. The only difference is you smoke a little grass. I have had dinner with the doctor I told you about. Other than that the dates are few and far between.

The basic rule I have for dates now is no dates at all except with friends of friends or people who are gay. I can never tell in advance how involved it is going to get, and I'd just as soon avoid those kinds of situations. I just can't see myself going through all kinds of emotional hell if the guy finds out. If I went out with an average college kid on campus and he found out from someone else who knew me, it would blow the guy's mind. That's playing very dirty pool—I wouldn't want to do that to anybody.

When you get down to it, I am very puritanical. As I said earlier, I would never think of using any sexual devices, or prosthetic devices—like the ones they sell in the stores in New York City. I never realized there were those kind of things, as a matter of fact, until I met with that group of transsexuals a few years back. I might have read about them before that, but it's very different reading about it and knowing people that use it. It's two different things entirely. I don't know why, but I think those kinds of things are vulgar, that's basically it. It just seems weird. I didn't like the whole idea of it. I don't force my views on anybody else, but I have a very strong code of ethics and I'm very unbendable about certain things. I consider myself fully heterosexual, and I believe in behaving within the guidelines of heterosexuality. I think devices aren't normal. They don't turn me on. I also think they would only frustrate me worse. If someone is making love to a device that I have, they aren't making love to me—there is nothing going on with me. How can you make love to a piece of rubber or plastic.

Although I'm strict about my code of ethics for myself, I think generally that any two people that make love and that both of them get something out of it, are well and happy, that that's an OK sexual relationship.

One thing that bothers me a lot is my voice. I have such a deep voice. If I had a voice to match my appearance, it wouldn't be bad. I have less hair on my legs, arms, and chest than most females, and what hair I have on my face is concentrated on my chin. I have hip and breast development, but my voice is very masculine, especially over the telephone. It's real bad—the operators call me "sir," which really pisses me off. I tell them "Jane Fry" and even spell it out for them, but they still call me "sir." I'm trying to change my voice by taping it and listening, but it just blows my ego totally. There is a procedure that I refuse to go through that is supposed to raise my voice, but it's dangerous because it involves scraping the vocal cords, and I don't feel like losing my voice. When I was in Boston, some people were talking about one of the universities giving voice instruction free of charge, and they were willing to work with transsexuals. In Boston everybody seemed to know everybody else, and there was a kind of referral system. It's going to be nice to live there. I met a man who said that the main thing about the voice was not the deepness of it but the accent that you put on words. A female's voice goes up and down more. Mine is a monotone which makes it more like a man's. I tried to bring my voice up and down, and it sounded like I was walking around falsetto—like a drag queen or something, which I couldn't take.

I never watch TV and never read the paper, either. I feel that if it's going to affect me I'm going to find out about it anyway pretty damn soon, and if it's not going to affect me there is no sense in worrying about it. Mostly, all I do is read paperbacks—science fiction. I don't remember the authors—I just read them. One author I like is the one who wrote *Stranger in a Strange Land*. Better than that one is *Starship Troopers*. I usually have four or five books going in all parts of the house. Wherever I sit down there's a book.

One book that I don't suggest that you read is *Myra Breckenridge*. I burn every copy I can get. It's about a real sick person who happens to get an operation to become a female, and then at the very end of the book she decides that she doesn't like being a female after all and goes back to being a male. It's totally absurd.

One book that I've read twice is Christine Jorgensen's, which I think is damn good considering it was the first. She wasn't the first to have the operation, but she was the first to have the publicity and the first to stand up

in front of everybody after having it. She had to be supermiddle-class conservative to be first, because in order to get where she got she had to convince
the majority of people that she was all right. If she was anything else, nobody
would have understood. She could have never walked the road that I am
walking, which is the freak life. Most transsexuals can't afford anything else
but to be middle class. It's easier to get the operation that way. Spending all
their time thinking about the operation, they don't want to take any chances.
People look at me and say that I'm not even acting my age. They have to be
conformists, because they are so nonconformist in one thing they have to conform in everything else—in many ways they're overconformists.

I use to be real down on homosexuals, and many transsexuals are; but I've
been around so many that my normal fears are gone. In some respects I am
comfortable around them, but in others I'm not. I don't like having to
associate with a subculture in order to be accepted. I would like to be just
myself. It made me angry when I used to go to Gay Liberation meetings that I
was part of that subculture, even though I knew that I wasn't one of them.
Even people in Gay Liberation knew that I wasn't one of them, but society
didn't know where to put me so they shoved me there. Society makes subcultures—people don't willingly go into them. The majority of homosexuals I
know don't want to hang around only with others like themselves. They would
just as soon live a normal, healthy, active life—love who they please without
having society bother them. But since they do love the same sex, people say
they are sick—abnormal—and they get pushed into hanging around together
in bars and places. The majority of homosexuals hate the bars.

All they, and the majority of transsexuals, want is to live as close to normal
as possible, with the same alternatives as everbody else. But society says that
we can't. People are just forced to act in ways they don't want to.

I still have my ups and downs. I get real depressed, but after a few days it
wears off and after it wears off I'm like at a different plane than I was before.
It's like going up a ladder, step by step. You shake at each step, but you're
moving on. The closer I come to getting the operation emotionally and
physically the more I feel like a woman, but then the more I feel neglected because I am still a male. That's what I mainly get depressed about now. Psy-
chially and emotionally I am ready for the operation, yet it is not in sight.

Of course that's an important reason that I am going to Boston, so I can get
a job and fulfill the two-year working requirement. I try to see their side of it
about proving that I can function as a woman by working, but I think I am
functioning as well as any other freak at the University. But they don't
consider freaks at the University people, so therefore I've got to be a nice, middle-class, young lady for awhile. The people who you think are liberal are very
hung-up, too. You have got to find out their hang-ups and play their game.

They're not all hung-up. I think Dr. Meed is OK. She wrote me a fantastic letter of recommendation, saying something to the effect that I had been through so many years of therapy and that she wholeheartedly recommended surgery. Very few physicians come out and put it in such straightforward language like she did. Actually, before that letter I had never seen a psychiatrist wholeheartedly recommend anything. They are very tentative, so that no one can come back and say they were wrong. You have to learn to play games with them—learn their moods and their idiosyncrasies. That's fascinating—it's like playing chess with yourself.

I just talked to my wife recently. We are like old friends who haven't seen each other for a long time and have lost interest in each other. I don't see my son. I don't want to, because I don't want to get involved with him. It's not a good idea for him to see me either. He is the only child I will ever have, so I don't think any child could be as close to me as he is. I don't want my emotions to start running wild, and I'll want to take him to the park and do things like that. It wouldn't be a good idea for him to know that the woman he is with is his father. I think it might confuse him—especially at four years old.

There was a period of time when I denied that I had a child, at least I denied it to other people. I didn't deny it to myself. I used not to mention him, or if somebody found out I would say somebody else was the father. The reason for that is that it was a lot easier for people to deal with me, which made it a lot easier on my head. If I told people he was mine, it would bring up all kinds of questions in people's minds about me sexually and it would be upsetting, but I've learned to handle it now. I kind of matured. There are lots of things that I wouldn't tell people that I tell them now. Before I would just tell people the very basics about me, and it was much easier not having people thinking about the child. If I mentioned my son, people would start relating to him and asking me about why I got married and thinking that I must have been physically normal to do that, and then it would be harder for them to accept. It's easier for people to accept if they can understand it as totally biological, but it's much harder for them to handle it if the biological isn't clear. It's not difficult for me to talk about my son now, but it's harder than talking about my wife.

My wife and I are legally separated, according to the Church. We did that when I was still in the VA, which I forgot to tell you about. The Church usually doesn't grant annulments, but they granted me one. Legally we're not divorced, but according to the Catholic Church we are. I wanted to do it for Joan because I felt that I owed her that much—she had always been very religious. The priest that we talked to was very understanding, which kind of surprised me. He was the first professional person that I met who knew about transsexuals without having to go into a long rap. He started right off the bat with, "Why did you get married?" It didn't even seem to bother him that I was a transsexual, which was really nice. He didn't even slip a cog. Usually people start slipping gears when I'm around, especially middle-class straight people.

After I got out of the VA I looked into a divorce, but it was too expensive. I went down to see my lawyer, and I wore a skirt and blouse. He came out looking for John Fry, which was tough for him to handle because there was nobody else in the waiting room. He said, "Are you here for John Fry?" I said, "Yes, I'm John Fry." We got inside and he asked what was going on, and I told him I was changing from a male to a female and it was going to be kind of ridiculous me being married to my wife. He was pretty cool about the whole thing. A friend recommended him. He told me that if I went before a judge I should look as straight as possible—get my hair cut and wear a suit. I went over to Crisis and asked anybody if they own a suit. They just thought it was a big laugh, me wearing a suit.

One thing that still blows my mind, and that's why I don't go much, is going to the VA. They still call me Mr. Fry. I told them that my name was Jane, and that there is no law in the book that states you can't change your name. You can use another name just as long as it's not for felonious purposes. If anybody wants to know my real name, I carry it stashed away in my wallet. They won't change. I even get my prescriptions filled privately.

After I got out of Central, I thought of bringing a lawsuit against Long and Regan for committing me when I wasn't a danger to myself or others. I knew some people who were starting a chapter of Mental Patients' Liberation in Central City,and they knew a lawyer who specialized in malpractice suits. I went down and talked with him and gave him all the information I had. And he told me that it looked like I had a fairly good case, but he wasn't sure so he didn't want to waste my money with proceeding without an investigation. He told me to come back in a week, and then he told me he could do an investigation to search out the possibilities of winning the suit and that he could do that in 10 hours, and he got $50 an hour. That $500 wouldn't cover any of the work on the suit itself, just the investigation. I couldn't go through the Legal Aid Society, because I would get a financial reimbursement from it, and nobody wants to touch this kind of thing if they're working gratis. I had to have $500 just to get started. If you don't have money, nobody wants to touch you.

Most lawyers work on a percentage of the case, but this lawyer didn't mention that. I'm sure the transsexual thing makes the case all that more complicated. I didn't like the way the lawyer treated me in the first place. When I got up to leave, he gave me the eye and said, "Yes, I think I will call you Jane." I felt like saying, "What the hell else do you think you are going to call me!" but I didn't. I didn't want to get him angry. I saw this guy's partner also. We had an appointment, and I rode up in the same elevator with him. I was wearing hot pants, and I looked fairly nice. I didn't even open my mouth until we got in the office, and then he found out I was his client. Shook him up.

When I talked to the lawyer he told me that they would bring up everything about the transsexualism if I went on the stand, which might be difficult for me to take. He also said that there would be a lot of publicity. It would be on the front page of *The Tattler* or *Midnight,* or something like that. That is the way people would look at it. It would be like the case of that school teacher recently who is trying to get her job back. She had the operation, and the school board fired her. I am sympathetic in certain respects to the people that fired her in that, while she's in her legal rights, she made a lousy decision to try to go back there and work. Not in the same school and in the same class. She must have known that she would upset the school. Even though I can see their side, I don't think that that is any reason for firing her. Well, anyway, when I thought about the trial, I thought it was going to be very rough psychologically. But I really didn't care. I could handle it. I felt that nobody can do more to me than what has already been done.

I thought that the jury might rule against me, but I felt that if they got the full facts and deliberated on them that it would be hard for them not to rule in my favor. The jury would have their prejudices, though. Let's face it, anybody in this society that wants to change his sex is automatically sick. They might think about it like: "Here we have these two doctors that sent this poor sick person to a hospital to get him help, and here this ungrateful person is turning around and suing them." The jury would be made up of people from Central County, but if my lawyers were smart enough, they would let me on the stand long enough so they could see that I wasn't sick. If they got over being uptight and could understand transsexualism, they could see the malpractice in an honest light—which is what I would hope for.

I wouldn't expect to find a jury of my peers, even if you considered my peers broadly as being college students and lower-income people. I guess the only people that could judge me honestly would be freaks. People condemn freaks, but they are honest. They don't let prejudice cloud their minds. And if they are prejudiced they know it and will admit it. If they don't like blacks, they say it—they are totally open about it rather than playing games. I'd probably get Archie Bunker on the jury. Actually, the lawyer said he was afraid of a jury trial and was going to try to do it another way if he took it.

I'm very pessimistic about the lawsuit now. I have no way to get the money. Here the lawyers and doctors are supposed to serve you. They are supposed to have some professional ethics about fees and things. I feel about lawyers the way I feel about doctors. They're after their own good. The reason I was filing suit for monetary gain was for one thing; it would have been a helluva boost to me. I would use the money for the operation, and that would just fuck right over those doctors' heads so bad. Can you imagine me using their money for my own thing. That would really be beautiful.

I've mentioned going to Boston a couple of times, so I should fill you in on that. I visited there a month or so after I got out of Central State, and I'm planning to move there any day now. The reason I went was, for one thing, Dr. Meed is in Boston now and I wanted to see her again. When I went, I thought that I would like to live in the same city as she; in case I got into any trouble, I would like her to be around to bail me out. I wouldn't like another Central State to happen. She is working in the Medical Center in the Adolescent Unit. So that was the main reason why I chose to go. But also I had heard some nice things about Boston, so I wanted to check it out. I wanted to move out of Central, so I was trying to choose a place. I have an aunt that lives there, but I wasn't planning to see her because I'm sure I'd freak her out. I had gone there a couple of times when I was a kid, but I liked it more this time than any other.

I arrived in Boston late on a Friday night. I took a bus from Central City. I had no place to go, so I figured the best thing to do was to get my head together, which means I got a hotel room and some sleep, and generally re-laxed. I got a hotel walking distance from the bus station, because I didn't know how to use the MTA and didn't want to spend money on a taxi. I woke up and tried to make up my mind what kind of action to take from there.

I knew this organization existed in Boston called BUR which is a kind of conservative organization run by homosexuals to help homosexuals. It is a ho-mosexual liberation kind of thing, but it's one of the oldest in the United States besides Vanishing Society. It's run by middle-aged guys that are not radical or anything. That's kind of bad in my estimation, but they were serving a very good function. There was an article in a paper I was reading at Crisis that mentioned this group and what they were doing. So that's how I knew about them. When I went there I had no inclination to call them, but I was stuck and wanting someone to talk to and help me find a place to stay, and what have you. It was Saturday, and I tried to look up their phone number but couldn't find it at first. I called one number and there wasn't any answer, and then I called another and it was their crisis line. It's a 24-hour thing for ho-mosexuals. I talked to this guy and said I needed some help locating, and he told me to go out to their office. They gave me directions, and I went out to their place in Mansfield by the MTA. When I got there, they were really nice and we rapped awhile. Then we started calling around trying to find me a place to stay, without any luck. One of the people that was there and helping me call all day was Paul. He said that I could come spend the night at his house. The next morning another member came over, and he and I drove all over Boston looking for a place to live, but it was Sunday and we didn't have much luck. So I went back to his house and stayed there that night. We looked again on Monday, with no luck, so I stayed there one more night, and then he left me off at the bus stop on Tuesday. By this time I was really low on money. I didn't have much to start with, but it goes fast in a place like Boston. I decided that rather than go right back to Central City I would give looking one more try.

I went to the Salvation Army, figuring they might have a list of rooming houses, or at least help me by telling me a way to get some finances together, or something. They gave me a really hard time. Pissed me off, too, because I was in their youth organization once. They told me to get lost because I was a woman. I said, "Look, I happen to be a female, but quit the bullshit. All I'm asking you for is a list with rooming houses on it." He said, "Well, we don't have any." I told him that the only reason I went there was because my parents were Salvationists, but that didn't impress him.

The guys from BUR had told me about the New Life Health Service, so I thought that I would give it one more try and call them to see if they could come up with something. I called and this person answered the phone, and I told her I was transsexual in from Central City and she said, "Hey—it's really great hearing from you—come on over and talk." Their office was like walking distance from the bus stop where I made the call from, so I just walked over. They had just opened a week before and were in the process of organizing it. There was a social worker there whom I rapped with for awhile, and then she said, "There is a person here we would really like you to talk to. Her name is Sally." She came over and, come to find out, she was a transsexual in the same phase that I'm in and we had a lot in common. We all got rapping, and she introduced me to someone else whose name I forgot, who was a transsexual. We just got really talking—really interesting. They were glad to see me, and everything, and made me feel at home.

I wound up spending three hours with Sally and we really got rapping. Sally is like me in many ways. She is a transsexual and a freak—you know, a hippie. Most transsexuals are conservative and hung up on middle-class values, but she isn't. Other people there were like that, too. They are like me in that they are fairly comfortable in their roles—they're comfortable with what they are. They are working toward an end, and their heads weren't screwed up. They weren't masquerading as something; they were something which is entirely different.

The way Sally is, is she refuses to wear falsies or hip pads or a lot of makeup, or anything like that. She feels the way I do:"If people don't want to accept me, then to hell with them." I want to be able to say that whatever I am it's all me, and not something someone manufactured. That's exactly the way the transsexuals I met in New York weren't.

Sally and the others told me about the plans they had for starting like a commune for transsexuals, and that a gender identity clinic was open in one of the Boston universities which would be run by bonafide community health people what will be free. They have social workers, psychiatrists, and doctors working there. It seems fantastic—like a free clinic basically for homosexuals, but recently they added transsexuals to it.

I would have stayed in Boston, but my finances were down to nothing. Rents in Boston are sky high, and there is also this health law that says that in rooming houses you have to pay one week's rent in advance, plus a one-week deposit, plus a key deposit. The law is to keep hippies from making dope pads, which of course doesn't work anyway. Rooms were something like $25 a week, which I couldn't pay for by that time.

I might have stayed with Sally but I had only $15 left, and I either had to buy a ticket home or stay, since I had to buy food and everything. I decided to come back here and refinance myself and then come back. Sally couldn't keep me until I got some money, because she had a straight roommate at the time and it was getting touchy between them. She was making her roommate nervous, and so she told me that if the two of us were in the house it would really blow it. Sally needed her share of the rent to pay for the apartment, so that's the reason I didn't move in. We agreed though that when I got back to Boston we would get together and we would go from there—kind of play it by ear. They were talking about getting a group of about six together, but you know how things go, you're never totally clear until you get started.

Sally was the kind of person I could really relate to, and it was wonderful to find someone like that. Actually, I had met one other transsexual a long time ago that I felt I might have a lot in common with, but I never got to know her. It was in Dr. Rider's office in New York in the waiting room. She had already had the operation.

Well, anyway, I plan to go back to Boston as soon as I can get some money together. Probably that will be at the end of the month when my welfare check comes—it's actually aid to the disabled. It's not because of the transsexual thing that I get it, but because of the complications. I get it from the county, not the VA. Jill says I ought to go now, and that she would cash the check for me and send me the money, but I don't want to go without it, besides that's illegal and I don't want to get her into any trouble. I've also got a hole in my pocket, so the money I have now wouldn't last me.

I think it will be easier in Boston getting a job than it is here. I think my major problem is going to be my education. When I apply for a job I'll just tell them that I'm a girl who has been living with my parents 'till then. There's nothing wrong with that. I tell them I'm still staying with my mother and father, and my mother has been very sick and I've been taking care of her.

It's lying, but what are you going to do? The major problem is going to be getting a job I can stick with that's not boring. I would go bananas sitting on a production line or something like that. That's one reason I haven't worked 'till now. I just couldn't handle it and the transsexual thing at the same time. I think I could handle school, but I don't know if schools would accept me, and then there's the problem of getting the GI bill as Jane. If they accepted me at the University in Central City and I could afford it, I would stay right here. It would be better in Boston, because no one would know about me at the school there. There are people who would know, and it might spread around. I wouldn't mind coping with that, but I would like to be accepted for myself.

I don't know, moving to Boston will be like starting all over again. I might get a clerk job or a waitress job, but it will be like a new life. I won't get a good job, because I don't have any letters of reference. All my old references check out as John Fry, which is another reason I haven't gotten a job here. I won't show my social security card when I go look. I have it memorized, so there is no reason to show my card. I'll just tell them what it is. I can't remember telephone numbers; I have a block against that.

One thing that I would really like to get going when I get to Boston is a transsexual newsletter written by transsexuals for transsexuals. I would also like to start a counseling service for transsexuals. There are many courses being taught now for paraprofessional counselors. Matter of fact, I had a few sessions at the Gay Liberation League.

I've got clothes and books spread all over three different places. I've got some stuff at my old place, some at Crisis, some stuff at my parents, and some stuff at the place I went to right after Central State. So I want to round it all up and bring it to my folks' house, go through it and pick out what I want to take to Boston, and repackage it, and everything.

17

Reflections and The Future

My wildest dreams are getting a doctorate, getting my own house, working on my own at things that I like to do, and being my own boss—not having somebody hanging over me and telling me what to do every five minutes. I would like to make a decent living, so I don't have to worry about money the way I do now. Having the operation of course comes first in my dreams, and having a boyfriend—which is something I keep myself from getting involved in now. I would like to be married sometime but not right off the bat, not for quite awhile, I think. I am just not into the normal marriage game right away. I'm kind of a liberated woman in that respect. I am a modern person, and I wouldn't want to be tied down. I would like to go out with whom I want, and after awhile I might feel like settling down—once I find the right person.

I'm very much concerned about school. I'm almost 27 years old and feel that it's getting kind of late. I had better get back to school pretty soon; otherwise I'll end up being a waitress someplace for the rest of my life. I would like to have some kind of a career, and if not a career at least some education behind me. I know school isn't all heaven—it's got its trials and tribulations—but it has a lot of good parts and I would just like to be a part of it. I would like to do it while I'm still young enough to enjoy it.

I don't know if Dr. Roper or the other doctors would consider my going to college as fulfilling the working as a female requirement. It's crazy. I could call her up, but I've generally put it off. The last time she knew about me I was heading toward the Medical Center—she was the one who got me in. Lately, I've canceled quite a few appointments with her. I haven't had the money to go, for one thing. It costs me $35 just for the busfare there and back. It also takes a whole day. I don't mind the time—I enjoy traveling, but it gets expensive, especially when you're on welfare. It takes just about a whole month's check. I went to her three times, but I haven't been since fall. I just don't want to call her because she will know about Central State, and I'll probably have to do the psychological tests all over again and I don't want to go through that again. They always come out right, but you just can't convince them. I would have to prove to her that I was extra sane, because of Central State. I have to keep proving myself to everybody else. I also don't want to tell her about my educational plans. I wouldn't want to tell them what I'm interested in majoring in—psychology. They will tell me that if you have too many problems you shouldn't go into a field like that.

If I had been born with female organs, I don't know what I would be now. For sure, I would be doing a lot more things than I am doing now; I would be enjoying life a lot more. I wouldn't be concentrating on just one thing all the time. That takes up so much of my energy and time. I have so very little time to live.

I like working with people, so I might be doing that. It seems to be my calling. I get a great amount of personal satisfaction in doing things like that, like working at Crisis. I worked there a year and never got a cent. They never paid me even expenses, but I was paid a thousand times over by just my self-gratification.

Being a transsexual hasn't been all negative; it has broadened my experience a lot. I've learned quite a few things, you might say. Also I feel that when I got rid of my masculine mask I was able to be reborn—like swapping lives. I could think about who I wanted and what I wanted to be and almost rebuild my personality and life the way I wanted it. I think that was a helluva advantage, but something that I had to pay very dearly for.

If it weren't for being a transsexual, I don't think I would be as conscious a person as I am now. I know about people, and my playing roles, and the way people react in situations. I'm much more conscious and critical of my life, and life in general. People aren't as aware of role playing and being phony as I am, because I have been through it.

I also think that I am more sure of myself. I am not as worried about petty things as other people are. Little problems that people have mean nothing to me. What they get shook-up about doesn't bother me at all. The transsexual thing is so overwhelming—it is such a problem that nothing can be tougher—that nothing shakes me up. Once you have faced what I have faced, you're either a stable personality who is strong or you crack up.

Since I've changed from male to female, masks are obvious to me—I've become superconscious of taking them off and putting them on. It's very obvious to me, swapping roles, like putting on a new suit of clothes, or something like that. Talking to different people is like getting dressed for different meetings. Thoughts like that are in the forefront of my mind. Since I am so conscious of it, it makes it easier for me. When I first meet someone I have a neutral role, and then I start getting feedback. It's not on a verbal level, it's more feeling—feeling how people want you to relate to them. I just fit into the role that they feel comfortable in. I'm so busy finding the role they want me to play, I can't remember the names of anybody I meet.

After the operation I won't consider myself a transsexual. I will consider myself a normal female, and I perhaps might be angry or it might bother me if someone called me that. Some doctors misused the term and said that you're only a transsexual after the operation. That just isn't so.

You know, it's really funny. I have yelled at people for help; I have screamed from rooftops, "I want help," and everybody says, "Yes, I will help you." They ask you how they can help: "What is the problem?" And then they always end up doing to you what they wanted to do in the first place. They don't give you what you want, but what they think you want. I don't know why they bothered to ask what I want in the first place. My whole outlook on society is that everybody in the society is just a super-egotist. They can't be wrong. People and society seem to feel definitely that they have to help you whether you want it their way or not. "I'm going to help you this way, and come hell or high water I am going to cure you one way or the other." This isn't only true of transsexuals, it's true of most mental patients and anybody who is very different. They don't look at you and say, "Wow, this is a really beautiful person the way she is." Very few people take that approach. Their approach is that they are going to cure "it"—and by curing you they mess you up more than you were before, especially in "hospitals."

People just aren't sensitive enough to help you when and how you need it. You have to be off the wall before they listen to your asking for help, and then the treatment is worse than the pain. When I was back in school, I think I asked people for help in subtle ways. I think I kind of yelled to my teachers that I was in trouble, but they ignored it. People don't like to get involved.

I think professionals should more or less accept people as they are and not as what they think they are or should be. I've seen so many people who sit around and read books about people and don't know anything about them. Some garbage collectors know more about people than some PhD's—so it's not the education. It's the ability to accept people for what they are for themselves.

I think that the main thing is that they should meet clients at their own level, which they seldom do. Quite a few social workers, psychiatrists, and whoever that I have met take the attitude that you are sick. They don't treat people where they are at and as human beings; they treat them like some diagnosis.

I don't think I am very different from other people who have been excluded from society and generally fucked over, but what is unique is my ability to see it from a distance Many of the people I talk to who have been on the fringes take everything very personally and don't see the ludicrousness of the whole system.

People are the funniest animals alive—they don't realize it though. In my position you can sit back and see it better. Society puts you on the outside, and you're not quite as involved as the mainstream so you can see it pretty clearly. You watch the hustle and the bustle and you start to wonder—you really say to yourself, "Wow, do I want to get sane?" I know many times I have been in hospitals and the patients say, "You know, I don't want to get sane." They take a look at the nurses and all the hassles they have; the nurse comes in all shook-up because she had a fight with her husband the night before and he had to sleep on the couch, and all the rest of it—all that petty shit. She is frustrated and bitchy. You sit back and say, "I don't want to get involved with that anymore." You start taking on a "the hell with" attitude, and it's easier to make it. They can't do a damn thing to you, so you just sit back and laugh at it.

Society doesn't give me the operation; it puts up so many barriers that I can't get it and then considers me totally insane. They may stick me away in an institution for the rest of my life. They don't know what I would have amounted to. They don't know the value I could have been to society. So they lose me, and they lose all the money they are paying for my upkeep.

Society says you're sick and having to fight, that if you're not sick you become sick. You have 50 different problems that you have to deal with because of the frustration you have in dealing with other people. It becomes very hard for a person to reach his potential or to get ahead in any way—economically, socially, psychologically.

A society in which I wouldn't have to suffer the way I have is a society made up of human beings instead of plastic images; a society in which being human comes before being in a role. The way society is now, if you don't wear a mask or if you don't wear the right one, you'd better watch out. Sometimes I don't wear a mask. In rejecting my masculine mask I find that being myself is more comfortable than wearing a mask. It gets me in trouble all the time, because people can't relate to me. They can't figure where I'm at, because I don't have a sign on me that says what I am. People can't take you just as a human being, they have to take you as a mask. Like, people have to know what you do before they start talking to you. They have to know whether you are a student or a professional or a housewife, or whatever. If people can't put you in the right pigeonhole—the right category—they can't handle you. People have in their minds that there are two categories of sex, male and female, and if they can't put you in one of those, they don't know what to do.

I've learned to fight society differently than the way I started. If you consider society a brook and each person a small boat, if you try to row against the current, you get washed away; but if you kind of float and go with the stream part way and still pull over to the side, you can probably make it. At least you won't get swamped. I think I will have to conform some to get a job—much to my dismay—I would like to go to school, but I doubt very much whether it is going to be possible. I've learned that you just don't fight society directly. I just try to go along with some things without getting too shook-up, and to make it easier. The way it is now, people can do anything they want to me, but they can never change what I am. I am still me. I will keep fighting the current, but I'll go along with it part way so as not to make it too rough on myself. That's what I did when I went to Central State Hospital. That's what kept me sane there—it was knowing the fact that no matter what they did to me I am still Jane.

So here we are. Who am I? Why am I what I am? At the beginning of this book I told you how I feel about people trying to find reasons for me. I am what I am, and I fully embrace that. I'm just riding with the punches. I am human—much to the amazement of some people. Because people still place themselves on a pedestal and think they have the right to judge the inner feelings of another, that's why I have had some tough times. People told me I was sick because I was not like them, and then proceeded to convince me of it and cure me at the same time. To tell you the truth, I was convinced for awhile. Our system is set up to make the unsual like the usual. I fight against this. I am me, and the only person who carries the thoughts and actions the way that I do. Not that there are not other transsexuals—there are. But I am the only one exactly like me, and I'm damn proud of it. But why does the world rebel against the fact that some people are different than they are? Why must I be punished for the failings of society?

PART

III

Conclusion:
On the Records

Jane's story stands by itself as a rich source of sociological understanding and probably does not warrant a lengthy conclusion. Therefore I will close by presenting the reader with additional data relevant to Jane's story, and with a short discussion of a few of the questions it raises.

After completing the first two parts of this volume, I visited the VA Hospital and the Medical Center where Jane had been a resident. The data quoted throughout this section were obtained from the medical records of these institutions.

The Politics of Perspective

In Part I it is suggested that an autobiography is valuable because it makes available the author's own perspective on his of her situation unaltered by the interpretations of professionals. Let me briefly review Jane's perspective and compare it with those of some of the professionals who came in contact with her.

According to Jane, most of her problems are not internal, but rather are imposed by others. She accepts her gender feelings not as a psychological disorder but as just a part of her: "I know what I am. I like it. . . . " According to her viewpoint, her problems do not stem directly from the fact that she wants to be a woman, but from the reactions others have to that desire. They are the wounds suffered from living in a society that does not accept her definitions. This lack of acceptance makes it difficult for her to feel good about herself. Her problems are compounded by having to deal with a system of authority and power which systematically prevents her from becoming what she knows she is.

While society is reluctant to accept her as a woman, various members of the professional community do, but mostly only through interpretation. That is, they believe that she feels she is a woman, but they do not accept it at face value. They do not consider her feelings real and valid, but manifestations of a psychological disorder. *She is the problem.* They devalue her definition of the situation by characterizing it as a symptom of mental illness. One psychiatrist observed:

> . . . inmature verbalizations around the topic of a new sexual identity . . . a pattern of character disorder of a very primitive nature.

Another reported:

> . . . the patient vigorously denies his suppression of masculine identity as a defense against castration anxiety. [4/68]

According to a psychologist:

> Mr. Fry displayed a psychotic profile evidenced by strong expressions of unconventional values, intense lack of self acceptance, and a great need for more affection and support. . . . He displays overt sexual inversion, is non-conforming and feels hurt if one doesn't pay attention to him.

A summary report written in January 1971 after Jane's discharge from the VA Hospital after a long stay states:

> It is obvious that Jane has problems with sexual identity. It seemed to many of the staff that one of the core conflicts was around excessive dependency needs. She has been able to see that her creating crisis situations—taking overdoses—are often attempts on her part to have others express love and concern for her. In addition the role of "poor Jane trapped in a man's body" is part of her repertoire. Underneath this, one might suggest that being a woman means being passive, being taken care of and not being active in satisfying one's need but getting that need satisfied indirectly. [1/72]

Jane accepts her gender feelings "for what they are," that is, she takes them for granted. The professionals, however, see them as "immature verbalizations," a "character disorder," "castration anxiety," a "psychotic profile," and part of a "repertoire" for the resolution of "core conflicts."

Differences between Jane's perspective and the one presented in the medical records revolve around the issue of "cause." Jane, presenting her story, does not seem to be concerned about "cause." In speculating in the area of cause, she suggests that biological factors may be at the root of her problem,[1] but in her words, "I'm not interested in reasons anymore . . . all I want to do is get it fixed." In rejecting the search for cause, she suggests that there is no more reason to *explain* herself than to *explain* anyone else. To use the term *cause* is to make her opinions less valid than those of others. Her refusal to worry about cause is self-affirmation. But Jane is constantly led into discussions of *cause* in her contacts with professionals. In doing this they start with an assumption that she has come to reject—that she is "mentally ill," "sick"— that she has to be explained.

Jane is particularly annoyed by professional theories that point to early trauma or an abnormal childhood with parental deprivation as the root of her feminine feelings. In the story of her childhood, she indicates problems at home. On occasion her father drank and was absent from the home. But she also describes pleasant experiences with her parents around the dinner table, on summer outings, on bus rides, and participating in a variety of other activities. According to Jane and in view of our own examination of her story, it seems that her background was not too different from that of many poor children, most of whom are not "transsexual." In regard to linking her childhood to her gender identity, Jane states:

> Sure, if you look hard enough into my childhood you would find things, just as if I looked into yours I could find things, if I wanted to.

Early in her psychiatric career, the medical records reveal strong emphasis on the theory that a "cause" was rooted in her childhood. A psychiatrist's report, written after one short interview with Jane in 1967 during her hospitalization for abdominal pains, notes:

> The patient's early life pattern was schizoid. Father was apparently an alcoholic with large dependency need. Mother thoughts described as guilt— probably controls life. No doubt his male identification was imperfect—his father presenting a confusing image of passivity and violence. . . . [5/67]

This statement is a contradiction in some respects, and an exaggeration in others, of what we know from reading her story.

In the records Jane's father appears again and again; he becomes a subject the doctors appear to fixate upon. Her reluctance to accept their interpretation of her relationship with him is not seen as a difference in opinion, but rather is devalued as being a manifestation of her inability to accept the "cause" of her problems and is considered further evidence of her illness.[2] Her first VA Hospital psychiatrist wrote:

> . . . comes up with denial that he hates his father or that his father is a sadist.
> He keeps insisting that his father corrects him because he loves him. [2/68]

There are many other areas where we see contradictions. Her suicide attempts provide a clear illustration. Jane explains the motivation behind her early attempts as strong guilt feelings concerning her desire to be a woman. Prior to her first attempt these feelings were intensified when she discovered that the hospital staff knew of her gender desires. She felt that she was being looked down upon as a "pervert" and as an "immoral creature." Jane relates her later suicide attempts to extreme depression resulting from her frustrated attempts to obtain the operation, and to the decreased possibility that the operation would be available. The professionals paint a very different picture. Her doctor at the VA Hospital explained Jane's first suicide attempts, on the one hand, as being "highly manipulative" [2/68] and, on the other, as "intense anger toward [a] punitive father which is blocked"; this is "imbedded in his self destructive tendencies." [3/68] Jane's suicide attempt after leaving the VA Hospital is understood by the psychiatrist who saw her to be the result of the "war in herself between the 'bad' he—a hard hat like father—and the good 'she.'" The doctor went on to explain that "this fantasy is represented in the current scene by the increasing probability that he will be able to have his conversion operation. The possibility of this seems to make the bad 'he' anxious to kill the 'worthless' 'she'—which helps to explain some of his suicidal behavior."

We can see, as in previous examples, that Jane's explanations are not taken seriously by professionals. Her frustrations, suffering, and torment aren't considered the "real" reason for her behavior. Her perspective is devalued by being discussed as symptoms, or "incoherent rumblings."

In these quotations and in virtually hundreds more, some of which are mentioned later, we see glaring contradictions between Jane's definitions and those of the professionals. The many pages of Jane's story that have preceded this discussion have acquainted us with Jane's vocabulary and views before confronting those of the experts. Having spent more time with her and having more first-hand information about her than all the professionals whose comments have been presented here,[3] we are in a position to look at them more skeptically and to give the patient's perspective more credence. Seldom are we given an opportunity to see, in such detail, the position of the "client" juxtaposed with that of the professional, be the client a "juvenile deliquent," a "retardate," a "welfare recipient," or a "transsexual." This is a very important consideration in developing an understanding of the politics of service organizations. The professional, because of his position and his status, and the years of training and experience through which this position was acquired, is deemed to have the answers, the explanations, and the prescription. The professional is seldom effectively challenged, and more rarely are the assumptions based on his training and experience publicly examined or questioned. Jane's perspective enables us to question inductively diagnostic labels, psychological constructs, and the way mental illness and various forms of so-called "deviant behavior" are conceptualized.

Jane sees her situation, in part, as a power struggle between her definition and that of society. By and large she considers psychiatric professionals her antagonists. Some are supportive and helpful, but in general they, like the other laymen, deny that her definition is valid. Jane sees the situation as a political one (that is, a matter of who has the power to define her). She begins to act in such a way as to manipulate the system and, in other ways, to fight the battle of perspective by employing various underdog tactics. She first verbalizes this view that power is at the root of her difficulties after the case conference in which the staff decides not to give her female hormones as she had requested. After this experience she states:

> The way I looked at the doctors and the other staff members was that they were either for me or against me . . . It's good to find out who is on your side and who isn't. Jane, on the nursing staff, passed the word on to me about what physician felt what way. She'd say "Don't freak out while this physician's on duty—just stay clear of him. . . . "
>
> . . . I was very angry and frustrated about the conference. . . . You're fighting all these people, and you know you're right. At the time I didn't know that much about psychiatry—the ins and outs of it. They snow you with fancy words that don't mean anything. They play word games with you, and you end up getting the shaft every time.

The professionals even denied that there was a conflict; they suggest that her definition of the war is a symptom of paranoia. In their self-assuredness and position of power, nurtured by years of contact with other professionals who share the same vocabulary and conceptualize in similar ways, the doctors and psychiatrists saw Jane's conflict with them as further evidence of her pathology. Her unwillingness to accept their viewpoint was seen as a symptom of mental illness.

Support for the position just stated can be found in numerous places in the medical records. For example, during Jane's hospitalization at the VA, she angrily confronted her psychiatrist when he failed to support her desire to receive female hormone injections. The doctor described this encounter as a "transference of hostility that originated from his father." After Jane requested hormone shots, was denied them, and was being put under close watch because of a possible suicide attempt, her psychiatrist wrote the following statement in which he indicated that he considered her belief that she was being coerced by the hospital to be a manifestation of her sickness.

> Felt that he was being watched and was defensively angry about this . . hopefully he will view present authority figures as less malevolent than before . . . imagined coercion. [4/68]

Similarly, the psychiatrists considered Jane's feelings of being tormented, teased, and persecuted symptomatic rather than genuine and realistic.

> Mr. Fry exhibits an excess of introspection and has feelings of being picked on. Furthermore, he is passive, dependent, has family problems and blames others for his problems. [7/69]

Jane later went to the Medical Center for treatment of appendicitis and was subjected to ridicule. When she went to the same facility for psychiatric care, it was observed that:

> She has the sensation that people are talking about her as if she is transparent. [1/69]

Jane's definition of the power relationships in the hospital is thrown back at her in the medical record. As I've already suggested, the professionals in the hospital never see their relationship with Jane as one of conflict. Their accounts of her are so negative as to suggest that she is seen as having little personal worth. The records mainly contain a series of episodic accounts of mostly negative behavior. Only on very rare occasions when reading the medical records is there any suggestion of the feeling that you get when reading her own story; that is, that she is a bright and sensitive human being. Even though nurses' reports occasionally included comments such as "always willing to help others," "socializing well," "very helpful when one patient has a seizure," and Jane's own story tells of many positive relations with hospital staff, the summary report of her long stay at the VA describes her as an individual who is not valued as a person or as a source of understanding:

> Very early in his hospitalization staff became very much aware of the
> manipulative aspects of Mr. Fry's behavior and over the course of the many
> months feelings toward the patient solidified in a very negative direction. Mr.
> Fry seemed dedicated to 'turning off' those around him. . . . Mr. Fry's
> general demeanor combined sullenness, an almost paranoid attitude toward
> others. . . . [1/71]

The continuous use of masculine nouns and the tone of these remarks support
the suggestion that it is useful to understand Jane's view that her relationship
with the hospital is a power relationship, albeit one that is not acknowledged
by staff.

The doctors believe in the ideology of service, and that everything they do
for Jane, whether she agrees with it or not, is in her best interest. In her story
she recalls numerous incidents in which she feels that the actions of hospital of-
ficials contradict her best interests; yet the records indicate a constant effort to
help Jane. The grossest example of this, Jane's involuntary commitment to
Central State Hospital, is even viewed by the psychiatrist as a form of help.

> She cannot stay here [Medical Center] and I feel that at this point she could
> act destructively to herself in a serious way. I recommend commitment to
> Central State Hospital . . . to have her stay condones and supports her de-
> structive behavior. [3/72]

It should be noted that at no time is Jane allowed to enter her uncensored
comments in the record. The denial of her perspective is so complete that she is
never given an opportunity to challenge the professional opinions entered in
the hospital record.

We do not know if the doctor knew what it was like at Central State Hospital when he sent her there for her own protection, but through Jane's
description of that facility, and of the commitment process, we can seriously
question the doctor's judgment, and, more importantly, we can begin to
seriously question whose view of reality is distorted.[4]

How can we further understand the conflicting views just presented? We
might see them as the result of Jane's misfortune in meeting incompetent
professionals. However, the reputations of the hospitals whose records we have
seen are good, and we have no reason to believe that the professionals she dealt
with are any way less competent than others in the field. We might see the
conflict as a result of Jane's incompetence. However, our discussion and Jane's
own story challenge that simplistic explanation which is often used in

explaining criticism of the service professions. We could see the conflict as the expected outcome of a situation in which a person with an extremely unusual difficulty, the nature of which is highly controversial and the origins of which have not been discovered by science, requests medical and psychiatric help. While this is a seductive way of understanding the controversy in that it can be dealt with as an unfortunate mistake, it ignores the fact that such conflicts exist just as often between children who are "trouble makers" in school and their teachers, between "juvenile delinquents" and the police, between welfare recipients and social workers, between skid row inhabitants and "missionaries," between the blind and Lighthouse employees, and between the "mentally retarded" and special educators.[5] This is not to say that a conflict exists in all relationships between clients and professionals concerning the nature of the client's problem. In many of these relationships there is agreement between the defined and the definer as to "the problem." When the authority structure is strong enough, that is, when people believe that other individuals in certain positions (such as doctors and other professionals) have the right and the knowledge to apply definitions, the politics of perspective become obscured by a veil of consensus. The politics of perspective become apparent when there are conflicting definitions of a situation, neither of which can be acted upon without interfering with the other. The writings of others (already cited), and Jane's story, suggest that the conscensus model of professional-client relationships may be at times a facade hiding a continuing conflict.

Jane's story provides data which allow us to explore the relationship between the client and the professional in new ways. If we look at her story as a means of shedding light on society, rather than on an individual, perhaps we can go beyond questions of who is right and who is wrong in Jane's specific case and begin to develop a conceptual framework that characterizes reality not in terms of objects and behavior but as an individual's perception of objects and behavior.[6] Through her story we can begin to move from a conceptual framework that emphasizes etiology, nomenclature, normality, and abnormality toward one that explores the rhetoric of science and the politics of diagnosis.[7]

The Exception to the Rule Trap

As has been suggested one way people deal with Jane is to consider her an exception to the rule. That is, they do not question the concept of "mental illness," but see her as not being "mentally ill," as being incorrectly diagnosed. If the reader spent many hours talking, with respect, to others labeled "mentally ill," he probably would see them in a similar way. This can also be extended to other categories of "deviants," and this has been my experience with various categories of labeled people, including those whose labels suggest an extremely low level of symbolic functioning, the "mentally retarded." After having a long, pleasant conversation with a person who is a resident of a state school for the "mentally retarded," there was a tendency on my part to think that the person I had conversed with was not really "retarded," rather than question the whole concept of "retardation."

As we have seen, according to her records and to psychiatric definitions and judgments, there is no question that Jane fits the concept of "mental illness" as it is used. The inability to accept her as an "authentic" case attests to our inability to abandon old concepts and our belief in professionalism and psychiatry. Having been close to the subject in a relationship in which she was in control, some of the mystery of being "mentally ill" evaporates and we are left with a person. Words such as schizophrenic, hallucination, psychotic, paranoia, and transsexual seem pretentious. The vocabulary of the professionals has painted such a captivating picture that when we are confronted with Jane, whom their phrases are supposed to describe, but who is not at all illuminated by them, we tend to discard the example rather than the vocabulary. We believe so much in the images we have created that we cannot desert them in the face of a different reality.

The View from the Bottom

Jane's story has led us to question diagnostic categories and to be skeptical about the way in which we conceptualize mental illness. It can also lead us to question the way in which service organizations are presented in the social science literature. By traveling with Jane through her encounters with schools and hospitals, we see picture of these facilities different from that which is often presented in the professional literature.

From Jane's perspective, and apparently from the viewpoint of other hospital patients, serious criticism could be made of organizations that traditionally have been viewed as rational instruments for goal attainment—which is the way they are defined by sociologists and administrators.[8] It is clear that what the client-professional relationship in these hospitals meant to Jane was very different from what it meant to the professionals. In Jane's story there are numerous other examples of different perspectives on various aspects of hospital life. The basic premise that hospitals cure people has been questioned, and perhaps undermined, by her story. While cure and treatment dominate the official view of the facility, boredom, manipulation, and coercion constitute her view. From the perspective of the staff, phenomena such as seclusion and tranquilizing medication serve therapeutic ends, but from the viewpoint of the patient they are seen as a break in boredom in the case of seclusion, and a method of punishment and behavior control in the case of tranquilizers. Another illustration of different views of the same activity can be found in regard to the recreation program. Many of the staff-supported recreation activities, such as those carried out by volunteers, are seen as demeaning by Jane, while the staff sees them as therapeutic. Similarly, patient and staff look differently on "patient government." Jane describes patient government cynically: "It made you feel like a fool . . . doing all that for nothing. . . . " Her remarks illustrate the contradiction between the vocabulary of the therapist and the vocabulary of the patient, and bring into bold relief the fact that the hospital is a far different place for the patient than it is for the staff.[9]

Jane responds to the hospital according to how she perceives it, not according to how the professional staff perceives it. This point is critical and very often forgotten in examining service organizations. Clients have their own views of their problems and needs; they have their own concerns and agendas. How clients behave and the meaning they give to that behavior can only be understood by observing the world from their point of view.[10] To act as if clients do not have a perspective, or to fail to understand their perspective, is to view service organizations superficially and naively.

Stories like Jane's allow us to understand an organization not from the viewpoint of its administrators but from the perspective of those who deal with it. In order to develop programs that have the desired effect, one must realize that the individuals participating in the programs define their involvement. These definitions, rather than the ideas and wishes of the program planners, determine how participants respond to a program and the effect of that program on them.[11] Devaluing an individual's perspective by viewing it as naive, unsophisticated, immature, or a symptom of pathology may serve those in power, but it also makes a service organization a place where one-sided rituals are performed in the name of science.

Sexism

We cannot understand Jane without taking into account the nature of sex roles in our society, and how those who do not fit them are treated. We discuss some of the specifies of this in relation to her life later, but a few general remarks are necessary at this point. We might see Jane's experience, as she points out, only as an exaggerated example of what anyone feels who grows up in a society that emphasizes a strictly dichotomous image of sex roles and, through the mass media, holds up clearly defined prototypes of these roles. The existence of these prototypes in the form of tightly constructed sex images insures that most people will feel inadequate in their attempts to measure themselves with in these terms. Some individuals suffer only mildly because of the tyranny of these images. Jane has spent her life on the rack. Nowhere in Jane's story do the gender images appear more coercively than in public school and in the Navy. After living with her through some of her encounters with these institutions, we can begin to understand the debilitating effect, of sexism on someone who falls outside the present concept of "male" or "female."

Jane's story allows us to understand sexism, because through her we can experience it in its grossest form—we can experience it vicariously but then not vicariously—she is a paradigm that enlightens us all. We not only learn how sexism affects her life, but by examining our own reaction to her we can begin to understand our own taken-for-granted concept of sexuality. We can explore the nature of the discomfort she may make us feel, leading us to understand what society has planted in us.

Jane's Career as a Mental Patient

It was suggested earlier that the autobiography is valuable resource because it permits us to view the individual in the context of his whole life. This can lead to a fuller understanding of the stages and the critical events in the development of a person's self-concept. We will examine Jane's career[12] as a mental patient in the context of her whole life in order to illustrate the importance of the holistic approach and so that we can discuss the process of becoming and the nature of mental illness. This discussion is merely an illustration of one approach to understanding Jane's life, and is not proof of any theory.

Undoubtedly, Jane had a good deal of contact with the concept of "mental illness" or "craziness" in her early life. I say "undoubtedly," because it is difficult to imagine anyone growing up in a society in which so many references are made to "crazy," "wild," "insane" not to be sensitive to the concept.[13] In Jane's discussion of her childhood, she mentions "mental illness,'" or a related term, only twice. She spoke of her father's "breakdown" which occurred while they were living in Chester, New Jersey, and of playing on the grounds of the mental hospital in Vermont. We cannot say whether this contact with her father or with mental institutions left her more disposed to describe herself as mentally ill later in life, but a person who has had intimate contact with people considered "mentally ill" is perhaps more likely to apply the same phrase to himself.

In Jane's early years she does not apply the term "mentally ill" to herself, nor do others apply it to her, but she reports feeling "different" for as long as she can remember. Her earliest memories are of wanting to be a girl, and she makes it clear that, as far as she was concerned, wanting to be a girl was not unusual until she learned that others defined it as such. That is, she learned from others that her feelings were different, and to make special note of them. She reports mentioning her feelings to the girls she played with and being teased about them: "I found out quickly that you shouldn't mention it." She explains:

> I don't know when it all started. As far back as I can remember, when I was four or five years old, I knew I was a female and was angry for not being built like one. At the same time I didn't have the sense to say, "Why am I different?" or "How am I different?" but I just knew I was different; mostly I got feelings that I was different from people around me.

She remembers being teased and harassed by the children in her school.

Over time her conception of how she was different began to crystallize:

> Very few families in America sit down and tell their sons at a very early age that homosexuality is very bad and people that are sexually different are freaks, but it's such an ingrained thing that you learn it from snide comments and jokes that you hear.

Through reading her story we can sense the influence of such words as "faggot," "queer," and "fairy" in shaping the way she came to define herself. As she combined her feelings about being a girl with the information she received from others about sexual differences, she began to value her feelings negatively and to develop strategies for hiding them.

In discussing her school days, Jane speaks of developing tactics for self-preservation, mainly withdrawing into herself. She saw no alternatives open to her at the time. We can begin to understand that these behavior patterns might have been realistic adjustments to intolerable situations.[15] One might ask why Jane did not seek professional help in her youth. Jane, however, was ashamed of her feelings and to seek outside help would have revealed a secret she did not want to share. She saw, and perhaps correctly, that seeking help can often create more suffering than the problem itself. To discuss the problem with someone was to lose control of the information and would complicate her situation. As her story illustrates, seeking treatment is a double-edged sword.

Jane's puberty was a very difficult time for her. Her light beard and other secondary sex characteristics were clearly not the same as those of the boys around her. This, combined with other physical sensations which were difficult to define, made her very self-conscious about her body. In Jane's story we see how an apparently benign rule such as requiring students to take showers after gym classes, can have a profoundly upsetting effect on those to whom it applies. Such forced activities made a great deal of difference in Jane's experiences in schools and in other institutions. What a teacher may consider a childish fear that can best be dealt with directly by coercion is to her a matter of utmost concern involving her identity and personal dignity.

It is not until she moves to Central City that Jane purchases women's clothes. Here we can see the effect of custom and taboos on the formation of Jane's perception of her own behavior. In observing how strongly Jane reacts to her own desires, we can see the influence of sex roles; we can begin to understand how basically trite and benign acts (at least trite and benign from the point of view of the cultural relativist) can be matters of life and death for some members of a society.

Throughout her early life Jane felt that she was different but hid her feelings from others. She did not see her differences as signs of mental illness. She had guilt feelings about her thoughts and about her dressing, but she described them as "bad" or "immoral" rather than "crazy" or "insane."

Jane's enlistment in the Navy, according to her story, was in part an attempt to force herself to be a man. She soon found herself singled out in bootcamp and was called a "queer" and a "fairy." Again, she interprets these comments more as being a reflection of her personal worth than a judgment on her sanity. As Jane's unhappy experiences in the Navy increase she realizes that what she saw once as a means of proving her masculinity is having the opposite effect. The Navy, with its predominant sexist themes, finds Jane dominated by her feminine thoughts. While she is still in bootcamp she has her first contact with a psychiatrist, whom she consults upon the recommendation of the company commander. This encounter was the first time her being an "oddball" brought her in contact with the mental health profession. In discussing her visit to the psychiatrist, she indicates that the regimentation and, more importantly, being kidded by the other men were "getting to" her, but the visit is still not taken by her as an indication of insanity. She hides her feelings about wanting to be a woman from the psychiatrist for fear that she might be dismissed from the Navy.

Throughout her Navy years Jane searches for a definition of herself and of her sexuality. But this search is not characterized by doubts concerning her state of mind, at least not until the later part of her tour of duty. In her early searching she questions whether or not she is a homosexual: "I started asking myself if I was a homosexual or not. I just came to the attitude—no I'm not." As part of her search she has an affair with a man, dresses as a woman in public, and visits a woman prostitute in Puerto Rico. She attempts to confirm her masculinity by joining the submarine service and becoming "one of the boys," but she is often humilated in this attempt. An especially memorable incident from her story is the time she falls asleep in another sailor's bed only to have him come in and tell her that he does not want any "queers" sleeping in his bunk. During this period Jane felt depressed and hurt, and continued to feel guilty about her feelings; she was also concerned about being caught. She states: "The whole idea of it was dirty in my mind, and bad, and therefore I was a bad person . . . guilt and fear of being caught were synonymous."

Not until late in her naval career did she seriously begin to doubt her sanity. It is clear that she observes the reactions of others in attempting to understand her own doubts. In the discussion of her trip to Puerto Rico the first signs of this questioning become evident. When she helped a drunken shipmate into a taxi, he said to her: "Friend, I don't like what they are doing to you, but try to stick it out." Commenting on this she says:

> It made me feel good that he had said that. After a while I started developing feelings. Like, I was wondering if all that was happening around me—the tormenting, the joking—wasn't just all in my head.

Soon after that, after she requests a transfer from the submarine, Jane clearly questions her "mental condition":

> In a situation like that, a person in my position starts saying to himself, "Am I wrong? Am I sick? Or is everybody else sick? . . . I started doubting my own sanity. I started wondering what was actually happening. I never really doubted my sanity until this point . . . .

Jane, while on the *Star,* has seizures and is sent to a psychiatrist for an examination. At this point she seemed to have begun to feel that she was in need of psychiatric help, as her comment indicates: ". . . the whole seizure thing was not psychological, [but] it would give me a chance to talk to a psychiatrist . . ." At this point Jane was ready to accept for herself, as others were willing to bestow, the label "mentally ill;" this is what happens when she is sent to the Naval Hospital and finds herself being sent to the Neuropsychiatry Unit. She thought she was going to the unit to have her seizures investigated, however:

> After a long time [waiting] someone came up to me and said, "Fry, come with me." . . . When I got there "clank"—the door shut after me and was

locked . . . I just really got cold inside and thought, "Oh, my God—what did
I get myself into? It was the locked psychiatric ward of the Naval Hospital.
The nut house. I said to myself, "Maybe I'm totally nuts."

Up to this point in her story she had not mentioned suicide, but she is told at
the hospital: "Give me all your sharp instruments . . . ." On the locked ward,
with all her possessions confiscated, Jane is ready for the worst, including a
mental illness diagnosis. She is then told: "You don't belong here. We'll put
you in the open ward." After being on the brink of incarceration, she embraces
the opportunity to be something less than a "total nut," and accepts her
placement with relief. During her brief stay at this psychiatric facility, her
first, Jane finds some comfort: "It was the only place in the Navy that nobody
bothered me."

    While not completely comfortable as a mental patient, she begins to see
some benefits:

> I felt a little ill at ease at first because I was a nut, but then I began taking
> advantage of it. If anybody wanted to talk, I told them I was crazy and don't
> bother me. That's when I took on a philosophy about being nuts. . . . It's not
> so bad being nuts because nobody bothers you . . . . They don't expect you to
> play their silly games.

The stress of Navy life and the occurrence of repeated seizures added up to an
intolerable situation. As a means of retreat, she defined herself as being
mentally ill. In the hospital, as her comment indicates, she finds advantages in
being ill, the most important of which was the opportunity to leave the Navy.

    At the time of her discharge Jane seems to have accepted the label "mentally
ill," but it is not completely clear whether she ever fully embraces the term as
a description of her condition or whether she sees it as a convenient umbrella
under which to hide. It was at this point that the professionals decided to
define her as "mentally ill." Jane soon finds out that what at one time may be
an umbrella is also a stigma which will affect job opportunities and future
experiences adversely.

    The first indication of this came in August of 1964 when, two months after
being discharged from the Navy, she goes to Central City VA Hospital to complain of headaches and sleeping difficulties. She believes her symptons are related to the blow on the head she suffered in bootcamp, but the medical records
list the primary diagnosis as "headaches of undetermined etiology" [8/64].
According to one examining physician, her problems were interpreted as "psychiatric problem—passive aggressive personality" [8/64]. There is no indication in the records why this diagnosis was made: there is evidence that her
psychiatric condition was mentioned only because a "previous psychiatric

evaluation" had been made. Jane had been categorized. Evidence to suggest that her diagnosis at that point was based solely on her earlier diagnosis is indicated in the report of the psychiatrist who was consulted on the case. He stated:

> Was recently discharged from service—psychiatric reasons—was labeled "Schizoid personality—marked." There has been no reason for requesting psychiatric consultation on the basis of his stay so far. In interview was friendly, co-operative, coherent—not anxious or depressed. Nothing idiosyncratic about his communcation.
>
> *Impression*: I can add nothing to what is already in the record. There is no specific problem now. With regard to diagnosis, I can make no certain diagnosis. He might be considered as: possible adolescent adjustment reaction or questionable schizoid personality. [8/64]

On her second visit to the VA after being discharged from the Navy, Jane complained of abdominal pains. After several tests were administered, a psychiatrist was again summoned; he diagnosed the pains as a "psychophysiological reaction" [1/67] and suggested that:

> ... if he were to enter psychotherapy he might be able to find out the cause of his pain and that might help him feel more comfortable. [1/67]

It is clear that Jane's previous encounter with the psychiatrist in the Navy, which led to her discharge, and that the appearance of "schizoid personality" on her medical record launched her career as a patient. At this point in her life even though, she indicates that she has again rejected the definition of being mentally ill by not consulting a psychiatrist and by viewing her headaches as organic in origin, she cannot persuade others to define her in a similar way. The diagnosis from the Navy would be her calling card throughout her hospital career.

It should be noted that while Jane felt that the most crucial event in her visit to the hospital was being asked to present herself nude to a group of residents and interns, this traumatic experience is never mentioned in the records. The records indicate only that an endocrinologist noticed what he seemed to feel were physical abnormalities.

> ... immature physical development ... little facial hair—shaves only once a week ... abnormality in pubic hair pattern ... chest ... some obesity and mild gynecomastia.

Jane reports that these findings were never fully discussed with her. To the contrary, when she goes to her doctor crying, after the would-be presentation, and tells him of her feminine feelings, he suggests she go to a psychiatric clinic. She states: "I didn't think it was a psychiatric problem, but after doctors kept telling me I had a psychiatric problem I began to think I did." By juxtaposing Jane's story with the records we can see that some of the most significant events in her life are probably not included in, and perhaps were systematically excluded from, the official documents.

Jane's third visit to the VA was prompted by several bizarre events. Her story and the report in the medical records are in general agreement:

> . . . my mother came home and found that I had filled the bathtub with cocoa and water and had taken out all the light bulbs in the house. . . . I sat there trying to butter my cigarette lighter and eat it. . . When my mother saw me, she thought that I had had a total nervous breakdown, so she called my father, who rushed home. . . . The sheriff came but said there was nothing they could do because I wasn't endangering the public. They finally talked me into going to the VA, convincing me that there was something wrong with my stomach. . . . After this doctor wouldn't admit me, my father demanded that I see a psychiatrist.

At this point in the story we see her family enter into her hospital career in such a way as to suggest they were perhaps beginning to believe that her difficulties were related to "mental illness."

The medical records indicate, as Jane's own story states, that this visit to the hospital was for treatment of a "psychotic reaction to scopolamine" [5/67], a drug found in over-the-counter sleeping tablets. During this visit, unknown to her, a secondary diagnosis of "acute paranoid schizophrenia" was officially entered in her medical record.

Jane was later examined by a neurologist for headaches and stomach pains, and he wrote:

> I suspect his symptoms are not due to any organic cause but are associated with his schizophrenic manifestations. No need for any further workup. [5/67]

Even long after this she experienced repeated blackouts which she defined as seizures; these seizures were repeatedly considered psychosomatic. Not until almost four years later were the blackouts revealed by a neurologist to be " . . . temporal as well as major motor seizures . . ." The tone of his statement suggests that other doctors had ignored this possibility:

> I have said a number of times in my consultations and in conversations with members of the department that this patient does have a seizure disorder. The etiology of the seizure disorder is unknown but it certainly could be re-

lated to frequent head trauma. You must not take this patient off anti convulsant medication. I repeat again, it is a mistake to take this patient off anti convulsant medicine. [4/71]

Before her marriage Jane had been in the VA Hospital three times and had been referred to several psychiatrists. Her job history during this whole period was marked with difficulties, many of which were related to sexism. She hoped that marriage would provide companionship and confirmation of her masculinity, however, she found living with Joan, her wife, an intolerable situation, especially as the time of the birth of the child came closer. Jane was clearly in distress: "I just couldn't hack it anymore." Having no alternative source of help, she sought admission to the psychiatric ward of the VA Hospital. Her story suggests that her decision to commit herself was a logical one, and very much in line with a partial acceptance of some of her problems as being related to "mental illness." She states:

> I chose to go to the VA because it was a place I had been before. If I had had friends in the city I could trust or a place I could go I probably would have gone there, but I didn't. The only place I thought of was the VA.

The fact that she was in need of help, or defined herself as such, cannot be questioned, but whether the concept of mental illness merely provided her with a direction in which to seek help, or whether the term described, in any way, the nature of her suffering and needs is not clear.

The first paragraph in Chapter VII, "Entering the VA Psychiatric," raises questions about psychiatric and pseudopsychiatric terminology and about the role vocabulary plays in creating "mental illness." Jane reports:

> In February of 1968 I had the breakdown. I don't know if I would call it that but that's the term they would lump this kind of thing I went through under.

This statement suggests that the term "breakdown" and its application to her experience is problematic for Jane. Apparently it is the availability rather than the appropriateness of the term that leads her to apply it in defining her condition. Jane's story also raises questions about how we learn to attach words to our feelings and to what degree these words change or alter the meaning of that which we experience. Terms like "breakdown," "hallucination," "paranoia," "psychotic break," "schizophrenia," and "mental illness" provide closure and a false sense of understanding to certain very diverse experiences which we know little about.[16] To name an experience is to put it in a category. To be a member of a category reduces anxiety, in that it produces a sense of having a community and an illusion of knowing. To name an experience engenders in people the confidence that what they have named is discrete and tangible; to categorize is to reify. While meaning may be gained through terminology, terminology puts distance between the experience and its understanding and inhibits our pursuit of knowledge. This seems to apply equally well to the individuals who experience the problems and to the people who use the terminology to discuss others. Naming replaces knowing.

Upon being admitted to the psychiatric ward of the VA Hospital for a long stay, Jane apparently accepted herself as being "mentally ill." While she was staying at the hospital, however, she came to define her relationship with the staff more as a power relationship and less as a therapeutic one. An important element in the changing of her definition was, first, the conflict with the hospital staff, and, second, the availability of other definitions, namely, terms found in the Christine Jorgensen story, the term "transsexual," and terms discovered in subsequent contacts with professionals in New York City. Dr. Campbell's first letter to her provided her with a definition different from those available at the VA. The letter stated: "You are evidently a transsexual who has had the same sad experience with the medical professional as so many others."

Jane, of course, could not define herself as a "transsexual" until she knew the term existed. This statement raises questions similar to the ones raised in our brief discussion of terms such as "breakdown:" Is a person a "transsexual," or of any other similar designation, for that matter, before they define themselves as such or before others define them as being of "that kind"? While Jane reports having feelings about being a woman as far back as she can remember, identifying her feelings with a specific diagnosis or "scientific" label served to solidiify her concept of herself. The questions are: What is the effect of diagnostic and classificatory vocabularies on recruiting for these categories? And to what extent does the existence of these categories lead people to conceptualize themselves and others within limited parameters once they are created. Societies are constantly in the process of creating new diagnoses and new categories within which to place their members. (At present we are solidifying the parameters under such designations as "elderly" and "child abusers.") The term "transsexual" was not coined until the early 1950s. Doctors report an outpouring of letters from people who, after having the concept and then the term made available to them through the popularization of the Christine Jorgensen story, began to define themselves under it.[17] As Jane's story reveals, the availability of definitions, concepts, and terms is central in understanding how people come to define their feelings and themselves. It is the control of these definitions that is central in understanding the politics of being different.

In understanding Jane's acceptance of herself as a woman, and her rejection "mentally illness," one has to take into account her physical characteristics. Although Jane is physically a male (Jane's sexuality has nothing to do with hermaphroditism), she did not have strong masculine secondary sex characteristics. This made her a more likely target for ridicule in her earlier life, which undoubtedly caused her to question her masculinity and at the same time supported the notion that she was "a woman trapped in the body of a man." Later in her life these characteristics contributed to her success in being mistaken for and in being accepted as a woman. The importance of this in crystallizing her feminine identity and in supporting her definition as a woman is illustrated in her story by the many references to those events in her life in which she received feedback from others regarding her femininity. An example of this is the time the nurse at the VA Hospital told Jane that the doctor who had seen her in female attire had referred to her as "a typical Vassar coed." About this Jane says: "I went right out of my tree. It was really a great boost for me to hear that." When Jane tells of her visit to Jimmy, her childhood friend, she emphasizes his mistaking her for her sister, Harmony. While Jane might be seen as selectively perceiving and exaggerating others' reactions to her that confirm her femininity, her physical characteristics undoubtedly called forth some of these responses, and her interpretation of them and must be taken into account in understanding her experiences.

In tracing her changing perception of herself, the period immediately following her leave from the VA Hospital after her long stay is very important. How she conceptualizes herself at the end of her story cannot be understood without taking into account the presence of groups of individuals in the university area whose views of sex and mental illness were not those prevalent in the larger society or those that dominate the medical profession. These people, members of the youth "counterculture," provided Jane with a kind of support and acceptance that allowed her isolated definitions of reality to gain strength Jane is very clear about the importance of this period in her discussion of Grand Street:

> All these peole were interesting and understanding. They knew what was going on with me, and it didn't blow their minds.They were very accepting people, and that's why I was probably able to come out in the open with them. These are the people who taught me to be open about myself.

The members of the "counterculture" who befriended Jane were important in supporting and reifying her sense of reality. Through the Gay Liberation League and the Crisis Center she came to be more adamant and to articulate a more political definition of her difficulties. In examining social movements in Jane's life, we can see the relationship between an individual's struggle with reality and the collective struggles on a group level. We see how the presence of an organization can unite people and facilitate the development of the perspectives in individuals who would otherwise be isolated in their struggles.

We have followed Jane's career far enough. Studying her life history cannot provide us with definitive conclusions about the nature of "mental illness," but her life story illustrates the process by which a person can come to be defined as "mentally ill." Through it we can grasp the complexities and the contingencies involved.

Jane's story can help us question and perhaps challenge the complicated and esoteric vocabulary of the mental health profession. Her account describes "mental illness" as a powerful ideological monopoly. There is a dearth of definitions in our society and few divergent agencies that provide individuals, especially those who are struggling and suffering, with ways of conceptualizing themselves other than in the terminology of "mental illness." The various social movements mentioned in Jane's story are perhaps a means of challenging this monopoly. And those who helped create the monopoly, the professionals, can contribute to its demise too.

Social science holds an ever-increasing position of importance in providing our definitions of reality, since they typologies, definitions, and diagnoses it creates provide sources from which individuals and groups may choose definitions for themselves and others. Social scientists must realize that they are now and will be in a position to construct the definitions of reality that form the basis of therapies and other policies. The politics of perspective will be discussed in the vocabulary that social science creates. It is important for social scientists to understand their position, that they manufacture realities. The creation of perspectives with their reifying vocabularies is not a scientific issue. It is a moral and political issue. Yet, in the age of science, morality and politics are discussed as science. Ideology—new perspectives and new definitions—will allow people who have been characterized as "sick," "perverted," or "immoral" to see themselves in new ways and to unite to make their perspectives politically viable in the arena in which reality is defined. Only when people become aware that the human situation is a matter of "define" or "be defined" will there be choice.

NOTES

1. It should be noted that the doctor who first prescribed hormones for Jane, as well as many highly regarded medical experts, believes that transsexualism very likely as physiological roots. Many experts take a psychological stand in terms of explanation, and some take a sociological stand. In this area, however, there is little agreement as to "cause," as is true in all areas of "deviant behavior" theory. The volume edited by Richard Green and John

Money presents the contradictory opinions *Transsexualism and Sex Reassignment,* (Baltimore: The Johns Hopkins Press, 1969). For a sociological approach, see James P. Driscoll, "Transsexuals," in *Trans-Action* (March–April 1971). The highly emotional nature of the controversy among professionals over cause is evident in the letters written in response to Driscoll's article in the October 1971 issue of *Trans-Action.* A more subtle example of emotionalism appears in Edward Sagarin, *Odd Man In* (Chicago: Quadrangle Books, 1969), Chapter 5.

2. See Erving Goffman, *Asylums* (Garden City, N.Y.: Anchor Books, 1961), pp. 35–43, for a discussion of "looping." Many of the points made by Goffman throughout his book are illustrated in Jane's story.

3. Dr. Meed spent more time with Jane than I did in interviewing her, but none of the comments presented here are hers. She made very few notes in the records, and her handwriting was close to indecipherable.

4. Others who have questioned this in regard to the psychiatric profession include: R. D. Laing, *The Divided Self* (Baltimore: Penguin Books, 1965), *The Politics of Experience* (New York: Ballantine Books, 1968); and Thomas Szasz, *The Myth of Mental Illness* (New York: Harper and Row, 1961), *The Manufacture of Madness* (New York: Harper and Row, 1970). Szasz's discussion of the psychiatric profession as a moral policeman has been particularly influential in this discussion.

5. For examples of studies that illustrate the conflicts between clients and professionals, see: Robert A. Scott, *The Making of Blind Men* (New York: Russell Sage Foundation, 1969), Chapter 7; Julius Roth, *Timetables* (Indianapolis: The Bobbs-Merrill Company, 1963); Samuel Wallace, *Skid Row as a Way of Life* (New York: Harper Torchbooks, 1965), Chapter 4; Dorothea Braginsky and Benjamin Braginsky, *Hansels and Gretels* (New York: Holt, Rinehart and Winston, 1971); Gresham M. Sykes and David Matza, "Techniques of Neutralization: A Theory of Delinquency," *The American Journal of Sociology*, Vol. V, no. 22 (December 1957); Goffman, *op. cit.*

6. See Herbert Blumer, *Symbolic Interactionism: Perspective and Method* (Englewood Cliffs, N.J.: Prentice-Hall, 1969).

7. Refer again to the works of Thomas Szasz.

8. See Amitai Etzioni, *Complex Organizations* (New York: Holt, Rinehart and Winston, 1962), p. 143; Theodore Caplow, *Principles of Organization* (New York: Harcourt, Brace and World, 1964), p. 119; Talcott Parasons, "Suggestions for a Sociological Approach to the Theory of Organizations," *Administrative Science Quarterly*, Vol. I (1956), p. 64.

9. Goffman, *op. cit.* Also see Burton Blatt (Ed.), *Souls in Extremis,* (Boston: Allyn and Bacon, 1973) especially the article by Douglas Biklen.

10. Blumer, *op. cit.*

11. See Robert Bogdan, *A Forgotten Organizational Type* (Ann Arbor: University Microfilms, 1970).

12. See Erving Goffman, "The Moral Career of the Mental Patient," *op. cit.*, and Robert Bogdan, *Participant Observation in Organizational Settings* (Syracuse, N.Y.: Syracuse University Press, 1972), pp. 68–70.

13. See Thomas Scheff, *Being Mentally Ill* (Chicago: Aldine Publishing Company, 1966).

15. See R. D. Laing, *The Politics of Experience, op. cit.*, pp. 114–115.

16. After reviewing the literature on the causes of mental disorder, Thomas Scheff remarks: "Many investigators, not only in the field of schizophrenia, but from all the studies of func-

tional mental disorder, apparently now agree; not only have systematic studies failed to
provide answers to the problem of causation but there is considerable feeling that the
problem itself has not been formulated correctly." (*Being Mentally Ill*, Chicago: Aldine
Publishing Company, 1966, p. 9.) In a review of the literature on schizophrenia, Don D.
Jackson observes: "There is no agreement among therapists and investigators as to the underlying nature of schizophrenia and its cause." (Schizophrenia," in Stanley Coopersmith
(Ed.), *Frontiers of Psychological Research* (San Francisco: W. H. Freeman and Company,
1966). Some articles dealing with such subjects start by claiming that mental illness cannot
be defined and yet go on to discuss a topic that falls under this genetic term. For example, in
a recent article by Willard Gaylin, a professor of clinical psychiatry, states: " . . . Psychiatry
is not at a stage where it is capable of defining mental illness." ("What's Normal?" *The
New York Times Magazine*, April 1, 1973, p. 54).

17. See Harry Benjamin, *The Transsexual Phenomenon* (New York: The Julian Press, 1966),
pp. vii and 16. Also see Harry Benjamin's introduction to Richard Green and John Money
(Eds.), *Transsexualism and Sex Reassignment* (Baltimore: The Johns Hopkins Press, 1969).